ISLAM

PAUL LUNDE

DORLING KINDERSLEY
LONDON · NEW YORK · MUNICH · MELBOURNE · DELHI
www.dk.com

A DORLING KINDERSLEY BOOK
www.dk.com

ART EDITOR
Paul Jackson

SENIOR EDITOR
Ferdie McDonald

SENIOR DESIGNERS
Karen Gregory, Edward Kinsey

SENIOR CARTOGRAPHIC EDITOR
Simon Mumford

DESIGNERS
Peter Bailey, Victoria Clark,
Nicola Liddiard

EDITORS
Sam Atkinson, Debra Clapson,
Ailsa Heritage

DIGITAL MAPS - DK CARTOPIA
Rob Stokes

SYSTEMS COORDINATOR
Phil Rowles

PRODUCTION
Michelle Thomas, Melanie Dowland

DK PICTURE LIBRARY
Fergus Muir, Hayley Smith

PICTURE RESEARCH
Anna Grapes, Carolyn Clerkin

DIGITAL SCANNING - DK
Dave Almond

EDITORIAL DIRECTION
Andrew Heritage

PROJECT MANAGER
David Roberts

Reproduced by GRB, Italy

Printed and bound in Italy by L.E.G.O

First published in Great Britain in 2002
by Dorling Kindersley Limited,
80 Strand, London WC2R 0RL

A Penguin Company

Revised 2003. Copyright © 2002, 2003 Dorling Kindersley Limited, London

A CIP catalogue record for this book is available from the British Library.

ISBN: 1 4053 0404 9

CONTENTS

PREFACE

THE TRAGEDY OF SEPTEMBER 11, 2001, the toppling within the last two years of both the theocratic Taliban regime in Afghanistan and Saddam Hussein's secular socialist regime in Iraq are events that make it urgently necessary for Muslims and non-Muslims to confront and overcome the barriers that separate them and establish a common ground for mutual understanding.

The destinies of the Islamic world and the West have been intertwined since the expansion of Islam in the 7th and early 8th centuries radically changed the political map of the world. Medieval and Renaissance European civilization took shape in the shadow of powerful Islamic empires, and modern Islamic states were formed in the shadow of European imperial powers.

Islam is not coterminous with the borders of nation states. It is a global religion, with adherents throughout Europe, the Americas and Africa, as well as in its traditional heartlands. In the modern global village, it is of vital importance to learn from the failures and achievements of one's neighbours. The ethical systems of the world's religions are in remarkable agreement, and it is on this common ground that the future must be built. It is hoped that the following brief account of Islam will serve to correct misconceptions and contribute to this urgent necessity.

Paul Lunde, Seville, April 2003

OPPOSITE

A Mauritanian scholar *displays a medieval parchment legal text. The scholars of this region played a key role in the diffusion of Islam to Africa south of the Sahara.*

ISLAM IN CONTEXT

The imprint of Islamic culture on the modern geopolitical map is enormous. Confined for the most part to the Old World of Afro-Eurasia, the Islamic domain stretches from the Atlantic to the Pacific Rim, encompassing some of the richest countries in the world, and some of the poorest, some of the most fertile and densely populated, and some of the most harsh and desolate.

A Shi'ite Muslim *faces Mecca to pray at a mosque in Isfahan, Iran.*

ISLAM TODAY

THE POPULATION OF THE WORLD stands at about 6.2 billion. As many as 1.2 billion are Muslim, one-fifth of mankind. There are 44 countries with majority Muslim populations. They form a continuum from the Atlantic coast of Africa south of the Sahara to the shores of the Mediterranean, through the Middle East, Iran and Afghanistan to Pakistan's border with India, then north to Kazakhstan, the northernmost Muslim country.

This modern mosque in Rome was finally built after much controversy. Its presence on the Gianicolo hill overlooking the Vatican makes it a symbol of the globalization of Islam.

Beyond India, with its Muslim minority of some 120 million, is Bangladesh, with a population of 127 million Muslims. South, separating the Indian Ocean from the Pacific, is Indonesia, with some 200 million Muslims. There is a substantial Muslim minority in the Philippines.

Islam is currently spreading in Africa south of the Sahara, a process that began in the Middle Ages and accelerated in the 19th and 20th. Perhaps as many as one-fifth of the world's Muslims now inhabit sub-Saharan Africa. North Africa has been Muslim territory since the 8th century, and East Africa has had a steadily growing Muslim presence since about the same time.

There are large numbers of Muslims in China. Nobody knows exactly how many, but the figure of 40 million is probably closer to the truth than the 17 million of the official Chinese figure. There is a large mosque in Christchurch, New Zealand. There is a community of Muslims of Algerian decent in Fiji.

Between five and six million Muslims live in Europe, seven or eight million in America. Most large towns in England, France and Germany, have mosques. English Muslims of Indian and Pakistani origins have made major economic and social contributions to post-war Britain. Turkish workers have contributed substantially to German post-war prosperity, some settling permanently in Germany, while retaining contacts with their homeland, others returning to Turkey to finance businesses and build homes. Most Muslim workers in France, predominantly from North Africa, maintain close ties with their countries of origin, returning to visit friends and relations whenever they can.

The pan–Islamic World

Percentage of Muslims in population
- 91–100%
- 51–90%
- 21–50%
- 6–20%
- 1–5%
- less than 1%

Official status of Islam
- ☪ formally designated Islamic republic
- ● secular state where population is more then 50% Muslim
- 𝕀 established religion is Islam
- ✳ membership of Organization of the Islamic Conference (OIC)

MULTICULTURALISM IN THE WEST

Europe and America became multicultural in the years following the Second World War. Buddhist, Hindu, Sikh and Muslim communities, the latter from a variety of different homelands, were established in most European countries as well as in the Americas. Food improved everywhere. New words entered our vocabularies. Academic historians began to devote themselves to non-Western cultures, global history flourished and even percolated into school curriculums, hundreds of new academic journals devoted to non-western languages and cultures appeared. The classic academic reference work on Islam, the Encyclopedia of Islam, the first edition of which was completed in 1926, comprised four thick volumes; the second edition, still incomplete, so far fills ten substantial volumes. The Encyclopedia Iranica, in the course of publication, will be even longer when completed.

Almost every major university in Europe has Muslim academics of the most varied origins, teaching and researching in every conceivable field. Male and female students from the Muslim world, many of them studying the sciences, are to be found in every major university in Europe and America. There are excellent universities in the Muslim world too, and almost everywhere education is considered a top government priority.

The globalization of Islam is immediately apparent in this map of the modern world. All Muslims share the same essential beliefs, but Islam has many different cultural expressions.

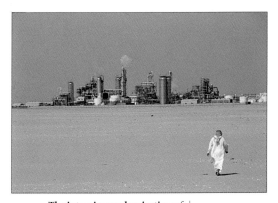

The intensive modernization of oil-producing countries such as Saudi Arabia and the Gulf States has taken place within a strongly traditional structure.

There are Muslim writers, scientists, doctors, engineers, IT geeks, academics, students, actors, pop-stars, television presenters, journalists, firemen, film-makers, taxi drivers, fashion-designers, fruit-pickers, steel workers – you name it. Many of them are leaders in their chosen field. An Egyptian novelist, Naguib Mahfouz, won the Nobel Prize for Literature in 1988. The Nobel Prize for Physics went to a Muslim scientist, Abdus Salam, in 1979 and the Nobel Prize for Chemistry in 1999 was awarded to the Egyptian Ahmed Zewail. I even know of a young Saudi woman who is taking part in scientific research in Antarctica.

Anyone who has travelled in the Muslim world has met men and women from all walks of life with a perfect command of one or more European languages, mastered either in Europe or America or in their own country. One does occasionally meet a European who speaks Arabic, Swahili, Hausa, Berber, Urdu, Uzbek, Pashtun, Persian, Tajik, Turkish, Malay or Chechen, but it is rare, and regarded as an eccentricity of little utility, like collecting old flat irons.

Thousands of Americans and Europeans live and work in Islamic lands, particularly in Saudi Arabia and the oil-rich Gulf States. Americans connected with the petroleum industry have been working in Saudi Arabia since before the Second World War, and some working there now are the third generation of their families to do so. Yet it is easier to find an American or European who knows all about Zen Buddhism than it is to meet someone who knows anything at all about the basic beliefs, ethical principles and history of Islam.

TRADITIONAL LIFESTYLES

The nomadic pastoralists *of Arabia provided the manpower for the Islamic conquests and Turkish and Mongol nomads were the state-builders of classical Islamic civilization. Although today nomadic pastoralists constitute an infinitesimal part of the world's population, many are still found in the North Africa, Arabia and Central Asia.*

IMPRESSIONS OF ISLAM

Countries such as Morocco, Tunisia, Egypt, Jordan and Turkey have long been major destinations for European tourists. Even tourists who visit these countries without any particular interest in their

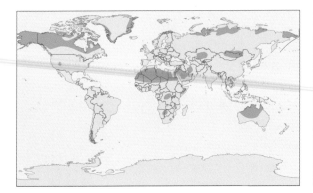

Nomadic population

☐ Nomadic population area

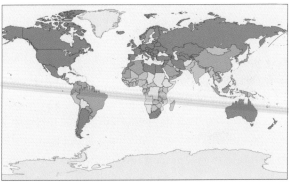

Daily calorie intake per capita

☐ above 3,000 ☐ 2,000–2,499 ☐ data not available
☐ 2,500–2,999 ☐ below 2,000

cultures learn something of local customs and get a feel for architecture, landscape and cuisine. Bookshops in the West are filled with good books on Islamic art and architecture and it is now much easier than it once was to find authoritative books on Islamic history and culture. For those who have the time and inclination to learn one of the three classic languages of Islamic culture – Arabic, Persian and Turkish – excellent grammars and tapes are available.

Despite these reciprocal opportunities for learning about one another, more Muslims are familiar with European and American culture than Europeans and Americans are with Islamic culture.

The images of the Islamic world that appear in the European and American press are almost invariably negative and associated with violence. The fact that the vast majority of Muslims lead normal lives and follow an eminently rational faith notable for its emphasis on kindness, brotherhood, clemency, social justice and peace has been obscured by the political events of recent years.

The picture most Muslims receive of the West is often similarly skewed. The West is consistently portrayed as bent on the exploitation of the rest of the world, a supporter of the enemies of Islam and an oppressor of the poor. The export image of Western society, derived from films and television, is lamentable, and needs no commentary. There is a generalized feeling among Muslims from all parts of the world of resentment and hostility towards the West. Its extreme manifestations in the form of internal and international terrorism are as lamented by Muslims as they are by non-Muslims, but Muslims comprehend the motivations of such actions in a way that non-Muslims seldom do.

Kurdish refugees flee across the mountains from Iraq to Turkey in 1991 to escape persecution by the forces of Saddam Hussein. Sadly the Western media turn their attention to the Islamic world only in such times of war or disaster.

STANDARDS OF LIVING

The disparity in calorie intake, life expectancy and infant mortality between industrial and non-industrial nations is shown on the maps below. For the most part figures for Islamic countries lie somewhere in the middle range, but there are exceptions, notably among the oil-rich nations and poor war-torn regions, such as Afghanistan.

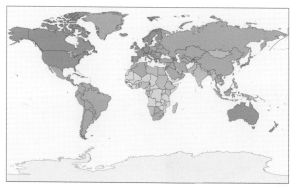

Life expectancy at birth

above 75 years	55–64 years
65–74 years	45–54 years

below 44 years
data not available

World infant mortality rates (deaths per 1,000 live births)

above 125	35–74
75–124	15–43

below 15
data not available

OPPOSITE

A market scene *in Pakistan shows the persistence of traditional dress, albeit in a modern form, and the striking absence of women in public places, which are traditionally male preserves.*

Much of this resentment has to do with specific recent events – the bombing of Afghanistan, the violent means employed by the Israelis to crush the Palestinian intifada, American support for Israel, the presence, until very recently, of American troops in Saudi Arabia, the long-standing sanctions against Iraq and the American-led "war of liberation" which brought Saddam Hussein's regime to an end in April, 2003. These are all cases where many non-Muslims share the outrage felt by Muslims.

At a deeper level, however, hostility derives from the impact of modernization on Islamic societies and the crisis of authority that arose from the actions of secularizing regimes based on Western models. The legitimacy of these regimes, frequently established by secularized military elites, is questioned by many devout Muslims and often opposed by militant revivalist movements. This has in turn led to the suppression of such movements despite their wide popular followings. Establishing an acceptable balance between the demands of a modern state and the Islamic concept of a just, consultative government is one of the challenges facing the Muslim world.

RELATIVE PROSPERITY

Disparities in wealth *between rich and poor nations have come into sharper focus as a result of globalization. This is particularly true of the Islamic world, where the oil-producing states enjoy per capita incomes undreamt of in poorer, more populous nations.*

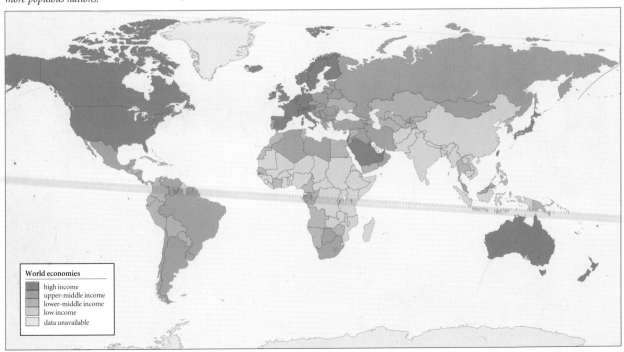

World economies

- high income
- upper-middle income
- lower-middle income
- low income
- data unavailable

THE ISLAMIC FAITH

Some 1.2 billion people in the world today are Muslim – about one-fifth of the world's population. The youngest of the three great monotheistic religions, Islam reveres the scriptures of its precursors, but regards the Holy Qur'an as the complete and final revelation of the One God to humanity.

The spiritual heart of the Muslim world *lies, as it has done since the 7th century, in the Haram, the sacred enclosure in Mecca, the birthplace of the Prophet. Hundreds of thousands of the faithful make the annual pilgrimage, the hajj, to Mecca each year.*

ORIGINS

The Islamic faith encourages festivals and celebrations that involve the whole community. In this medieval illumination, a colourful procession celebrates the end of Ramadan, the month of fasting.

I N THE EARLY 7TH CENTURY the Byzantine and the Persian empires dominated the heartlands of the Old World. The Byzantine empire was the Christian successor to the Roman empire, its territories reaching from Constantinople to the Atlantic. Since the reign of Constantine the Great, Christianity had been the official religion. Paganism was a thing of the past.

The religion of the other great empire, Sasanid Persia, was a form of Zoroastrianism, an ancient and complex religious system that had a profound influence on both Judaism and early Christianity. Both Byzantium and Sasanid Persia were theocracies with hierarchically-organized priesthoods. Zoroastrian Persia and Christian Byzantium were bitter enemies and, during the lifetime of the Prophet Muhammad, engaged in a long war that exhausted the resources of both.

The last area in the region with a significant pagan presence was the Arabian Peninsula. Arabia was a vast land of desert and steppe, three times the size of France. Its interior was *terra incognita* to the ancient world. Indeed, it was not precisely mapped until the 1950s. It was inhabited by Arabic-speaking nomadic pastoralists who could survive in this hostile environment only by the presence of a few scattered oases and jealously protected wells. Without the camel, with its ability to travel long distances between waterings and to recycle desert shrubs and brackish water in the form of milk, these deserts would have been impassable.

Yemen, the Arabia Felix of the classical world, received the tail end of the monsoon rains and could therefore support agriculture. This mountainous land had been home to highly developed civilizations dating back to at least the early 2nd millenium BCE. These civilizations, speaking languages closely related to Arabic and with their own writing system, developed ingenious irrigation systems based on catchment dams that stored seasonal rainfall. The last of these civilizations, that of Himyar, came to an end shortly before the rise of Islam. Christianity had penetrated here, and at the time of the Prophet Muhammad there was a bishopric at Najran, not far south of Mecca. Across the Red Sea was another Christian kingdom,

Inscriptions in a Semitic language survive on the ruins of a dam at Ma'rib in Yemen. This alphabet was in use almost until the Islamic era and is the origin of the Ethiopian script.

Ethiopia, which, according to Arab tradition, invaded Yemen in 570 and then attempted to attack Mecca. Arabian tribes in the north, close to the Byzantine border, had been influenced by both Christianity and Judaism, and some pre-Islamic tribal poets, whose verses were later collected from the oral tradition, were avowedly Jewish or Christian. Central and western Arabia, however, were still pagan. Yet even here there were small islands of monotheism. One was Yathrib, later called Medina, which was inhabited by Jewish tribes, though what form of Judaism they professed is unknown.

The religions of West Asia c.600

- area converted to Christianity by 600
- area of Jewish settlement
- area predominantly Zoroastrian
- principal trade routes

MECCA

Mecca was a pagan cult centre to which surrounding tribes made pilgrimage during stipulated months of the year in which a truce was observed, guaranteed by the ruling oligarchy, the tribe of Quraysh. The object of pilgrimage was the Ka'ba, a square edifice built of black stone with an inner chamber containing images of pre-Islamic deities. It occupied the centre of a taboo precinct, called the *haram*, in which it was forbidden to spill blood or even to pluck a blade of grass during the pilgrimage season. Near the Ka'ba were various sites associated with events in the life of Abraham *(Ibrahim)*. According to the Qur'an, Abraham originally built the Ka'ba to honour the One God, calling it the House of God, *bayt Allah*, and it was there that he offered to sacrifice his son in obedience to God's command. As time went on, polytheism once more took hold and idols were introduced into the Ka'ba.

Mecca lay just west of the ancient Incense Road from Yemen and south Arabia to Palestine and Syria. By the late 6th century the collapse of the irrigation system in Yemen and wars between Persia and Byzantium had probably reduced the trade in frankincense and myrrh to a trickle. They are scarcely mentioned in early Islamic tradition. Mecca nevertheless traded with the frontier cities of Byzantium and Persia, and this trade was significant enough to create a comparatively wealthy class in Mecca. This class was composed of members of the leading clans of the tribe of Quraysh.

Christianity, Judaism and Zoroastrianism *were the three principal religions of West Asia at the time of Muhammad.*

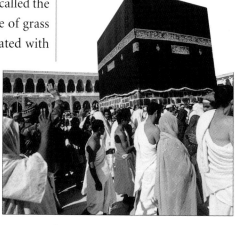

The Ka'ba, *in pre-Islamic times centre of a pagan cult, is now the focus of the hajj, the annual pilgrimage to Mecca. Here pilgrims perform the tawaf, seven circuits of Ka'ba.*

THE CLAN OF HASHIM
The Prophet Muhammad, 'Ali and the caliphs of the 'Abbasid dynasty were all members of the Meccan clan of Hashim, a clan of the tribe of Quraysh. The present king of Jordan is descended from the clan.

Hashim
|
'Abd al-Muttalib
|
al-'Abbas   'Abd Allah   Abu Talib
|
MUHAMMAD
|
Fatima *(married)* 'Ali
|
Hasan   Husayn

'Abbasids

MUHAMMAD, THE MESSENGER OF GOD
Muhammad ibn 'Abd Allah, the Prophet of Islam, belonged to a clan of Quraysh called Hashim. The date of his birth is generally agreed to have been 570. His father died when he was very young, his mother Amina when he was a boy of six. He was raised first by his grandfather, chief of the clan, then by his uncle Abu Talib. Like the vast majority of his compatriots, he was illiterate. When he was 25 he married a wealthy widow named Khadija, who was involved with the caravan trade and for whom he worked as a commercial agent. Almost nothing else is known of Muhammad's life before he received the first revelation of the Qur'an at the age of 40. He died in 632.

Tradition records the presence in Mecca at this time of a group called *hanif*, men dissatisfied with the prevailing pagan environment who made a practice of going on retreat in caves on the surrounding mountainsides. Muhammad apparently went on retreat to a cave on a nearby mountainside for a month each year, and it was while he was there that the first verses of the Qur'an were revealed to him.

THE FIRST REVELATION
This first revelation occurred on the slope of Mount Hira outside the town of Mecca in western Arabia in the year 610. The archangel Gabriel (Jibra'il) appeared to Muhammad holding a scroll in his hand and commanded him to read it, saying iqra'! (Read!).

Terrified, Muhammad pleaded that he was unable to. Gabriel reiterated his command, and Muhammad repeated the words after him, reciting the first five verses of what is now the 96th chapter of the Qur'an:

The archangel Gabriel (Jibra'il)
was the intermediary between God and the Prophet, delivering the Qur'an in a series of revelations between 610 and 632.

Recite, in the name of the Lord who created,
Created humanity from a blood clot!
Recite, for your Lord is most generous,
Who taught by the pen,
taught humanity what it knew not.

[QUR'AN 96:1-5]

Shaken by his experience and doubting his own senses, Muhammad returned to his home and confided in his wife Khadija, who questioned him closely about the circumstances. Had the revelation come from an angel or from a devil? Convinced of the reality of what had occurred, and that the revelation was indeed divine, she reassured her husband. Other revelations followed, at irregular intervals, asserting the Oneness of God, demanding that mankind abandon polytheistic beliefs, warning of dreadful punishments for those who did not hearken. These first revelations are short, densely worded and urgent. There is only one God. He has no associates. He is the same for all humanity. All humanity must submit to the One God *(Allah)* and repent before the imminent end of the world. It is from the verb meaning "submit" that the noun Islam, meaning "submission (to the will of God)", is derived.

For a time Muhammad confided the continuing revelations only to his family and closest friends. After Khadija, the first to accept the faith was Muhammad's cousin 'Ali, later to become the fourth caliph *(khalifa)* of the Muslim community. Then followed Zayd, a slave he had manumitted and adopted as his son. Other early converts were Abu Bakr, 'Umar and 'Uthman, all to number among the successors to Muhammad at the head of the Muslim community.

Three years after the initial revelation, Gabriel commanded Muhammad to preach openly, and he began to make public attacks on polytheism. He gained new adherents, and news of Islam began to spread throughout Arabia. Leaders of the tribe of Quraysh became worried, for they were the custodians of the Ka'ba and the haram, and while they had no objection to the idea of a new religion, they feared both for their authority and the revenues they derived from the cult centre they controlled. Muhammad's followers began to be actively persecuted, and a number of them fled across the Red Sea and took refuge with the Negus, the Christian ruler of Ethiopia. Muhammad himself was protected by his relationship to his uncle Abu Talib, but his humbler followers, like the Ethiopian slave Bilal, the first to give the *adhan*, the call to prayer that summons the faithful to their devotions, suffered greatly. The *adhan* given by Bilal is unchanged to this day:

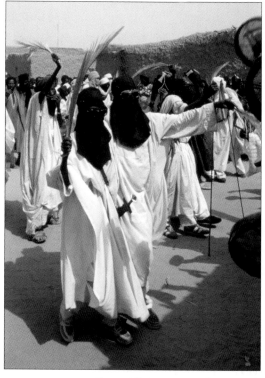

Tuareg tribesmen *carry palm fronds as part of the annual celebration of* mawlid, *the birthday of the Prophet, held on the 12th day of Rabi' al-Awwal.*

God is the most Great! I testify that there is no god but God. I testify that Muhammad is the Messenger of God. Come to prayer! Come to salvation! God is the most Great! There is no god but God!

THE NIGHT OF POWER

The Night of Power, *Laylat al-Qadr*, the night the Prophet received the first revelation, is traditionally identified as the 27th day of Ramadan, the month of fasting.

Behold, We sent it down on the Night of Power;
And what shall teach thee is the Night of Power?
The Night of Power is better than a few months;
in it the angels and the Spirit descend,
by the leave of their Lord, upon every command.
Peace it is, till the rising of dawn.

Quran 97:1–5

THE MUSLIM LUNAR CALENDAR

Muslims regulate time by the moon, rather than the sun. The day begins at sunset, rather than dawn. This means that as the sun sets on Thursday evening, Friday begins.

Months are reckoned from crescent moon *(hilal)* to crescent moon. The lunar year is about 11 days shorter than the solar year, so there is a discrepancy between solar and lunar calendars. The lunar year contains 354 days, rather than 365. This means that, in relation to the solar year, the lunar calendar retrogresses through the seasons at the rate of 11 days a year. For agricultural and fiscal purposes, however, a solar year was used, so that it would march in accordance with the seasons.

The names of the months are:

- **Muharram**
- **Safar**
- **Rabi' I**
- **Rabi' II**
- **Jumada I**
- **Jumada II**
- **Rajab**
- **Sha'ban**
- **Ramadan**
- **Shawwal**
- **Dhu al-Qa'da**
- **Dhu al-Hijja**

The festival of 'Id al-Fitr *marks the end of the 30 days of fasting in Ramadan, the seventh month.*

THE HIJRA (HEGIRA)

As Muhammad refused to cease preaching monotheism and attacking the pagan gods, his position in Mecca became increasingly untenable. Then his uncle Abu Talib died, and he lost the protection of his clan. The death of Abu Talib was quickly followed by that of his beloved wife, Khadija, also a powerful source of comfort and protection. He considered emigrating to Ta'if, in the mountains near Mecca, but here too there was a pagan cult centre and he was driven out by its devotees. Around this time Muhammad met a group of men from one of the Arab tribes from Yathrib. Impressed by his message, they offered him their protection if he should need it. Fearing for the safety of his followers, Muhammad sent them, 70 men and women, to take refuge in Yathrib, an oasis some 215 miles (350 km) to the north.

On the night of July 16, 622, Muhammad and his friend Abu Bakr left Mecca for Yathrib, closely followed by a detachment of Meccans bent on killing them. They passed the night in a cave and while they slept a spider spun its web across the mouth. Spotting the unbroken web the Meccans rode on and Muhammad and Abu Bakr were able to elude their pursuers and reach Yathrib safely.

This exodus from Mecca is known as the *hijra*, a word that means "migration". Those who migrated from Mecca to Yathrib in 622 are therefore called the *muhajirun*, "those who made the hijra". Islamic tradition has lovingly preserved their names, for they are the nucleus of the first Muslim community and a primary source for the deeds and sayings of the Prophet.

The hijra marks the shift from a persecuted minority religion to an organized autonomous Islamic community. Muslims very early recognized the hijra as the turning point in their history, and 622 was taken as the first year of the Muslim lunar calendar, known from the event with which it begins as the *hijri* calendar.

THE CONSTITUTION OF MEDINA

The earliest Islamic political document is known as the Constitution of Medina, for this was the name by which Yathrib would henceforth be known. The full form in Arabic is Madinat al-Nabi, "The City of the Prophet", for it was here that Muhammad resided until his death. The Constitution of Medina, the text of which has been preserved in the biography of the Prophet by Ibn Ishaq,

The map shows *the approximate route of Muhammad's journey* (hijra) *from Mecca to Medina in 622 .*

regulated relationships between the muhajirun and the inhabitants of the oasis of Medina. Those who extended their hospitality to the immigrants from Mecca and accepted Islam are called the *ansar* or "helpers". The ansar were for the most part from the two Arab tribes which dominated the oasis. Like the muhajirun, they are an important source for tradition. The Jewish tribes formed part of the community, or *umma*, and like the Muslims were required to contribute to the cost of military campaigns and fight against external enemies. A major part of the document concerns what might be termed rules of engagement and division of booty. The Muslims of Medina were on a war footing because of the threat from the Quraysh of Mecca. All disputes were to be referred to God and Muhammad.

This document marks a radical break with the tribal past. Tribal loyalties are replaced by loyalty to the umma. It is no longer blood-relationship which defines the group, but faith. All Muslims, whatever their origins, are equal. Those who could not accept this new state of affairs were expelled. Relationships with the Jewish tribes rapidly soured. One tribe was expelled two years after the hijra for doubting Muhammad's mission. Two years later another tribe was expelled for plotting his assassination. Finally, in 627, the men of the last Jewish tribe of the oasis were exterminated for collaborating with the enemies of the umma and their womenfolk enslaved.

The Arab conquerors *travelled in much the same way as these present-day Bedouin, covering vast distances on swift camels. However, they fought on foot or from horseback.*

It was around this time that tradition places the composition of the letters Muhammad sent to the rulers of Persia, Byzantium, Ethiopia and the Governor of Egypt, inviting them to embrace Islam, or suffer the consequences.

MUHAMMAD'S WIVES

Soon after reaching Medina, Muhammad married 'A'isha, the daughter of his friend Abu Bakr. 'A'isha was the Prophet's favourite wife, and it was she who tended him on his deathbed. Because of her closeness to him she is the authority for many essential *hadith*, the first-hand accounts of the deeds and sayings of the Prophet. After Muhammad's death 'A'isha played a brief political role, taking part in the Battle of the Camel. The Prophet married many times; some of these marriages were political, in order to forge alliances, some to provide support for women who had lost their husbands, some were love matches. He married daughters of his friends 'Umar and 'Uthman, the second and third caliph respectively. His own daughter by Khadija, Fatima, married his cousin 'Ali, the fourth caliph.

WAR WITH THE MECCANS

In 624 the Muslims defeated the Meccans and their tribal allies at the battle of Badr, capturing an important caravan and gaining much prestige among the neighbouring tribes for doing so. The Meccans counter-attacked the following year, winning the battle of Uhud. It is a tribute to Muhammad's leadership and authority that this defeat did not dishearten his followers. The Meccans besieged Medina for forty days in 627, but finally withdrew. This was the famous battle of the Ditch. A Persian convert to Islam named Salman al-Farsi suggested digging a deep trench to stymie the Meccan cavalry, and this was effective.

The kiswa *is a beautifully embroidered covering that is hung over the Ka'ba in Mecca. The doorway below it in the picture above leads to the chamber where the pagan idols were kept before Muhammad destroyed them in 628.*

The Muslims retaliated by moving on Mecca. Quraysh saved their city by negotiating a treaty at a place outside Mecca called Hudaybiyya. The treaty allowed the Muslims to come to Mecca for three days the following year to perform the pilgrimage. A truce of ten years was agreed. Meccan caravans could pass freely through Muslim territory, and in return the Muslim community of Medina was recognized as an autonomous legitimate political entity.

In accordance with the terms of the treaty of Hudaybiyya, the Muslims of Medina made the pilgrimage to Mecca the following year. The prayers and actions of the Prophet during this first Islamic pilgrimage, established these rites for all time.

During the course of this pilgrimage, Muhammad destroyed the idols inside the Ka'ba, restoring it to its pristine Abrahamic purity.

In 629 the Muslims were strong enough to take Mecca, even though they numbered no more than about 1500. The city was surrendered by a wealthy leader of Quraysh named Abu Sufyan. His son Mu'awiya would in time become the first Muslim governor of Syria and the first caliph of the Umayyad dynasty. Two of Muhammad's bitterest opponents, 'Amr ibn al-'As and Khalid ibn al-Walid, embraced Islam. This was a momentous event for the faith, for in a few short years these two men were to lead the armies that conquered the Byzantine empire and Sasanid Persia. The rapid rise to prominence in the Muslim community of men of Quraysh (who had recently been bitter enemies) gave rise to natural resentments among the muhajirun and the ansar. It is a mark of Muhammad's skill as a leader and his authority that he was able to overcome these resentments. If Islam was to survive and triumph over its enemies, it needed as many competent supporters as possible.

The taking of Mecca took place without bloodshed. Since the city surrendered, it was granted immunity from looting and only a few executions were carried out. This established a legal precedent for dealing with enemies who did not take up arms against the Muslim armies.

Having consolidated the Muslim grip on Medina and Mecca, the main danger to the umma now came from the tribes. Several of these had been allies of Quraysh, others had already shown their loyalty to Muhammad. Alliances with these nomadic tribes was personal, between leaders, and according to custom such agreements terminated on the death of the leaders who had made them. Some tribes converted to Islam, at least nominally, new alliances were formed with others, some were defeated militarily and submitted to Islamic rule.

THE DEATH OF MUHAMMAD

On June 8, 632, three years after the occupation of Mecca, Muhammad died after a short illness. His death meant the end of revelation and direct divine guidance. The community had suddenly lost its Prophet, leader, friend, guide and counsellor.

Muhammad died at noon. No one knew what to do. Some refused to believe that he could be dead. Finally, Abu Bakr, Muhammad's closest friend, father of his favourite wife 'A'isha, who had been with him when he died, stepped forward and addressed the crowd that had gathered before the humble dwelling in which the Messenger of God had died. "Whoever worshipped Muhammad, let him know that Muhammad is dead, but whoever worshipped God, let him know that God lives and dies not!"

That evening the closest friends and relatives of Muhammad met to discuss the succession to the leadership of the community. Among them were Abu Bakr, 'Umar ibn al-Khattab, 'Uthman ibn 'Affan of the clan of Umayya, and the Prophet's son-in-law 'Ali ibn Abi Talib. All four of these men were related to Muhammad either by blood or by marriage. At a certain point in the discussion, 'Umar clasped Abu Bakr's hand, signifying that he had been chosen to succeed Muhammad at the head of the Muslim community. The word for "successor" in Arabic is *khalifa*, literally, someone who takes the place of someone else. The fact that during Muhammad's last illness Abu Bakr had taken his place as leader of the communal prayers was a deciding factor.

The town of Mecca *in the time of the Prophet was dominated by the Haram, the sacred enclosure housing the Ka'ba. There were also various sites, such as the Well of Zamzam, associated with the life of Abraham (Ibrahim).*

THE QUR'AN

The opening page *of the Qur'an, as in this beautifully decorated Persian example, contains the Fatiha (the Opening) preceded, as is every sura but one, by the* basmala.

FOR ALL MUSLIMS THE QUR'AN (KORAN) is the word of God. It is the final and perfect revelation revealed in Arabic to His Prophet, Muhammad, through the archangel Gabriel in a series of revelations that took place in western Arabia between 610 and 632.

The word *Qur'an* is derived from the Arabic verb "to recite" or "to read", and means simply "recitations, readings". Islam means "submission", that is "submission to the will of God". A Muslim is one who has so submitted. Faith is *iman*, and hence a "believer" is a *mu'min*. The essence of the Islamic faith is stated in the *Fatiha*, the *Opening* of the Qur'an:

Praise belongs to God, the Lord of all Being, the All-merciful, the All-compassionate, the Master of the Day of Doom. Thee only we serve; to Thee alone we pray for succour. Guide us in the straight path, the path of those whom Thou hast blessed, not of those against whom Thou art wrathful nor of those who go astray.

[QUR'AN: FATIHA]

Islam is the last of the three monotheistic religions, the Qur'an is the final revelation, and Muhammad is the final Prophet. The Qur'an completes and supersedes the scriptures of the two earlier monotheisms, the Jewish Torah and the Christian Gospels, Tawrah and Injil, as they are called in Arabic, are referred to throughout the Qur'an and are accepted by Muslims as inspired.

Islam, Christianity and Judaism thus share a common body of reference. The Qur'an refers throughout to the prophets and patriarchs of the Old Testament and to Jesus in the New. Adam and Eve, Cain and Abel, Noah, Abraham, Moses, Aaron, Elijah, Isaac, Ishmael, Jacob, Jonah, Zachariah, Benjamin, Joseph, David and Solomon are as familiar to Muslims from the Qur'an as they are to practising Jews and Christians. They are all referred to in the Qur'an, sometimes glancingly, sometimes in detail. Sometimes the references to Biblical figures coincide with scripture, sometimes the Qur'anic versions differ slightly or substantially. Other prophets, unfamiliar to the Judeo-Christian tradition, are also mentioned, such as Dhu al-Qarnayn, Dhu al-Kifl, Salih and Shu'ayb.

Since the One God is the ultimate source for all three scriptures, these similarities are not surprising. Differences are accounted for by the partial nature of previous revelations and in some cases their careless transmission or even falsification. There is a fundamental difference between the Qur'an and its predecessors. The Qur'an is not "about" God, it is the very word of God, speaking directly to humanity or addressing His Messenger, Muhammad.

This explains the centrality of the Qur'an to Muslims. The Qur'an is the foundation stone of Islamic society, its constitution, and permeates all aspects of life. To try to live by the Qur'an is to obey God's will, and the ideal society is a society governed by its precepts.

> **Say, He is God, One, God, the Everlasting Refuge, who has not begotten, and has not been begotten, and equal to Him there is not any one.**
>
> **[QUR'AN 112]**

The central message of the Qur'an is to believe in The One God, and in Him alone. He is All-Powerful and All-Knowing. The word for God in Arabic is *Allah*, literally, "The God". There is no other, and to associate anything with God, thereby detracting from His uniqueness, is *shirk*, "polytheism". Time and again God has sent His prophets to humanity, warning them to abandon unbelief, but the warnings have been ignored, the prophets persecuted and driven away. The Qur'an presents a last chance for humanity to submit to the will of God, for Muhammad is the "Seal of the Prophets", and there will be no more warnings.

Believers will be rewarded with Paradise, while the unbelievers will be sent to Hell. The delights of Paradise and the torments of Hell are graphically described. God's mercy and compassion are infinite, and He guides whom He wills. There is a final judgement, in which humanity will be weighed in the balance and made to account for its sins.

DUTIES OF THE TRUE BELIEVER

Central virtues of the Islamic faith, after true belief in God and the Final Judgement, are charity and keeping one's word.

True piety is this: to believe in God, and the Last Day, the angels, the Book, and the Prophets, to give of one's substance, however cherished, to kinsmen, and orphans the needy, the traveller, beggars, and to ransom the slave, to perform the prayer, to pay the alms. And they who fulfil their covenant when they have engaged in a covenant, and endure with fortitude misfortune, hardship and peril, these are they who are true in their faith, these are the truly godfearing.

[Qur'an 2:177]

Providing water *for wayfarers by endowing roadside fountains is a common act of charity in the Islamic world.*

The Qur'an's famous Throne Verse incomparably presents the Islamic conception of God:

> God there is no god but He, the Living, the Everlasting, Slumber seizes Him not, neither sleep; to Him belongs all that is in the heavens and the earth. Who is there that shall intercede with Him save by His leave? He knows what lies before them and what is after them and they comprehend not anything of His knowledge save such as He wills. His Throne comprises the heavens and earth; the preserving of them oppresses Him not; He is the All-high, the All-glorious.

[QUR'AN 2:255]

THE TEXT OF THE QUR'AN

Muhammad could not read and write. He proclaimed the revelations he received to his followers, who learned them by heart. Arabian society knew of writing, and several members of the early Muslim community, such as Zayd ibn Thabit, the Prophet's scribe, were literate. They noted down the revelations as they came, using whatever writing materials were at hand – thin flat stones, pieces of leather, potsherds, the flat surfaces of the shoulder blades of camels. Oral transmission was nevertheless thought more reliable. Professional reciters were able to transmit without error large numbers of long, complex poems. Whereas a written document could contain scribal errors or even be forged, a text known by heart by a number of people was a guarantee of accuracy and authenticity. The greater confidence placed in oral rather than written transmission was reinforced by the ambiguities of the early Arabic script.

Even today, many Muslims have committed the entire text of the Qur'an to memory. Someone who does so is known as *hafiz*, "one who has preserved". If for some reason all printed copies of the Qur'an should vanish, the exact text could still be faithfully reproduced from the oral tradition.

Although the first two caliphs, Abu Bakr and 'Umar were concerned about the possibility of the loss of revelation by the deaths of men and women who had memorized portions of it, it was not until the third caliph 'Uthman, that all the materials were gathered together to produce a standard written text. This was completed by 650 and all subsequent Qur'ans reflect this text.

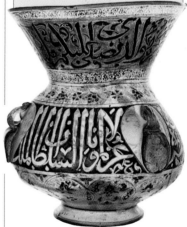

This mosque lamp *is beautifully decorated with verses from the Qur'an and calligraphy giving the name of the ruler.*

OPPOSITE

A young man *in Mauritania studies a portion of the Qur'an. Writing boards are used in regions where paper is scarce.*

Muslim children *throughout the world learn to recite the Qur'an in special schools.*

STYLE

The concise, allusive, elliptical style of the Qur'an is very unlike that of the Old or New Testaments. A single *sura* will often contain many different rhythmic modes, sudden shifts from first to third person, equally sudden shifts of subject, verbal and rhythmic echoes of what has gone before or is to come. End rhyme often occurs in linked passages, but the verses do not fit the metrical schemes of Arabic poetry, and are not poetry. Nor are they prose. The depth and range of allusion, both in sound and sense cannot be reproduced in translation, but can be appreciated even by those unfamiliar with Arabic by listening to a recording of a Qur'an recitation.

Although narratives occur, such as the stories of Joseph and Noah, even these are highly allusive and presuppose a familiarity with the story. The Qur'an therefore needed commentary to be properly understood, and commentaries, sometimes of great extent, were produced by scholars from earliest times. Called *tafsir*, they are still a major area of scholarly endeavour today.

The style of the Qur'an is so striking and so different from other literary works that it is characterized as inimitable. The inimitability of the Qur'an is technically termed *i'jaz*, and the concept was elaborated in the 10th century. The Qur'an cannot be imitated, and any attempt to do so is doomed to failure. The Qur'an is also untranslatable. This is why all Muslims, whatever their native language, must learn to read the Qur'an in the original. Versions of the Qur'an in other languages can of course be used to understand the meaning of the text, and there are early examples of Qur'ans written in Iran and Turkey with interlinear versions in Persian and Turkish, but these are simply aids to understanding and not the Qur'an.

FORM

The Qur'an contains 114 chapters, called suras. Each sura is divided into verses, called *ayus*, literally "signs". In modern editions of the Qur'an these are numbered, as in the Bible, but traditionally they were marked off by rosettes and sometimes numbered by fives. The suras are arranged in order of length, with the exception of the first, the *Fatiha*, the "Opening". This sura, repeated five times a day by every Muslim at the beginning of prayers, is the condensation of the message of the Qur'an into eight short verses. After the Fatiha, all the other suras are arranged by order of length, with the

---

PATRIARCHS AND PROPHETS
The Qur'an makes frequent allusions to the lives of the major figures of the Old Testament and the New.

We raise up in degrees whom We will; surely thy Lord is All-wise, All-knowing. And We gave to him Isaac and Jacob – each one We guided. And Noah We guided before; and of his seed David and Solomon, Job and Joseph, Moses and Aaron – even so We recompense the good-doers – Zachariah and John, Jesus and Elias; each was of the righteous – Ishmael and Elisha, Jonah and Lot – each one We preferred above all beings; and of their fathers, and of their seed and of their brethren; and We elected them, and We guided them to a straight path.

[Qur'an 6: 81-85]

longest placed at the beginning of the book and the shortest at the end. This arrangement goes back to the original 'Uthmanic codex of 650.

Each sura has a name, usually chosen from a striking word or expression in one of the verses. Thus the very long second sura of the Qur'an, immediately following the Fatiha, is called the "Sura of the Cow", *surat al-baqara*, after the story of the unblemished cow sacrificed by the Children of Israel in the wilderness at the command of Moses, which occurs in this chapter. Some suras, such as the "Sura of Abraham", have straightforward, self-explanatory names, others are more intriguingly titled, for example the "Sura of the Ant" or the "Sura of the Elephant".

As the revelation of the Qur'an took place over a period of 22 years, during which Muhammad preached first in Mecca, then in Medina, and because very often verses could not be understood without some knowledge of the circumstances that called them forth, it became customary to add, after the name of the sura, the city in which it was revealed – Mecca or Medina.

MANUSCRIPT OF THE QUR'AN

This superb early Ottoman Qur'an with its rich but restrained decoration and meticulously exact calligraphy shows the skill and devotion of the copyist and illuminator. To make beautiful the Word of God is held to be an act of worship and thanksgiving. Because the Qur'an is the Word of God, care is always taken to avoid even the smallest slip in copying.

The need to read and study the Qur'an in its original language spread literacy throughout the Islamic world.

The script of this Qur'an is naskhi, *developed by Ibn al-Bawwab in the 10th century and brought to perfection by Ottoman calligraphers*

The flap protects the manuscript from dust

Glazed and polished, hand-made paper

The heading gives the name of the sura and often the number of verses it contains and whether it was revealed at Mecca or Medina

THE SURAS OF MECCA

This short sura of just twelve lines is a good example of the more passionate, mysterious style of the revelations made at Mecca.

By the white afternoon and the brooding night! Thy Lord has neither forsaken thee nor hates thee and the Last shall be better for thee than the First. Thy Lord shall give thee, and thou shalt be satisfied. Did He not find thee an orphan, and shelter thee? Did He not find thee erring, and guide thee? Did He not find thee needy, and suffice thee?
As for the orphan, do not oppress him, and as for the beggar, scold him not; and as for thy Lord's blessing, declare it.
[Qur'an 93: 1-12]

This inscription is the basmala, *"In the name of God, the Merciful, the Compassionate", beautifully reproduced on Iznik tiles at the Kiliç Ali Pasha Mosque in Istanbul.*

Generally speaking, the suras revealed in Mecca are short, highly charged and deeply moving. The suras revealed in Medina, where the first Muslim community became a political as well as religious entity, are longer and frequently contain, as well as passages of great beauty, more prosaic passages containing material on marriage, divorce, inheritance and other subjects of concern to the ordering of a Muslim society.

Every sura but one is preceded by the *basmala*; "In the Name of God, the Merciful, the Compassionate" *(bi-smi llah al-rahman al-rahim)*. This phrase is still written at the head of every document, even personal letters, and is repeated before undertaking almost any activity. The emphasis upon God's mercy and compassion is the quintessence of Islam. Because this phrase occurs with such frequency in written documents, Muslims are always careful not to tread on paper with Arabic script, and will very often pick up scraps of paper with writing upon them and place them in a niche in a wall to guard them from possible desecration.

Copies of the Qur'an can only be touched by someone in a state of ritual purity, that is, who has just performed the ritual washing that precedes prayer. Non-Muslims are naturally never in this state, and should therefore not touch the Qur'an. This prohibition does not extend to translations into other languages, for these of course are not the literal word of God.

The Qur'an is recited, or rather chanted, aloud when read. It is normally placed in a folding wooden support, the *kursi*, in order to elevate it above the knees of the reciter, who is generally seated on the floor.

There are seven traditionally accepted ways of "reading", that is, pronouncing the consonantal text. None of these affect the consonantal text itself, and in only a very few cases do they affect the sense. Early commentaries on the Qur'an will often cite "readings" from one or another of these different traditions, in order to throw light on the meaning of a particular passage and to show different ways in which it can be construed. Very rarely do these affect points of doctrine.

THE SCRIPT OF THE QUR'AN

The Arabic script in which the first exemplars of the Qur'an were written consisted of 14 basic letter forms which represented 28 different consonants.

Short vowels were not indicated at all and long vowels only infrequently. In the course of the 7th century this defective script was perfected, first by the addition of dots above or below letters to differentiate consonants of similar shape but different pronunciation, then by marks above and below the letters indicating the three short vowel sounds of the Arabic language – a, i and u. These aids to pronunciation brought the written text into line with the orally transmitted text, producing a canonical text that was accepted by all Muslims.

An essential difference between the Islamic and the Jewish and Christian revelations can be appreciated at a glance by opening scholarly editions of the Hebrew Bible and the Greek New Testament and comparing them to the Qur'an. The texts of both the Hebrew Bible and the Greek New Testament are accompanied by extensive notes at the bottom of the page, listing large numbers of variant readings from the manuscript tradition. Both have long and exceedingly complex textual histories. The text of the Qur'an, however, is presented with no scholarly apparatus whatsoever; no variant readings from divergent manuscript traditions are listed. The consonantal text has been fixed from the year 650, when the Caliph 'Uthman established the text we have today both from the fledgling written tradition and, more importantly, from the memories of those men and women, contemporaries of the Prophet Muhammad, who had learned verses of the Qur'an by heart as they were revealed.

A young British Muslim recites from the Qur'an. The text rests on a kursi, the traditional wooden stand used to hold the Qur'an.

KUFIC SCRIPT

The earliest Arabic script takes its name from the town of Kufa in what is now Iraq, though it was in use well before the town was founded. There are a number of regional forms, but all are bold and angular. A modern form of Kufic is used throughout North Africa. This Kufic Qur'an, written on vellum, the finest kind of parchment, dates from the 9th or 10th century.

The red dots indicate vowel sounds. The system used in this manuscript was later replaced by a more accurate notation

The skill of the calligrapher lay in spacing the letters attractively on the page

The letters are widely spaced, rather than closely joined, as in modern Arabic script

Early Kufic Qur'ans are written on parchment, often trimmed to this rectangular shape and size

Buraq is the winged, human-headed beast that carried the Prophet on the Night Journey to Jerusalem and the seven spheres of heaven.

> It is He who has sent His Messenger with the guidance and the religion of truth, that He may uplift it above every religion, though the unbelievers be averse.
>
> [QUR'AN 9:33]

THE MESSENGER

Muhammad was the *rasul*, or messenger, who delivered God's word to humanity. He is also a Prophet, *nabi*. In the Islamic prophetic typology, which as we have seen includes the Prophets of the Old Testament as well as Jesus, the Prophet is in touch with the supernatural, and can perform miracles. Muhammad too was able to multiply food, cause stones to speak, split the moon. But Islamic tradition does not lay particular stress upon these miracles, with the exception of the Night Journey to Jerusalem (*'isra*). The Prophet's journey to Jerusalem and his ascent into heaven (*mi'raj*) on the back of the miraculous steed Buraq are referred to in the Qur'an, in the sura called "The Night Journey". The "Further Mosque" (*al-masjid al-aqsa*) in the first verse of this sura was located by the commentators in Jerusalem. However, the true miracle of Islam is the Qur'an itself, which eclipses all others.

But Muhammad was not simply the passive receptor and transmitter of the Qur'an. He had total understanding of the meaning of the words he transmitted, and had been in close contact with the divine. He is the exemplar of the perfect man (*al-insan al-kamil*) and the perfect Muslim. Because of his contact with the divine, and the fact that he alone of all mankind was chosen as recipient of the revelation, he is considered free of error (*ma'sum*).

It is thus incumbent upon Muslims to try to model themselves upon him. Unlike the Christian ideal of *imitatio Christi*, this form of emulation is not limited to the spiritual, but for males can include externals, such as dress, comportment, dignity, even physical features such as length of beard.

THE PROHIBITION OF IMAGES

Although there is no specific prohibition of human images in the Qur'an, Islamic tradition has been reluctant to accept images of humans or living things. Non-Arabic speaking cultures were more tolerant. Timurid and Safavid Iran, the Ottoman Turks and Mughal India all had traditions of figural art, but not sculpture. Their manuscript illuminations sometimes include images of the Prophet, but his face is always hidden by a veil.

The Name of the Prophet can be formed into a decorative design.

SUNNA AND HADITH

The men and women of the first generation of Muslims to whom Muhammad repeated the verses of the Qur'an are known as the *sahaba*, "Companions". Since they had direct contact with the Prophet, they were not only sources for the exact wording of revelation itself, but for the day-to-day behaviour of the Prophet, his deeds, sayings, and even his silences. The *sahaba* are thus the source for the *sunna* ("precedent"), an immense corpus of eyewitness reports of the public and private behaviour of the Prophet and the men and women who knew him. Each of these reports is known as a *hadith*, a word that is often misleadingly translated as "tradition", but which in fact simply means "news, report". Each hadith is composed of two parts. It is introduced by an *isnad*, or "chain of authorities", the first link of which is the name of one of the sahaba. The succeeding names in the isnad are the names of the men and women who heard the hadith from the previous name in the chain.

The second part of the hadith is the actual report, called the *matn*. This may be a saying of the Prophet on a particular occasion, in which case the exact words are reported, or an account of something he did or did not do.

Because all four schools of law accepted the principal of the primacy of Prophetic hadith as a key source for legal rulings, it became imperative to winnow these from what scholars of the time called "the raging sea of hadith". In the early 9th century, the hadith were collected into six main collections, organized on slightly different principles. This material, gathered from the oral tradition, forms the sunna, and together of course with the Qur'an, is one of the four "roots" (*usul*), or principles, of the *shari'a*, the Holy Law of Islam.

The most famous and earliest collection is the *Sahih* of al-Bukhari. The title, meaning "The Sound", indicates that the hadith it contains are authentic according to the precepts of the hadith collectors. Hadith criticism centred not on the actual report, the matn, but on the chain of transmitters, the isnad.

The names that occurred in the isnad had to be those of reliable, upstanding men and women. Not only that, it had to be shown that they could in fact have coincided in time and place so that the hadith in question could be properly transmitted. On these and other similar critera, the hadith were classified as sound, good or weak (*sahih, hasan, da'if*).

Al-Bukhari classifies his material under headings that key into the legal literature. The range of topics shows how comprehensive Islamic law is: Revelation, faith, knowledge, prayer, charity, pilgrimage, fasting, social and economic relations, merits of the Prophets, the Qur'an, marriage, divorce, medicine, manners, apostasy, dreams, the Unity of God.

HADITH AND ISNAD (CHAIN OF AUTHORITIES)

• *Isnad* (chain of authorities):

'Ubayd Allah ibn Musa related to us: 'Hanzala ibn Abi Sufyan reported to us on the authority of 'Ikrima ibn Khalid on the authority of 'Umar (May God be content with them both!): He said the Messenger of God (May Prayers and Peace be upon him!) said:

• *Matn* (text of *hadith*):

"Islam is built on five (things): the testimony (There is no god but God and that Muhammad is the Messenger of God); the performance of prayer; giving alms; the pilgrimage; and the fast of Ramadan."

Ayyub al-Ansari, *the Prophet's standard-bearer and one of the* sahaba, *was killed at the first siege of Constantinople in the 7th century. His tomb* (above) *in Istanbul was erected in 1458.*

Founded by the Fatimids *in the 10th century, al-Azhar in Cairo is the oldest university in the world, with the highest reputation in the study of the religious sciences ('ulum al-din). A fatwa, or legal opinion, issued by the 'ulama of the university is considered authoritative throughout the sunni Muslim world.*

SIRA

The Prophet is referred to by name five times in the Qur'an, four times as Muhammad and once as Ahmad, a version of the same name. There are references to the fact that he was an orphan, but otherwise there are no materials in the Qur'an with which to reconstruct his biography. Nor would there be, for the Qur'an is not "about" Muhammad, but is God's message to humanity.

In order to understand that message, however, it was necessary to know, insofar as possible, the circumstances of the revelations of which the Qur'an is composed. It has already been pointed out that early Qur'ans divided the suras into two groups, those revealed in Mecca and those revealed in Medina. Many hadith with isnads reaching back to the sahaba recorded the exact circumstances under which a particular group of verses was revealed. In other words, a biography of the Prophet and the history of the first Muslim community could be reconstructed from the oral tradition. This would also allow a deeper understanding of the background of the revelation of the Qur'an and thus of the precise meaning of specific verses.

The earliest surviving biography *(sira)* of the Prophet is that of Ibn Ishaq, who died in 767. We do not possess Ibn Ishaq's original, but an edited version done in the early 9th century by a scholar named Ibn Hisham. Later biographies, some of which add new material, are for the most part based on Ibn Ishaq.

The *sira* of Ibn Ishaq is thus a primary source for the life of the Prophet. It is based on hadith, but includes poems and even documents, like the "Constitution of Medina", fundamental to an understanding of the earliest Muslim community.

'ILM AND FIQH

'Ilm, "knowledge", is the technical term for knowledge of the Qur'an and its exegesis as well as the legal decisions of the Prophet and the sahaba as recorded in the hadith. A scholar who has attained this knowledge through the demanding, lifetime's study required, is an *'alim* (plural *'ulama*). The 'ulama are custodians of the system of divine law which regulates the lives of Muslims. They have not hesitated to correct rulers and try to bring them back on the right course. Today the most revered institution for the training of 'ulama is al-Azhar in Cairo. The rulings of the 'ulama of al-Azhar have great authority throughout the Muslim world.

Fiqh is a Qur'anic term meaning "understanding". It refers to the task of understanding the duties incumbent upon Muslims as revealed in the Qur'an and the sunna, and the implications of these two sources for individual and social action. The specialist in this area of Islamic learning is a *faqih* (plural *fuqaha*). The standard compendia of fiqh are normally divided into two parts, one dealing with religious duties, the other with social duties and human relationships, including political theory.

SHARI'A

All aspects of the lives of Muslims, public and private, are in theory governed by divine law. The *shari'a* is the system of divine law that governs worship, ritual, conduct, and legal matters such as commercial contracts, marriage, divorce, and inheritance. The ultimate point of this system is entry to Paradise for the believer. The shari'a maps the road to salvation.

Like many other key words in Islam, shari'a has the original sense of "way, path". The systemization of the shari'a began in Umayyad times and was completed under the early 'Abbasids, slightly before the compilation of the canonical collections of hadith. The key figure in its elaboration appears to have been al-Shafi'i, who firmly based the shari'a on the sunna of the Prophet. Only Prophetical hadith were acceptable as legal proofs, that is hadith whose chains of authority led back to the Prophet himself.

SCHOOLS OF LAW

There are now four major mainstream schools (*madhahib*, singular *madhhab*): Malikiyya, Hanifiyya, Shafi'iyya, and Hanbaliyya, each named after its founder. Shi'a Islam follows the Ja'fariyya, which takes its name from the seventh Imam, Ja'far al-Siddiq.

DIETARY LAWS

The four categories of prohibited *(haram)* foods are carrion, blood, pork and offerings to pagan gods.

> These things only has He forbidden you: carrion, blood, the flesh of swine, what has been hallowed to other than God.
>
> [Qur'an 2:168]

The shari'a also prohibits the flesh of scavengers and carnivores, animals killed by a blow to the head or strangled, amphibious animals, insects and birds of prey with talons. Wine, and by extension, alcohol and other intoxicating substances are also forbidden. The Hanafi school of law prohibits shellfish. For meat to be lawful *(halal)*, it must be slaughtered under hygienic conditions by a mature Muslim of sound mind approved by the religious authorities. The animal's throat must be cleanly cut, severing respiratory tract, oesophagus and jugular. The name of God must be invoked before partaking of a meal.

These young men are studying the principles of fiqh *(Islamic jurisprudence) at a madrasa in Inner Mongolia, China.*

The Malikiyya, or Maliki, school is named after Malik ibn Anas, a *qadi*, from Medina, who died in 795. He is the author of the earliest law code, the *Muwatta'*. Malik recognizes four sources, or roots, of Holy Law: the Qur'an, sunna, customary law of Medina and the consensus *(ijma')* of the jurisconsults *(fuqaha)* of Medina. As the city of the first organized Muslim community, the practice of Medina was held to be closest to the Prophet and his Companions. This school of law is followed in Upper Egypt, North Africa except for Libya, parts of West Africa, the Sudan, Kuwait and Bahrain.

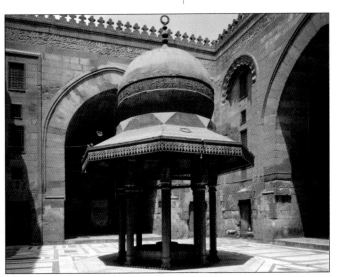

The four schools of law *in a madrasa are often arranged around the four sides of a courtyard, as here at the Sultan Barquq madrasa in Cairo.*

The second school is named after Abu Hanifa (699–767), a jurisconsult of Iranian origin. The Hanifiyya accepts the principle of reasoning by analogy, *qiyas*, basing a decision, in the absence of specific guidance from the Qur'an or sunna, on a similar case, guided by the principle of *istihsan*, "choosing the best solution". This school was the official school of law under the Ottoman empire. Today it rules the lives of Muslims in China, India, Pakistan, Afghanistan, Central Asia, the Caucasus, Turkey and the Balkans.

The founder of the third school was al-Shafi'i, who died in Cairo in 820. It was he who established a methodology for deriving law from the sunna, arguing that only Prophetical hadith could be used. Hadith from the Companions were disallowed. He held that the sunna served only to explain the Qur'an, and could not contradict it. He stressed the role of consensus *(ijma')*. Today the Shafi'iyya is the predominant school in Lower Egypt, Palestine, East Africa and Indonesia.

The Hanbaliyya, or Hanbali, school is named after Ahmad ibn Hanbal (780–855), a student of al-Shafi'i. He was even more rigorous than al-Shafi'i, rejecting all sources but Qur'an and sunna. This school was followed by the Wahhabi reform movement, and is today followed in Saudi Arabia, Oman and Qatar.

Towards the end of the 10th century it was felt that these four schools had effectively exhausted the possibilities of the Qur'an and sunna for the formulation of the shari'a. Only in modern times have scholars once again turned to the sources themselves with a fresh eye.

THE QADI

The shari'a is implemented by the *qadi* (from the verb *qada*, "to carry out"). The qadi must be learned in the shari'a and of recognized probity. He is appointed by the ruler. The institution took shape in Umayyad times, and was fully elaborated under the 'Abbasids. The Chief Qadi *(qadi al-qudat)*, residing in the metropolis, has authority over those in provincial towns. The qadi is assisted by official witnesses, whose task is to testify that correct procedures are followed. Plaintiffs have the right to be judged by the law of whichever school they follow. The shi'a, however, do not recognize the authority of sunni courts.

Pious men have always been concerned by the lack of separation between the executive and judiciary, fearing political interference. Even more worrying is the possibility of making a wrong judgement, and there are many cases in Islamic history of men refusing from moral scruples to accept the position of qadi.

PUNISHMENT

Human actions are classified by the specialists in Islamic law into five categories: obligatory, recommended, disapproved, forbidden and permissible. Obligatory actions are those that bring a reward in the afterlife, but punishment in the afterlife for omission. Recommended actions bring reward, but no punishment. Forbidden actions bring punishment, but reward for avoidance. Disapproved actions bring reward for avoidance, but no punishment for performance. Permissible actions are neutral, bringing neither reward nor punishment.

The punishments *(hudud)* for crimes like murder and theft are set out in the shari'a. Voluntary murder is punished by death, although this can be commuted if the offended parties agree to compensation. Involuntary murder or wounding is settled by compensation, theft by cutting off the right hand, brigandage by death, adultery by 100 lashes for both men and women, and the same for drinking wine and spirits. Stoning for adultery is based on the sunna, while the punishment of 100 lashes is Quran'ic. Standards of proof in a shari'a court are rigorous – four adult male witnesses are necessary to prove adultery. As a leading early jurist remarked, "Seldom do four witnesses come together on such a matter."

MARKET INSPECTORS [MUHTASIB]

Despite the comprehensive nature of the shari'a, it is limited by its sources, and there are many areas in which it is silent. The conflict between the ideal of rule by divine law and economic and political reality is a constant in Islamic history. Public order in the great Islamic cities was kept by the police. Markets were regulated by a *muhtasib*, a market inspector, who was responsible for keeping public order, testing weights and measures and checking the quality of goods. Several medieval manuals for market inspectors have survived, and give fascinating glimpses of urban life in medieval cities.

The market inspector *was in charge of public order and fair trading in the markets of traditional Islamic cities.*

WOMEN

The Qur'an specifically addresses both men and women, and women are as responsible for their actions before God as are men. They are legally inferior, however. A Muslim man may marry a non-Muslim, but the children must be raised in the Islamic faith; a Muslim woman may not marry a non-Muslim. In certain circumstances a woman's testimony in a shari'a court is worth half that of a man. The inheritance rights of women are guaranteed in the Qur'an, but a sister receives only half the portion received by her brothers. A woman's husband is obliged to provide for her and her children, but polygamy is accepted, and a man may take up to four wives, provided he looks after them equally. He may also take an unlimited number of concubines. In the modern world polygamy is rare and concubinage has vanished.

Marriage is a contract, sanctioned of course by divine law. In sunni Islam, the woman's guardian, usually her father, establishes the contract in her name. The shi'i, on the other hand, regard the contracted woman as a legal entity co-equal with the groom. The groom pays a dowry, the *mahr*, which is returned to the wife if divorced. The shari'a, following the Qur'an, discourages divorce, calling it "the worst of all possible things", but nevertheless recognizes that sometimes it is unavoidable as a last resort. A man may divorce his wife unilaterally, by pronouncing the *talaq*, the formula "I divorce thee!" three times. The first two pronouncements must be followed by a waiting period, in order to determine that the wife is or is not pregnant. If she is, she will have custody of male children until the age of 7 and female till the age of puberty, defined by the various schools of law as 15 or 18. The same rule applies to custody from the form of divorce known as *khul'*, which is divorce instituted by the wife. In this case, the wife forfeits the dowry received from her husband on marriage. This form of divorce can only be validated with the consent of the husband, except under Maliki law, which recognizes the authority of the court in this matter in cases of irreconcilable differences.

There is a famous verse in the Qur'an [4:34] which states that it is licit to beat a rebellious wife. Early jurisconsults softened the natural consequences of the text by concluding that beating was licit, but could only be done with the small stick used to clean the teeth – essentially a toothbrush. They thus brought the verse into line with the Prophet's well-attested kindness towards and respect for women.

The status of women varies enormously from country to country within the Islamic world. Here a group of young women attend a study group in a mosque in Morocco.

The Qur'an contains just one single reference to the veil: "and let them cast their veils over their bosoms and not reveal their adornments save to their husbands" [Qur'an 24:10]. This has been interpreted to mean anything from concealing the hair and obscuring the shape of the body to full concealment. The term *hijab*, veil, is often extended to mean the seclusion of women from the view of non-kin. The modern hijab is often a scarf covering the hair and tied under the chin, plus modest dress. The wearing of Islamic dress, *ziyy islami*, a mark of Muslim identity, is widespread among young Muslim women and men living in Europe.

The imam *delivers the Friday sermon from a pulpit called a* minbar *as in this illumination from a medieval manuscript showing a preacher in the mosque at Samarkand.*

THE PILLARS OF ISLAM

It is in the Sahih of al-Bukhari that the idea that there are five basic principles of the Islamic faith is first enunciated. They are the profession of faith, prayer, charity, fasting and pilgrimage. By the 10th century, these had come to be called the Five Pillars *(arkan)* of Islam.

THE PROFESSION OF FAITH [SHAHADA] The *shahada* is the Muslim profession of faith: "There is no god but God; Muhammad is His Messenger" *(la ilaha ila llah; Muhammadun rasul allah)*. The word shahada has a legal sense, "witness", and the pronunciation of this formula in Arabic, prefaced by a statement of intent and before qualified witnesses, is all that it takes formally to become a Muslim. This simple statement expresses total commitment to the message of Islam. Abu Hanifa, the founder of the Hanafiyya madhhab, gives the definition: "Faith is professing with the tongue, counting true with the mind and knowing with the heart."

PRAYER [SALAT] There are five daily prayers; dawn, noon, afternoon, sunset and evening. The worshipper faces towards the Ka'ba in Mecca as he prays. The worshipper must be in a state of ritual purity before praying, and this is accomplished by *wudu'*, "ablutions".

The direction of prayer is called the *qibla*, and is indicated in mosques by an empty niche in the wall called the *mihrab*. The correct way of performing ablutions, the wording of prayers, number of bows *(rak'at)*, position of the hands during prayer, are all meticulously laid out in the shar'ia. Worshippers normally repair to the mosque for the noon prayer. On Fridays, prayers are communal. They are led by an imam, literally "one who stands in front", who also delivers a sermon, called the *khutba*.

The mihrab *indicates the* qibla *or direction of Mecca and worshippers face it when they pray. This mihrab is in the Great Mosque of Córdoba.*

FASTING IN ISLAM

The aim of fasting is to attain, through the discipline of denial, a peaceful, devout state of mind, putting away all evil thoughts.

"O you who believe,
fasting has been
prescribed for you just
as it was prescribed for
those before you, so that
you will be godfearing."
[Qur'an 2:183]

A crowd of worshippers *in Cairo gives thanks at the festival of 'Id al-Fitr, which marks the end of the fast of Ramadan.*

OPPOSITE

Pilgrims *perform the* tawaf, *the sevenfold circumambulation of the Ka'ba, one of the key rites of the* hajj.

ALMS [ZAKAT] The giving of alms is fundamental to Islam, and charity is a form of worship. The *zakat* is obligatory, as the tithe was in medieval Christianity, and was levied in fixed proportions according to the wealth of the individual. The shari'a stipulated 10 percent of crops, 2 ½ percent of income. In the absence of any duly constituted authority to collect it, the *zakat* should be paid voluntarily. The alms are to be used for the relief of the poor, for the necessities of travellers, to ransom captives, to free debtors, and for other charitable purposes. In addition, all Muslims who can afford to should also give voluntary alms, called *sadaqa*.

FASTING [SAWM] The lunar month of Ramadan is set aside for fasting. The fast lasts from sunrise to sunset each day for thirty days. Adults must let nothing pass their lips during the hours of fasting. This applies not only to food and drink, but to tobacco smoke, for example. They must abstain from sexual contact and from all antisocial behaviour. The observance of the fast of Ramadan unites all Muslims in a common enterprise and creates great social cohesion. The object is to subdue the passions and draw nearer to God by purifying one's being through self-denial. The fast is broken after sunset and before dawn by meals, and the streets of any Muslim city are filled with joyous crowds at night during Ramadan. Many people perform *tarawih*, voluntary worship during the night hours. Very often the entire Qur'an is recited. For this purpose, the text is divided into thirty equal portions to correspond with the nights of Ramadan. Ramadan ends with 'Id al-Fitr, the "Festival of Fast Breaking", one of the two major festivals of the Islamic calendar, celebrated on the first day of the month of Shawwal. A special tax called the *zakat al-fitr* is levied to provide food or money to the poor so that they may particpate in the 'Id al-Fitr. This festival is also known as the 'Id al-Saghir, "The Little Festival", as opposed to the 'Id al-Kabir, "The Big Festival", which is celebrated at the completion of the pilgrimage.

PILGRIMAGE [HAJJ] The annual pilgrimage to Mecca re-enacts the Prophet's pilgrimage of 630, which in turn enacted events associated with the life of Abraham. It is incumbent upon every Muslim of sound health who can afford to do so to try to make the pilgrimage at least once in his lifetime, and it is the dream of all Muslims to make the hajj. The pilgrimage to Mecca is one of the most remarkable mass pilgrimages in the world, bringing pilgrims from all over the world to the city where the Prophet received the first revelation of the Qur'an. In the course of their lives, all of the pilgrims have faced the Ka'ba thousands of times while performing the daily five prayers, and to finally see the focus of those prayers is an event of tremendous emotional impact.

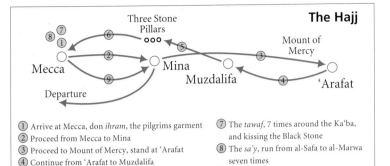

The Hajj

① Arrive at Mecca, don *ihram*, the pilgrims garment
② Proceed from Mecca to Mina
③ Proceed to Mount of Mercy, stand at 'Arafat
④ Continue from 'Arafat to Muzdalifa
⑤ Sacrifice, doffing the *ihram* and Stoning the Pillars
⑥ Proceed from Three Stone Pillars to Mecca
⑦ The *tawaf*, 7 times around the Ka'ba, and kissing the Black Stone
⑧ The *sa'y*, run from al-Safa to al-Marwa seven times
⑨ Return to Mina and departure

The Hajj, the pilgrimage to Mecca that all Muslims try to make at least once in their lives, takes place in the twelfth month of the Islamic calendar, Dhu al-Hijja. The route taken and actions performed are based on events in the life of the Prophet.

The Hajj takes place between the eighth and the thirteenth days of the last month of the lunar calendar, Dhu al-Hijja. Mecca is surrounded by a sacred precinct called the *haram*. When the pilgrim approaches the outer limit of the precinct, he must enter a state of ritual purity by bathing, having his hair and nails trimmed, removing jewellery and headgear and donning two seamless white garments, one wrapped around the waist and the other around the upper part of the body. This is called the *ihram*. As they don the ihram, the pilgrims declare their intention of making the pilgrimage and pronounce the *talbiya*, a phrase that declares their presence before God: "Here I am, O God, at thy service!"

The pilgrims now enter the haram and proceed to the Great Mosque in whose central courtyard stands the Ka'ba. Now they perform the *tawaf*, the circumambulation of the Ka'ba. They move at a rapid pace around the Ka'ba, which is draped in a black embroidered covering called the *kiswa*, seven times anticlockwise. They then perform the *sa'y*, the "Running", between two small hills called al-Safa and al-Marwa, now linked by an arcade.

The Hajj proper begins on the eighth day of Dhu al-Hijja. All the pilgrims proceed to Mina, outside Mecca, where again, following the practice of the Prophet, they meditate overnight. The next day they move on to the plain of 'Arafat, 9 miles (15 km) from Mecca, for the *wuquf*, "The Standing". They assemble at the base of *Jabal Rahma*, the "Mount of Mercy", where the Prophet delivered his farewell sermon. Here they again pray and meditate, from noon to sunset, examining their consciences and seeking God's mercy. The Prophet said: "The best of prayers is the prayer of the Day of 'Arafat", and for Muslims this is the culmination of their spiritual life.

After the sun has set, they proceed to Muzdalifa, about 4 miles (7 km) on the way back to Mina, where they pass the night. The next morning, the 13th of Dhu al-Hijja, they continue on to Mina, passing three pillars at which each pilgrim casts seven stones. One of the pillars represents Satan. The 'Id al-Adha, "Festival of Sacrifice" now commences. Camels, goats and sheep are ritually slaughtered and the pilgrims partake of a celebratory meal. (The festival, also called the 'Id al-Kabir, is celebrated throughout the Muslim world, and is the second major festival of the Islamic calendar.) Those pilgrims who have not already done so now return to Mecca to perform the *tawaf* and the

It is the custom in Aswan in Upper Egypt for returning pilgrims to decorate the fronts of their houses with scenes of Mecca and their pilgrimage.

sa'y. The pilgrimage is now officially over, and to indicate that the pilgrims have passed out of a state of ritual purity the men have their heads shaved and the women a lock cut from their hair.

JIHAD

Jihad is not one of the "pillars" of Islam, although the importance of the concept caused some early scholars to consider placing it among the primary Muslim duties, and it is sometimes considered "the sixth pillar". Jihad means "struggle, exertion". Two kinds are distinguished, the "Greater"and the "Lesser" Jihad. This distinction goes back to a Prophetical hadith. The "Greater Jihad" is the struggle against evil that all Muslims engage in throughout their lives, and it is this that is emphasized in the tradition.

The "Lesser Jihad" is "legal war", which unlike the Greater Jihad, is a collective, rather than personal, activity. The war must be legally declared by the Caliph. The enemy must be unbelievers whose territory borders on Islamic territory. Before the opening of hostilities, they must be invited to convert to Islam. If they accept, they then form part of the community of believers. If not, there are two possibilities. If they are conquered by force, the prisoners of war become the property of the leader. Movable property, after subtraction of the fifth part set aside for the poor, is divided among the warriors. Women and children must not be harmed. Trees must not be cut down, or herds upon which the livelihood of peasants depends driven off. "People of the Book", originally Jews and Christians, but later other groups with scriptures, have a privileged status and maintain the free exercise of their religion on payment of a head tax, the *jizya*. This codification of the rules of legally declared war is based on the practice of the Prophet in his wars against the pagan tribes of Arabia. The Muslim armies that conquered the Byzantine and Persian empires in the 7th century were on jihad. Accounts of their conquests make a point of showing that they observed the stipulations of the shari'a, particularly with regard to the treatment of subject populations and division of booty. At various times in Islamic history, groups within the Islamic community have declared jihad upon each other. The Isma'ilis, for example, declared their sunni enemies "unbelievers" in order to be able to wage war against them legally. So did the Almoravids in the 11th century, who declared the Muslim rulers of Spain "unbelievers" because of their failure to implement the shari'a. Since it is expressly forbidden in the sunna for Muslim to make war on Muslim, both these movements were discredited in the eyes of leading jurisconsults.

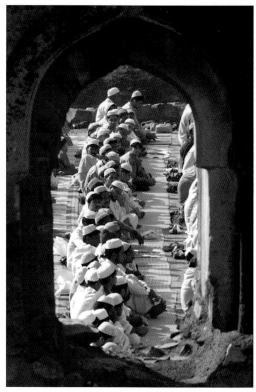

Muslims in Delhi *gather to pray at the festival of 'Id al-Adha, which marks the end of the Hajj.*

JIHAD
The duty of the believer is to spread the faith. This stern injunction is softened by the Qur'anic verse: "There is no compulsion in religion." This is taken to refer to the "people of the Book" who have protected status within the *umma*.

So let them fight in the way of
God who sell the present life
for the world to come; and
whosoever fights in the way of
God and is slain, or conquers, we
shall bring him a mighty wage.
[Qur'an 4:75]

THE MOSQUE

ALL MOSQUES, however grand in scale and richly decorated, conform to one simple basic pattern. The essential elements of a mosque are highlighted here on the great Selimiye Mosque in Edirne, built in 1569–75.

The muezzin mahfili is a raised platform, on which the muezzin stands when chanting responses to the imam (head of the mosque).

The mihrab, an ornate niche in the wall marks the direction of Mecca. The prayer hall is laid out so most people can see it.

The loge provided the Ottoman sultan with a screened-off balcony where he could pray, safe from would-be assassins.

The minbar is a lofty pulpit to the right of the mihrab. This is used by the imam to deliver the Friday sermon.

AUTHORITY IN ISLAM

Religious authority in the Muslim community resides in the Qur'an and sunna. There is no organized "church", with a hierarchy of authority, and there is nothing comparable to a priesthood, since there are no sacraments. Marriage is a contract. Mosques are places of worship, but are not consecrated ground. Islam is thus a "lay theocracy", and every Muslim is in a sense his own priest, as he himself carries out the obligations of his religion and has access to scripture.

Many mosques have a board outside, giving the times of prayer. These vary through the year with the times of sunrise and sunset

Minarets
The mosque's four slender minarets each have three balconies

Dome
The dome was the proudest achievement of Sinan, the great Ottoman architect. His aim was to surpass the dome of the great Byzantine church, the Hagia Sophia

Sultan's Loge
The loge is supported on green marble columns. It has its own ornately decorated mihrab

Mihrab
The niche is made of carved Marmara marble

Prayer Hall
The Selimiye's interior is exceptionally light because of the number of windows in the dome and surounding arcades

Ablutions Fountain
Intricate pierced carving decorates the top of the 16-sided open fountain.

Supporting Columns
The mosque's dome rests on eight massive pillars arranged in an octagon

Muezzin mahfili
Only very large mosques normally have a rostrum of this kind for the use of the muezzin

After the death of the Prophet in 632, political and religious leadership of the community passed to the caliphs. The word "caliph", *khalifa* in Arabic, simply means "successor". The first four caliphs – Abu Bakr, 'Umar, 'Uthman and 'Ali – were all related to the Prophet, the first three by marriage, 'Ali by blood. They are known as the "Rightly-Guided Caliphs" because all had direct access to the Prophet, and thus to the sunna. All were from the tribe of Quraysh, and all were elected to the caliphate *(khilafa)*. Jurists later codified the qualifications for the caliphate as any member of the tribe of Quraysh, of sound mind and body, who had been elected to the caliphate by his peers. Early divisions within the Muslim community centered on succession to the caliphate. The Shi'a, the "Party of 'Ali," believed that 'Ali was the natural successor to the caliphate by reason of his close kinship to the Prophet, and restricted the line of succession to his descendants.

Before performing *their five daily prayers, Muslims must ritually purify themselves by ablutions* (wudu').

By early 'Abbasid times, the major religious obligation of the caliph was to ensure that the shari'a was carried out. The class of men learned in the shari'a, the 'ulama, became the real authority in the Islamic empire. A scholarly elite, open to anyone with the requisite talents who had followed the gruelling course of study under recognized authorities, was formed and it was this elite that elaborated classical Islamic civilization.

THE UMMA

The word *umma* for the community of Muslims goes back to the establishment of the first Muslim community in Medina in 622. The fundamental concept, akin to the Greek idea of an oecumene, is that tribal, national and ethnic loyalties are subordinate to a larger concept, that of the brotherhood of all Muslims [Qur'an 49:10]. All members of the faith are equal, and this includes members of sectarian movements. This is why the use of words like "orthodoxy" borrowed from the Christian tradition make no sense in an Islamic context. Whatever their differences over the Caliphate, Shi'i and Sunni are equal before God.

The umma *embraces the whole worldwide community of Islam, from the wealthy Gulf states to the people shopping in this humble market in Gambia. The notion of a single Islamic community is in some ways similar to the the idea of Christendom invoked in medieval Europe.*

Outward signs proclaim the *umma*. The performance of the stipulated prayers at the stipulated times, the call to prayer itself, the shared fast of Ramadan, the Pilgrimage, the reading of the Qur'an and saying of prayers in the Arabic language, family structure, legal system, dietary laws, position of women and the custom of veiling, the use of the *hijri* calendar, urban organization and institutions – all these and many more serve to create an unmistakable Muslim identity. The flexibility and pragmatism of Islamic law has allowed great diversity in local practice, clear to anyone who has travelled in Muslim lands.

HISTORY OF THE ISLAMIC WORLD

The irruption of Arab armies from the Arabian Peninsula in the 7th century, bearing the message of Islam, remains one of the world's great epics. Within a few decades they had reached the Atlantic coast, entered Europe, and stood on the borders of China and India. The enduring legacy of this achievement is a tribute to the resilience of the Islamic social order.

Much of the history of Islam *is marked by fierce fighting for control of West and Central Asia. In this miniature painting (c.1591) the Mughal emperor Babur does battle with his cousin Tamal.*

Pre-Islamic Arabia

▨	Byzantine Empire
▨	Sasanid Empire
QURAYSH	Arabian tribe

THE CALIPHATE

WHEN MUHAMMAD DIED on June 8, 632, he had no living male heir. There were four candidates to succeed him as leader of the Muslim community: Abu Bakr, 'Umar, 'Uthman and 'Ali. As things turned out, each served in turn as successor (khalifa) to Muhammad. They are known as "The Rightly-Guided Caliphs" because they all had heard the revelation from the Prophet himself and been guided by his example.

Although 'Ali was most closely related to the Prophet, it was Abu Bakr who was elected Muhammad's successor. By a mixture of force and diplomacy, he brought the tribes of Arabia, who had renounced their allegiance to the Muslims on the death of the Prophet, back to obedience and sought a common enterprise to unite them. Following the Prophet's last wishes, he sent them, under Meccan leaders, against the Byzantine and Persian empires. Abu Bakr received news of the first victory shortly before his death in 634.

Under his successor, 'Umar, the Byzantine army was annihilated at Yarmuk in Palestine. In 638 'Umar entered Jerusalem, alone and simply clad, astonishing a populace used to the pomp of the Byzantine emperors. He was welcomed by the Patriarch Sophronios, and granted lenient terms to the city, guaranteeing that the Christian churches would not be destroyed or taken over by the Muslims. No effort was made to convert Christians and Jews, who enjoyed freedom of worship in protected communities governed by their own laws. While in Palestine, 'Umar set up the administration of the empire, organizing taxation of the conquered lands and pensions for Muslim warriors and their families. He retained local institutions, and for some years Greek in former Byzantine provinces and Pahlavi in former Sasanid provinces continued to be the languages of administration.

In the spring of 637, the Muslims won a major victory over the Sasanids at al-Qadisiyya, near Ctesiphon. In 642 another victory at Nehavend added all of Persia to the Muslim empire. The same year saw the fall of Alexandria, key to naval control of the Mediterranean. The Muslim armies that conquered Egypt were assisted by the Coptic population, who like the Nestorians and Monophysites of Iraq and Syria had suffered under Byzantine persecution.

'Umar was assassinated by a Persian Christian slave in 644. An advisory council chose 'Uthman to succeed him. Under 'Uthman, what is now Libya was added to the growing empire. Armenia was subjugated and Mu'awiya, whom 'Umar had appointed governor of Syria, built a navy and fought a number of naval battles against the Byzantines, at one point besieging Constantinople. 'Uthman's most enduring action was the establishment of the authorized text of the Qur'an. During his caliphate, 'Uthman was accused of showing undue favouritism to his own clan, that of Umayya. Disaffected troops from Egypt went to Medina to present their grievances, but negotiations broke down and 'Uthman was killed. The murder of 'Uthman and the choice of 'Ali to succeed him opened a rift among Muslims that persists to this day.

The Umayya clan, which included Mu'awiya, governor of Syria, refused recognition to 'Ali on the grounds his supporters had been implicated in the murder of 'Uthman. The conflict came to a head in 657 at Siffin, near the Euphrates. 'Ali and his partisans confronted Mu'awiya and his powerful army. Unwilling to spill the blood of fellow Muslims, 'Ali agreed to submit their differences to arbitration. The arbitrators decided against 'Ali, choosing Mu'awiya as caliph.

A 6th-century mosaic map of *Jerusalem, found at Madaba in Jordan, shows the city with its many Christian pilgrimage sites, as it would have appeared when 'Umar entered it in 638. The magnificent colonnaded main street was built by the Roman emperor Hadrian in the 2nd century CE.*

The Byzantines fought *many wars against the forces of Islam, Their secret weapon was Greek fire, the main ingredient of which was naphtha. It was propelled against enemy shipping from the nozzle of a plunger-driven device.*

**THE TWELVE
SHI'I IMAMS**

'Ali 656-661

Hasan 661-669

Husayn 669-680

Zayn al-'Abidin . . .680-712

Muhammad
al-Baqir 712-c.735

Ja'far al-Sadiq 735-765

Musa al-Kazim 765-799

'Ali al-Rida 799-818

Muhammad
al-Taqi al-Jawad . . .818-835

'Ali al-Hadi 835-868

Hasan al-'Askari . . .868-873

Muhammad al-Mahdi
*(The 12th imam vanished.
The shi'a, who call him the
"Awaited One", believe he will
return at the end of time as the
Mahdi to bring peace and
justice to the world.)*

**The Church of St John the
Baptist** *in Damascus was
transformed into a mosque in
Umayyad times. It is decorated
with magnificent mosaics sent by
the Byzantine emperor to
Damascus for the purpose.*

The supporters of 'Ali believed that he should have been the immediate successor of Muhammad, and that he had thrice been unfairly passed over. The schism of Islam into sunni and shi'i dates from Siffin. The sunni, or *ahl al-sunna wa l-jam'a*, "the people of custom and community" believe the caliph is Muhammad's successor only as ruler of the community, and that the caliphate is elective within the Prophet's tribe, Quraysh. The shi'i, (from *shi'at 'Ali* or partisans of 'Ali), believe the caliphate, which they call the imamate, is non-elective, and that the head of the Muslim community must be a descendant of Muhammad. They hold that the imam inherits the Prophet's spiritual knowledge and the ability to interpret Divine Law in its light.

Another faction was born out of the negotiations at Siffin. This was made up of those who refused recognition to either party. They considered the caliphate to be open to any observant Muslim of sound mind and body. They are called Kharijites *(khawarij)*, meaning "those who withdrew". They formed a radical egalitarian sect that for years caused havoc throughout the Muslim world.

In 661 'Ali was assassinated by a Kharijite in Kufa. The Kufans proclaimed his son Hasan caliph, but Hasan relinquished his rights to Mu'awiya, who had already been accepted by most Muslims as the legitimate caliph.

The Umayyads

Mu'awiya moved the capital from Medina to Damascus, from where he had governed Syria. The abandonment of the apostolic simplicity of the oasis of Medina, city of the Prophet, for a thriving, cosmopolitan city, filled with magnificent classical buildings and with a large Christian population, symbolized a fundamental change in the development of Islam.

Later Muslim historians accused the Umayyad caliphs, with one exception, of being kings, rather than caliphs. The word king, *malik*, had a pejorative sense in Arabic, for the Arabs had no tradition of kingship. Mu'awiya and his successors lived in palaces and built magnificent hunting lodges in the Syrian steppe. The ruling Arab military elite was proud of its Arab origins, cultivating the poetry and song of pre-Islamic times, at the same time adopting the luxuries of the civilizations they had conquered.

Mu'awiya maintained the unity of the empire, but could not eradicate the simmering discontent of the shi'i or the threat of the growing numbers of non-Arab voluntary converts to Islam *(mawali)* who felt excluded from the privileges enjoyed by Muslims of Arab descent. Before his death in 680, Mu'awiya obtained with great difficulty recognition from his advisory council of his son Yazid as his heir.

The shi'i refused to recognize Yazid as caliph, and urged 'Ali's son Husayn, grandson of the Prophet, to claim the caliphate by force. Yazid's army met him and his small band of followers at Karbala, not far from Kufa. Husayn lost his ten-year old nephew, two sons and six brothers, before he too, the last to die, met his fate. In 683, an Umayyad army invaded Arabia to crush another claimant to the caliphate. They sacked Medina and attacked Mecca. During the battle the Ka'ba caught fire, and Mecca was only saved from destruction by the death of Yazid.

In 685 the caliph 'Abd al-Malik came to power. He ruled for 20 years, creating an administrative structure, based on Byzantine models, that lasted, with modifications, throughout classical Islamic civilization. He made Arabic the language of administration, set up a postal system and issued the first Islamic coinage. He had the irrigation canals in the Tigris-Euphrates valley restored and introduced the Indian water buffalo to the Iraqi marshes. During his reign, Muslim armies reached the borders of Chinese territory, while in the west, the conqueror 'Uqba ibn Nafi' founded Kairouan and rode all the way to the Atlantic.

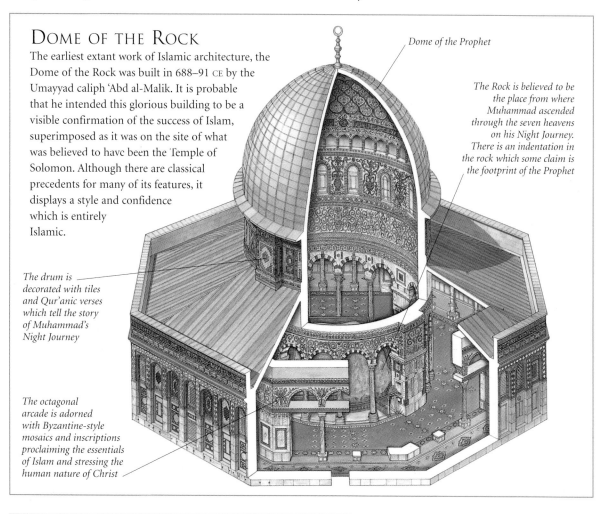

DOME OF THE ROCK

The earliest extant work of Islamic architecture, the Dome of the Rock was built in 688–91 CE by the Umayyad caliph 'Abd al-Malik. It is probable that he intended this glorious building to be a visible confirmation of the success of Islam, superimposed as it was on the site of what was believed to have been the Temple of Solomon. Although there are classical precedents for many of its features, it displays a style and confidence which is entirely Islamic.

Dome of the Prophet

The Rock is believed to be the place from where Muhammad ascended through the seven heavens on his Night Journey. There is an indentation in the rock which some claim is the footprint of the Prophet

The drum is decorated with tiles and Qur'anic verses which tell the story of Muhammad's Night Journey

The octagonal arcade is adorned with Byzantine-style mosaics and inscriptions proclaiming the essentials of Islam and stressing the human nature of Christ

THE SECOND WAVE OF CONQUESTS

The pacification of the central lands of the caliphate meant attention could be turned once more to conquest. The armies that had so recently been engaged in fighting each other, were now unleashed on North Africa, Spain, and the lands beyond the Oxus. In these regions, the Arabs were entering unfamiliar territory, far from the heartlands of the empire, and far from their supply bases.

In 710 a small group crossed the Strait of Gibraltar on reconnaissance. Meeting no opposition, the decision was taken to invade Visigothic Spain the following year. Led by a Berber convert to Islam named Tariq, a larger army crossed over in 711 and crushed the Visigothic army in a single battle. He was followed by his commander-in-chief, Musa ibn Nusayr, and by 713 all Spain, with the exception of Asturias in the far north, was in Muslim hands.

While the conquest of Spain was under way, another army, far to the east, crossed the Jaxartes River, having first subdued all of Transoxania, and fought all the way to Kashgar, on the borders of China. The year was 712. Simultaneously, yet another army reached the Indus and took Multan in the Punjab. It is said that the caliph received news of all three conquests on the same day. The territory of the empire had been doubled, and stretched from the Atlantic to the Indus.

In 718, Muslim forces crossed the Pyrenees and took Narbonne. In 725 they sacked Lyon and Vienne. A large force of Arabs and Berbers crossed the Pyrenees once more in 732, intent on sacking the shrine of St. Martin at Tours, one of the richest religious foundations in Gaul. They were finally turned back outside Poitiers by Charles Martel.

The conquest of Byzantine lands had not been completed. In 717, the year before the Muslims crossed the Pyrenees into Gaul, the Umayyad caliph Sulayman mounted a combined land and sea assault on Constantinople which ended in failure, due to the superb fortifications of the city, a bitter winter and the use of Greek fire by the defenders.

Umar II succeeded Sulayman on the latter's death in 717. He is the one Umayyad caliph of whom later chroniclers approved. He made a concerted effort to resolve the most serious social conflict in the empire, the position of the non-Arab converts to

This coin issued by 'Abd al-Malik shows the caliph imitating Byzantine usage. Later in his reign, 'Abd al-Malik removed images from coins, retaining only Arabic legends.

Islam. Despite the fact that they had accepted Islam, they were still forced to pay the taxes levied on non-Muslims. Umar rectified this situation, and ordered that they should be treated as equals of the Arabs. Those that had fought against the pagan Turks in Transoxania were granted state pensions. Unfortunately, these reforms, and others, came too late to stop the tide of discontent that was sweeping the empire. Umar II died after a reign of only three years, before his thoughtful and wide-ranging reforms could take effect.

In the last years of the Umayyads, a secret organization rallied to its cause various groups hostile to the ruling dynasty, among them many shi'i and non-Arab Muslims. In 747 the black flags of rebellion were unfurled in Khurasan in the name of a descendant of the Prophet's uncle, 'Abbas. The army of the last Umayyad caliph was defeated and all members and clients of the dynasty hunted down and exterminated. Only one young prince survived the debacle, 'Abd al-Rahman, who escaped to Spain, where he founded the brilliant dynasty of the Spanish Umayyads.

The growth of the Islamic world

- Muslim lands by 634
- Muslim lands by 656
- Muslim lands by 756
- → Muslim raid, with date
- ● new city founded by Muslims
- ▣ Muslim fortress
- ⚔ Muslim victory, with date
- ✕ Muslim defeat, with date
- 649 date of Muslim conquest
- Byzantine Empire c.610
- Sasanid Empire c.610
- Frankish Empire c.610

THE 'ABBASIDS

The 'Abbasids transformed the Arab empire of the Umayyads into a multiethnic Muslim empire. The government was no longer a *mulk*, a temporal kingdom, but a theocracy ruled by the Caliph, who was now styled "The Shadow of God Upon Earth". The cohesive factor in the empire was Islam, and all believers were equal. The *mawali* had finally come into their own, their original ethnic and cultural identity submerged in the *umma*. The power of the Arab aristocracy was over in the heartlands, although many of the older ways continued at the neo-Umayyad court in Cordoba. 'Abbasid society was dominated by Muslims of non-Arab origins, largely Persian.

BAGHDAD

To symbolize the change, the centre of power was shifted from Syria to Iraq, and a new capital built, Baghdad. The name of the city, significantly, is Persian, and means "Gift of God". It comes from the name of a small village that stood on the site of the new city. Baghdad is on the banks of the Tigris, not far from the Sasanid capital of Ctesiphon. Al-Mansur, the caliph who founded the city, chose the site because of the good air and the fact that the Tigris was a major commercial artery, linking the city to the Gulf and ultimately to the sea route to China, already opened by Muslim traders.

Baghdad was founded in 763, with due attention paid to the conjunction of the planets so the first stone could be laid on a propitious day. The core of the city, housing the caliph, his administrators, slaves and personal guard, was laid out according to cosmological principles, probably of Persian origin. It was circular, with concentric circuits of walls marking off the different quarters. In the centre was the Caliph's Palace. The walls were pierced by four gates, orientated to the four points of the compass. Beyond the outer wall of the Round City, suburbs grew up, and Baghdad shortly became one of the largest cities in the world, with a population larger than that of Constantinople. It was conventionally referred to as Madinat al-Salam, "The City of Peace".

The Umayyad caliphs had ruled like exalted Arab tribal leaders, and even the most autocratic of them had consulted councils of tribal and military leaders before taking important decisions. The 'Abbasid caliphs radically broke with Arab tradition in this and all other ways. The caliphs of Baghdad were absolute monarchs, holding the power of life and death over their subjects. Like the Sasanid Shahs, they were remote from the people, appearing only on ceremonial occasions, to lead the Friday prayers and the army on major campaigns.

The 'Abbasid caliphs all assumed throne names when they came to power, and these names all proclaim their dependence upon God, and at the same time divine support for their authority. They were descended from al-'Abbas, the

Prophet's uncle, and were therefore of the same clan, Hashim.

THE WAZIR

The *wazir*, anglicized as vizier, was the head of the bureaucracy, the *diwan*. The institution itself is almost certainly of Iranian origin, as is the word. The principal function of the vizier was to raise money and oversee the workings of an ever-expanding and complex bureaucracy. In early 'Abbasid times, the vizier was

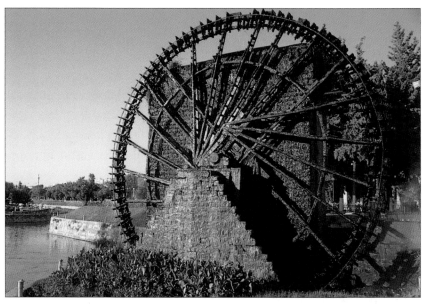

almost always a non-Arab. The famous Barmakid family, which provided a succession of viziers to the early caliphs, originated in Balkh, where they had been custodians of the famous Buddhist temple of Nawbahar.

This bureaucracy was staffed by clerks, *kuttab*, largely of Persian origin, and these formed an elite literate class that played an important cultural role, both producing and consuming the literary works that accompanied the 'Abbasid cultural renaissance. It was in early 'Abbasid times, coinciding with the foundation of the dynasty, that the Chinese technique of making rag paper was introduced first to Samarkand, then to Baghdad. The presence of a cheap, readily available writing material not only contributed to the growth of the bureaucracy itself, but to general literacy among the public. Baghdad and other metropolitan areas had well-stocked libraries, bookshops, popular authors and avid readers.

The army was formed largely of Persians and other non-Arabs, later predominantly of Turks. The volunteer tribal armies of the conquests were a thing of the past, and the commander-in-chief of the army, the *amir al-'umara*, became a powerful and often dangerous figure in the government.

The administration was modelled on that of Sasanid Persia, with many elements taken over from the Umayyads. The postal system, similar to the pony express of the American west, was used for official communications. Urgent messages were sent via pigeon-post. The postal system doubled as an intelligence service, for it linked all the provinces of the enormous empire to Baghdad and its agents regularly reported to central government on everything from the activities of dissident sects to the state of the harvest.

The noria (Arabic na'ura), *a device for lifting water from one level to another, is only one of the technologies that revolutionized agriculture in Islamic times.*

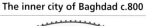

The inner city of Baghdad c.800

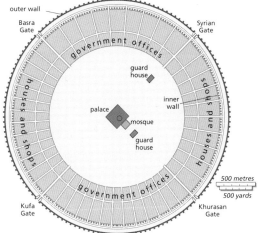

outer wall
Basra Gate
Syrian Gate
government offices
guard house
houses and shops
inner wall
shops and houses
palace
mosque
guard house
government offices
500 metres
500 yards
Kufa Gate
Khurasan Gate

Founded in 763, *the new 'Abbasid capital of Baghdad quickly became the commercial and cultural hub of the empire. The city was planned in every detail, with the caliph's palace and government offices at the centre.*

This 10th-century plate *from Nishapur, decorated with elegant Kufic script, shows the sophistication of 'Abbasid ceramics. Baghdad and other major cities had special quarters devoted to the various crafts: leatherworkers, metalworkers, bookbinders, jewellers, weavers, dyers, druggists and papermakers.*

TRADE AND PROSPERITY

Baghdad became the largest and wealthiest city in the world, rivalled only by Constantinople and far-off Xian, capital of T'ang China. The caliphate was ideally situated for the creation of a global trading network. Islamic shipping dominated both the Mediterranean and the Indian Ocean and colonies of Muslim merchants were established in the ports of western India, East Africa, Indonesia and China. Gradually Islam spread far beyond the political confines of the 'Abbasid empire.

The founding of the caravan city of Sijilmassa in southern Morocco in 757 opened up a trans-Saharan trade in the gold, ivory, slaves and ostrich feathers of sub-Saharan Africa, and this gold, together with silver and gold from mines in Central Asia, fuelled the economy of the empire.

Trade was encouraged by a stable bimetallic currency, the silver dirham and the gold dinar. These two coins, with a fixed weight that scarcely varied, became the standard for later European coinages and have been found in great quantities in archaeological excavations as far north as Scandinavia.

New ideas, technologies, plants and crafts flowed along the complex of land and sea routes which led to Baghdad and the provincial capitals. The expansion of commercial activity led to the development of sophisticated banking and exchange techniques. A letter of credit issued in Baghdad could be honoured in Sijilmassa or Samarkand. Trade stimulated crafts and craftsmen organized mutual-benefit societies which offered social services, caring for orphans, endowing schools and lodging travellers. Hospices for lodging travellers were built not only in cities, but along major trade routes.

During the reigns of Harun al-Rashid and his son al-Ma'mun Greek scientific and philosophical texts were systematically translated into Arabic, stimulating the development of Islamic science.

THE CALIPHATE IN DECLINE

Political decline, however, was already apparent even during the reign of Harun al-Rashid. Two years after he came to the throne in 786, an independent shi'i regime was established in far-off Morocco. The founder, Idris, was a great-grandson of Hasan. In 800, Harun al-Rashid granted another western dynasty, the Aghlabids in what is now Tunisia, virtual autonomy against an annual cash payment. This meant that the caliphate had virtually no authority west of Egypt, and in 868 a Turkish warlord, Ahmad ibn Tulun, seized that wealthy province.

Turkish slaves captured in Central Asia filled the ranks of the 'Abbasid army. Superb fighting men, they were indispensable but hard to control. As time went on they made and unmade caliphs at their will. They were so unruly in Baghdad that the caliph al-Mu'tasim built the city of Samarra to escape their violence.

OPPOSITE

The Mosque of Muhammad Ali, *the 19th-century ruler of Egypt, dominates the skyline of Cairo. The city was founded by the Fatimids in 963. With the eclipse of Baghdad, Cairo became the leading cultural, commercial and religious centre of the Arabic-speaking world.*

THE BREAK-UP OF THE 'ABBASID DYNASTY

In the 10th century, because of a combination of poor administration, inability to maintain the irrigation system upon which the agricultural prosperity of Iraq was based, growing salinity of the soil and above all the proliferation of independent dynasties, the revenues of the caliphate were much reduced.

In 945, an Iranian shi'i dynasty, the Buyids, occupied Baghdad. They were a Persian-speaking military elite, whose leaders only learned Arabic subsequent to their occupation of Baghdad. They took all economic and political power to themselves, even issuing coins in their own names with shi'i slogans.

Independent states proliferated: Tahirids, Saffarids, Samanids, Buwahids, Ziyarids and Ghaznavids in the east, Hamdanids in Syria, Tulunids followed by Fatimids in Egypt. Although this trend may have been regrettable from the point of view of Baghdad, it was beneficial for the spread of Islamic culture. Each of these dynasties emulated the court at Baghdad, attracting scholars, poets, musicians, architects and craftsmen. Under the Samanids, in Khurasan, Persian, written in the Arabic alphabet, reached the level of a literary language.

The idea of the caliphate, a united Islamic world, survived until 1926 when it was formally abolished. However, already in the second half of the 9th century political power was starting to pass from the caliph in Baghdad to dynasties of local rulers.

The Islamic imprint c.800–1200
- Islamic world c.1000
- 'Abbasid Caliphate at its greatest extent c.800
- campaigns of Seljuk Turks
- campaigns of Berbers
- further expansion of Islam
- ZIRIDS Muslim dynasty, with dates

1000 km
1000 miles

THE FATIMIDS

The sixth imam of the Shi'a, Ja'far al-Sadiq died in 765. His death led to a division in the Shi'a community that has lasted till the present. Ja'far had two sons, Isma'il and Musa. Isma'il was the elder, but his father disinherited him and appointed Musa heir to the imamate. The majority of shi'i recognized Musa, but a minority thought Isma'il was the legitimate imam. They are therefore known as Isma'ilis – one of the earliest, strangest and most successful of the dynasties that broke away from 'Abbasid control. They are also sometimes known as "Seveners", because Isma'il was the seventh in the line of succession that went back to 'Ali and Fatima, daughter of the Prophet, who gave her name to the Fatimid dynasty they founded.

The movement succeeded in establishing itself in Yemen, and from there sent agents to North Africa, where they mobilized a powerful army among the Berbers and in 903, in Kairouan, installed 'Ubayd Allah al-Mahdi as the first Fatimid caliph. The assumption of the title of succession to the Prophet was a direct challenge to the 'Abbasid caliphate.

'Ubayd Allah founded the port of Mahdiya, on the Tunisian coast, from where he and his followers almost succeeded in conquering the Islamic world. They took over much of North Africa and Sicily, then turned their eyes to Egypt. In 969, Jawhar, the general of al-Mu'izz, the fourth Fatimid caliph, conquered Egypt with an army of 100,000 men and began the construction of a splendid new capital: Cairo (al-Qahira).

In 868 Ahmad Ibn Tulun, the governor of Egypt, declared his independence from the 'Abbasids. The mosque he built at Fustat, now part of Cairo, is one of the glories of early Islamic architecture. When the Fatimids conquered Egypt in 969, they sited their capital al-Qahira (Cairo) nearby.

Under the Fatimid caliph al-Aziz (975–996) and his exceptionally competent wazir, Ya'qub ibn Killis, Egypt became the richest and most stable land in the Islamic world. The Fatimid navy dominated the Mediterranean, and Alexandria became once more the great market of the east. They also opened up the Red Sea route to India, diverting lucrative trade from the Gulf and Baghdad.

Al-Aziz was succeeded by his son, al-Hakim, whose cruel and erratic reign was marked by savage persecution of Jews and Christians and stern ordinances forbidding women to leave their homes. Some radical groups considered him semi-divine, and one of these has survived, the Druze of Lebanon and Syria.

The high point of Fatimid power was reached with the caliphate of al-Mustansir (1036–94). In 1057 a Fatimid general even briefly took Baghdad. Toward the end of al-Mustansir's long reign, Fatimid power decreased and overtaxation of the Egyptian population led to serious upheavals.

This ivory pyx depicting the pleasures of courtly life is from 10th-century Córdoba and is inscribed with the name of a son of the caliph 'Abd al-Rahman III.

THE UMAYYADS IN SPAIN

The only survivor of the 'Abbasid massacre of the Umayyads, 'Abd al-Rahman, called "The Immigrant", reached Spain, and in 756 was accepted by the various Arab factions as their ruler. Under the Umayyads al-Andalus, as the Arabs called the Iberian Peninsula, became the most heavily urbanized and richest country in Europe. They encouraged trade and agriculture, introducing sophisticated irrigation systems and new cash crops such as sugar, cotton, saffron and indigo.

In 929, 'Abd al-Rahman III took the title of caliph, an act of supreme defiance towards his 'Abbasid enemies. During his reign, his capital Córdoba became the richest and most sophisticated city in Europe, with a population of perhaps 500,000, at a time when Paris numbered some 38,000. Córdoba was famous for its mosques, palaces and libraries, one reportedly housing 500,000 manuscripts.

In the late 10th century, the brilliant and devious chamberlain (*hajib*), al-Mansur, led biannual campaigns against small Christian kingdoms in the north of the peninsula. In 997 he sacked and destroyed the shrine of Santiago de Compostela, the principal pilgrimage site in Europe, "the Mecca of the Christians". Al-Mansur died in 1002, and with him the military glory of the Umayyads. In 1018 Córdoba was sacked and burned by disaffected Berber troops. The dynasty effectively came to an end in 1031, when a group of prominent Cordobans simply abolished the Umayyad caliphate. Al-Andalus fragmented into numerous small kingdoms, each based on a provincial capital, some Arab, some Berber, and at least one Slavic – for numerous Slavs had served in the caliphal armies.

This scene of chess players is from a manuscript of the 13th-century Cantigas de Maria, a collection of songs in praise of the Virgin by Alfonso X, who set them to popular Arab melodies.

THE RECONQUISTA

By the 11th century, however, a small pocket of Christian resistance had begun to grow. Alfonso VI took Toledo, the former capital of the Visigoths, in 1085. It was the beginning of the period the Christians called the Reconquest (*Reconquista*), and it underlined a serious problem that marred this refined and graceful era: the inability of the numerous rulers of Islamic Spain to maintain their unity. This so weakened them that when the various Christian kingdoms began to pose a serious threat, they were forced to ask the Almoravids, a North African dynasty, to come to their aid.

The Almoravids (*al-murabitun*) were Sanhaja Berbers of the Sahara. Like their modern descendents the Touareg, the men of the Sanhaja veiled their faces, which contributed to the fear they instilled in their enemies. They were a puritan, reforming movement dedicated to jihad. In the years before they crossed into

Spain they had conquered large areas in Ghana. They then moved north and swept through Morocco. In 1086, led by the fearsome Yusuf ibn Tashufin, founder of Marrakesh, they crossed the Strait of Gibraltar and drove back the Christian armies. They then killed or exiled the Muslim rulers who had summoned their aid and established themselves in the splendid cities of al-Andalus, where the luxurious life quickly tempered their puritan zeal. The dynasty came to an end in 1147 at the hands of another Berber reforming dynasty, the Almohads.

The Christian victory *over the Almohads at Las Navas de Tolosa in 1212 marked the beginning of the end for the Muslim kingdoms of the Iberian Peninsula.*

This movement was founded by Ibn Tumart, a Masmuda Berber who proclaimed himself the Mahdi, "The Guided One". The Almohads (*al-muwahhidun,* "those who proclaim the unity of God") strove to restore Islam to its original purity. Ibn Tumart passed the torch of leadership to his companion and friend, 'Abd al-Mu'min, who took the title of caliph and declared jihad against all who opposed him. In 1146 he annihilated the Almoravid army at Tlemcen and the following year took Marrakesh, the Almoravid capital. His empire soon stretched from Spain to the Egyptian border.

In 1170, the Almohads chose Seville as their capital, and it is here that they produced two of their finest works of architecture, the Torre del Oro and the Giralda, transformed from minaret to bell-tower when the city was reconquered by the Christians in 1248. Like the Almoravids, the Almohads did not last long. Their army was virtually annihilated in the battle of Las Navas de Tolosa in 1212 by a coalition of Christian kings. The surviving Almohads fled Spain, and the *Reconquista* moved relentlessly forward.

GRANADA

In the last two centuries of their rule, the Muslims of Spain created the kingdom for which they are most famous: Granada. It seems as if they suddenly realized that they were a people without a country, and set about building a memorial: the Alhambra. This magnificent palace was begun in 1238 by Muhammad ibn al-Ahmar who, to buy safety for his people when King Ferdinand of Aragon laid siege to Granada, offered to become the king's vassal in return for peace.

The Alhambra, *built during the 13th and 14th centuries, is one of the most beautiful architectural complexes in the world, a fitting monument to the Muslim presence in Spain.*

His loyalty to Ferdinand eventually purchased another two and a half centuries for the kingdom of Granada. The last Muslim stronghold in Spain finally fell in 1492, the same year the New World was discovered by Columbus.

THE SELJUK TURKS

The arrival of the Seljuks in Islamic lands in the 11th century saved the Caliphate of Baghdad from succumbing to the Isma'ilis. The Seljuks were

The Ince Minare Madrasa in Konya, built in 1260, is so called for its "slender minaret", partly destroyed by lightning in 1900. Konya was the Anatolian capital of the Seljuk Turks. The facade of the madrasa is remarkable for its almost baroque decoration of intertwined stone ribbons bearing calligraphic inscriptions.

Oghuz Turks, whose original homeland lay in the vast steppe north of the Caspian and the Aral Sea. The Muslims had encountered the adept Turkish-speaking horsemen and archers of this region when they first crossed the Oxus in the 7th century. Many were recruited to the caliphal armies and some Turkish commanders were powerful enough to establish their own dynasties. The powerful Ghaznavid dynasty, whose most famous ruler was Mahmud of Ghazna, conqueror of northern India, was founded by a military commander who had served the Samanids.

Around 960, a group of Oghuz clans abandoned their shamanist beliefs and embraced sunni Islam. Their ancestral, semi-legendary leader was named Seljuk (*Saljuq*). After his death, power over the clans passed to his son Arslan, who began to push into the territory of Mahmud of Ghazna. Arslan's nephews, Tughril and Chaghri Beg crossed the Oxus and seized the key garrison town of Merv. In 1040 they defeated the armies of Mahmud of Ghazna. This victory marked the beginning of Seljuk power.

Between 1040 and 1060, the Seljuks fought bitterly against the Buyids, winning and then losing Baghdad several times. The Buyids went so far as to ally themselves with the Fatimids, their former enemy, but to no avail. The power of the sunni caliphate was restored and the staunch support of Tughril Beg and his troops put an end to Fatimid dreams of universal dominion.

In 1058 the caliph crowned Tughril Beg "King of the East and West", delegating the defence of the empire to him. His title was Sultan, a word that simply means "power". This power, and with it the responsibility of defending the Muslim community both from attack from without and schism from within, remained in the hands of Turkish-speaking peoples until the abolition of the caliphate in 1926.

The enemy without was the Byzantine empire, which had taken advantage of the weakness of Buyid rule to regain important territory in Anatolia, Armenia and Syria. The Byzantines were catastrophically defeated at the battle of Manzikert in 1071, and the emperor taken prisoner. The Byzantine defeat changed the demography of Anatolia forever. It ceased being a land of Greek speech, as Turkoman tribes and other Turkish groups sought new pastures in the wake of the Seljuk conquests, settled and eventually founded local dynasties. The loss of their richest territory was a blow from which Byzantium never recovered.

THE CRUSADES

Arab historians at the time considered the Crusades a minor irritant, dwarfed by the demographic, political and social transformation triggered by the coming of the Seljuks and the devastation wrought by the Mongols in the 13th century.

Threatened by Seljuk expansion after the battle of Manzikert, the Byzantines appealed to Pope Urban II for military aid. The Seljuk victory and the Almoravid invasion of Spain that occurred not long afterwards created a Christian reflex: Holy War. In 1095, Pope Urban II declared a "Truce of God", urging Christian leaders to lay aside their quarrels and unite in a crusade to recover the Holy Land.

The difficulty of the enterprise was daunting. The Christian armies, drawn from all over Europe, made up of volunteers, younger sons of noble houses, mercenaries, kings, adventurers and camp followers, had to cross thousands of miles of unfamiliar, hostile country to face an enemy of which they knew almost nothing. Yet these motley armies, driven by a combination of faith, greed and a desire for adventure, succeeded in taking Jerusalem in 1099. By this time, Seljuk power was waning, due to infighting over the succession, their inability to produce a durable political structure, and the invasion of yet another group of steppe nomads, the Kara Khitai, on their eastern frontier.

The crusaders were able to establish principalities along the Levantine coast, based in cities whose names still resound with romance: Aleppo, Antioch, Edessa, Tripoli and Acre. The Muslim response was at first confused and limited. When they did counter-attack, besieging Edessa in 1144 and retaking Aleppo, the Second Crusade was launched. It was a disaster. An attempt to take Damascus was repulsed, and the Emperor Conrad and King Louis VII returned in ignominy to Europe.

One of the leaders to oppose the crusaders was a Turkish commander, Zangi, who retook Edessa in 1144. His son Nur al-Din, famous in Arabic annals as a model of the just ruler, united Syria and Iraq, blocking the advance of the crusaders.

THE CRUSADES

- 1st Crusade (1096–9): Capture of Jerusalem.

- 2nd Crusade (1146–8): Siege of Damascus fails.

- 3rd Crusade (1189–92): Crusaders take Acre, but fail to retake Jerusalem.

- 4th Crusade (1202–4): Crusaders take Constantinople.

- 5th Crusade (1217–21): Attack launched on Egypt.

- Crusades of St. Louis (1248–54 & 1270): On first Louis IX of France is captured while attacking Egypt: on second he dies outside Tunis.

The capture of Jerusalem *by the crusaders in 1099 was a bloody affair, in which the mostly Christian population was put to the sword.*

Saladin was the most brilliant general to oppose the crusaders. His victory at Hattin in 1187 effectively broke crusader power.

The Ayyubids, *the dynasty founded by Saladin continued for some 60 years after his death in 1193, but as was often the case with military dynasties, in fragmented form.*

Nur al-Din had two trusted Kurdish generals, Shirukh and Ayyub. Ayyub was the father of perhaps the most famous Arab ruler of the time, Salah al-Din, "Saladin". When the crusaders, whom the Arab chroniclers always referred to as "Franks", a portmanteau term for all Europeans, decided to wrest Egypt from the hands of the now decadent Fatimid caliphate, Nur al-Din sent Shirukh and Saladin to prevent this. On Shirukh's death in 1169, power passed to his nephew, Saladin, founder of the Ayyubid dynasty. In 1171, Saladin abolished the Fatimid caliphate and restored the name of the 'Abbasid caliph in the public prayers. Sunni Islam was once more the official faith of Egypt.

With Egypt as his base, Saladin took the offensive against the crusaders. In 1187 he invaded Palestine, destroying the crusader army at the battle of Hattin. Jerusalem was occupied, and except for the coastal city of Tyre, the Holy Land was once more in Muslim hands. He eventually ruled not only Egypt, but Yemen, much of North Africa, Palestine, Syria and Armenia. He actively encouraged trade, which had declined during the last years of Fatimid rule, allowing Genoese and Venetian merchants to trade freely in Alexandria and other ports. The Red Sea route to India was under his control, and taxes on imports and exports formed an important part of his revenues. Saladin became a byword in medieval Europe for chivalry and bravery, often depicted as the bosom friend of Richard the Lionheart. Indeed much of the chivalric tradition, including heraldry, was brought to Europe by returning crusaders.

THE ASSASSINS

Isma'ili influence did not disappear with the Fatimids, but took a new form. At the death of the Fatimid caliph al-Mustansir, in 1094, another schism occurred, one group following his younger son, who succeeded him, the other his older, who had been put to death. Those who followed the older son, Nizar, formed a new, radical movement dedicated to destabilizing Seljuk rule by a campaign of assassination. These Nizari Isma'ilis, known to the crusaders as "Assassins", conducted a terror campaign, targeting for the most part sunni leaders. Their base was Alamut, in northern Persia, from where they sent agents to assassinate prominent sunni leaders. They twice made attempts on Saladin's life. The sect was led by Rashid al-Din Sinan, "The Old Man of the Mountain".

Map

BYZANTINE EMPIRE

SELJUKS OF RUM
Konya

Lake Van

LITTLE ARMENIA

Tarsus

Edessa

Mayyafariqin
1185: taken by Saladin

Antioch
PRINCIPALITY OF ANTIOCH

Aleppo
1183: taken by Saladin

Mosul

Mediterranean Sea

KINGDOM OF CYPRUS

Krak des Chevaliers

SYRIA

MESOPOTAMIA

Euphrates

Tigris

COUNTY OF TRIPOLI

Acre
8 Jul 1187: Surrenders to Saladin
1191: Recovered by Crusaders

Damascus
1174: taken by Saladin

Baghdad

Hattin
4 Jul 1187: Christians defeated by Saladin

to Tripoli and Gabes

Alexandria

KINGDOM OF JERUSALEM
Jerusalem
2 Oct 1187: taken by Saladin

Dead Sea

200 km
200 miles

Cairo
1169–71: Fatimid Caliphate overthrown by Saladin

EGYPT

Nile

HEJAZ

Red Sea

Qus

Aswan

Yenbo

Medina

to Ibrim

to Yemen

Saladin and the Ayyubid Sultanate 1169–1193

- maximum extent of Crusader states 1144
- Saladin's advance 1174–84
- other Ayyubid campaigns 1174–90
- routes of Third Crusade 1188–92
- Zangids 1127–1222
- dominions of Saladin 1193
- other Muslim states 1193
- Crusader states 1193
- other Christian states 1193

THE MONGOLS

In the 13th century, the Islamic heartlands faced yet another invasion of steppe nomads, more terrible than any that had gone before. These were the Mongols, led by Genghis Khan. They were a confederation of tribes, some Mongol and some Turkish, united by Genghis Khan in 1206. By 1218, he had succeeded in subduing the steppe peoples and turned west. The Mongols invaded the lands of the Kara Khitai, which brought them to the northern borders of Islamic territory, held by the Khwarizm Shahs. The following year, the Muslim Turkish Shah of Khwarizm massacred a party of 450 merchants on their way back from Mongolia. Genghis Khan considered this an attack on his own authority, and in 1220 led his armies into Khwarizm territory, taking Samarkand and Bukhara, then the two great cities of Merv and Nishapur.

Genghis Khan died in 1227, and two years later his son Ögödei was chosen as Khan of the Golden Horde. A new invasion of Muslim lands was launched, and by 1240 the Mongols had occupied western Iran, the Caucasus and much of Iraq. Three years later they defeated the Seljuk sultan of Anatolia.

In 1255, another Mongol army led by Hülegü Khan, grandson of Genghis, crossed the Oxus. He had been ordered to conquer Islamic lands as far as Egypt. In 1258 he sacked Baghdad, massacred the inhabitants and put the last 'Abbasid caliph, al-Musta'sim, and all the members of his family to death. Baghdad was looted, then burned to the ground. The ancient systems of irrigation were destroyed. The devastation was so complete that in many areas agricultural recovery is still incomplete.

In 1260 the Mongols turned towards Palestine and Egypt. Here they encountered the Mamluks, now the ruling dynasty of Egypt. Alerted to the danger facing them by a chain of signal fires stretching from Iraq to Egypt, the Mamluks had time to marshal their forces. They confronted the Mongols in Palestine, at 'Ayn Jalut, "The Well of Goliath" and defeated them – the first time a Mongol army had ever met defeat in the field.

A Mongol dynasty, the Il-Khans, ruled Iran until 1380, when they fell before yet another invasion from the steppes, that of Timur. With time, the Il-Khans embraced Islam and became patrons of art and architecture. The assimilative powers of Islam were as strong as ever.

MONGOL RULERS

Genghis Khan and his sons all led conquering armies westwards into Central Asia. This illustration is from a manuscript of Rashid al-Din's detailed history of the Mongol conquests.

The Mamluks learned much from Mongol methods. Their displays of archery from the back of a galloping horse were particularly impressive. This illustration is from a Mamluk manual of the equestrian arts.

THE MAMLUKS

The Mamluks who defeated the Mongols at 'Ayn Jalut in 1260 are remarkable not only for their military prowess. Mamluk means "possessed", hence "slave", and the rulers of this dynasty were of non-Muslim origin, purchased as slaves and often bearing the names of their owners. They were converted to Islam, educated and trained in the martial arts. Most were of Turkish, Mongol or Circassian origin, and retained their native languages.

There were two dynasties of Mamluks, which ruled in succession. The first were the Bahri Mamluks, who ruled from 1260, when Baybars took power after the victory of 'Ayn Jalut, until 1382. The Burji Mamluks who succeeded them were typically Circassian in origin, and ruled until their defeat by the Ottomans in 1517. The words *Bahri* and *Burji* (Nile and Tower) refer to the position in Cairo of the garrisons that housed them.

Baybars was perhaps greatest of the Mamluk rulers. He is one of the few Muslim rulers to be the subject of a romance, the *Sirat Baybars*, which can still, just, be heard recited in the coffee shops of Damascus. His many campaigns against the crusader states led to the final expulsion of the crusaders from Muslim territory under his successors. He repeatedly defeated Mongol assaults, but exchanged embassies with the Khan of the Golden Horde in his native Kipchak territory north of the Black Sea, and he and his successors forged commercial treaties with European monarchs, encouraging trade, which they taxed heavily.

In 1261 Baybars brought an uncle of the last 'Abbasid caliph to Cairo in order to confer legitimacy upon his reign. These shadow caliphs were given a pension and the task of supervising pious endowments *(awqaf)* and their income. Their presence was merely symbolic, and they were without power.

The Mamluks ruled Egypt and Syria, uniting them into a single state and the cities of Cairo, Jerusalem and Damascus are still studded with fine examples of Mamluk architecture. Baybars' magnificent tomb in Damascus still stands, as do his school and mosque in Cairo. The destruction of Baghdad and devastation of the Tigris-Euphrates valley shifted the focus of the Arabic-speaking world from Iraq to Egypt, with Cairo replacing Baghdad as the main centre of commerce and learning.

Timur invaded India in 1398, sacking Delhi in the same year. Babur, the 16th-century founder of the Mughal dynasty claimed descent from Timur, and through him from Genghis Khan.

TIMUR

Timur Lang ("Timur the Lame") was born in Transoxiana in 1336, into a Mongol tribe that had embraced Islam. He claimed, falsely, to be a descendant of Genghis Khan, although he did marry a princess related to the great conqueror. He led the last of the great Turko-Mongol nomad invasions – in many ways the most destructive of all. In 1380, having formed a coalition of Tatar, Mongol and Turkish nomads, he began a series of far-reaching campaigns that led him east as far as Delhi, where he massacred 80,000 people, and as far west as Russia.

Before putting the populations of the cities he conquered to the sword, he carefully set apart all those with special skills, and sent them to Samarkand, which was transformed into one of the loveliest cities in the world. Scholars, musicians, poets and artisans, brought to Central Asia to beautify Timur's capital, established a courtly style that spread throughout the region, reaching Afghanistan and India.

Timur's motives are hard to assess. He called himself the scourge of God, sent to punish men for their sins. He died in the town of Otrar in 1405, where the Khwarizm Shah had murdered merchants travelling under Mongol protection and unleashed the fury of Genghis Khan. At the time of his death, he was on his way to conquer China. The descendants of Timur were passionate lovers of architecture and science. Ulugh Beg, his grandson, founded a magnificent observatory at Samarkand and prepared a catalogue of the co-ordinates of the stars that was the most accurate yet to appear. The Mughal rulers of India traced their descent from Timur, and through him to Genghis Khan. They venerated their ancestor not only as world conqueror, but as a spiritual master.

Timur destroyed what was left of Baghdad in 1393, then sacked cities, killing their entire populations throughout Iraq. In 1400 he destroyed Aleppo, and many other of the principal cities of Syria, making huge towers of the heads of the dead, as was his custom. The following year Damascus fell, and the Umayyad mosque, one of the earliest and most beautiful Islamic buildings, was burned. 1402 found Timur in Anatolia, where he defeated and captured the Ottoman ruler Bayezid in the battle of Ankara.

The campaigns of Timur

- Empire of Timur
- Ottoman Empire
- Mamluk Sultanate

Campaigns of Timur: 1379–1405

- → against Khwarizm and Persia 1379–88
- → against Golden Horde 1388–91 and 1395
- → against Sultanate of Delhi 1398–99
- → against Mamluk Sultanate and Baghdad 1399–1401
- → against Ottomans 1402
- → planned invasion of China 1404–05
- ⚔ city sacked by Timur

OTTOMAN SULTANS

Mehmed II, *conqueror of Constantinople, painted by Sinan Bey in about 1480.*

(cont. p.70)

THE OTTOMANS

The Mongol invasions damaged the Seljuk empire in Anatolia beyond repair. Turkish nomadic tribes, fleeing before the Mongols, migrated into former Seljuk territories and small Turkish principalities arose in Anatolia, each centred on a former Byzantine city, and each dedicated to war against the Byzantines. The warriors who raided across the Byzantine frontier were called ghazi (raiders), but the word came to be almost an honorific, meaning a man who had risked his life and possessions to expand the Dar al-Islam, the Abode of Islam.

The westernmost of these principalities was founded in the early 14th century by Osman, whose name is commemorated by the empire that grew from this small beginning: Osmanli in Turkish, Ottoman in English.

The Ottomans captured Bursa in 1326 and this became their first capital. It became a major commercial centre, especially for the silk trade. Osman's son Orhan invaded Europe in 1354, taking Gallipoli. From this beachhead the Ottoman armies moved on to Adrianople, which became their European base for further expansion. They reinforced their position by transferring Turkish nomads and villagers to the European side of the Bosphorus. By 1372, the Ottomans had reduced the King of Bulgaria to vassalage and controlled the main routes through the Balkans.

It was during this period that the Janissaries, the elite corps of the Ottoman army, were formed. It was made up of Christian prisoners of war who embraced Islam and was under the command of the sultan himself. The name comes from the Turkish *yeni çeri* (new troops). The Janissaries were not allowed to marry, and were bound together through membership of the mystical Bektashi order. Personal mystical belief had been part of Islam since the beginning, but the formation of mystical sufi brotherhoods coincided with the rise of the Turkish ruling dynasties. These orders, devoted to mystical union with the divine through ecstatic practices, organized in strict hierarchies, proliferated and spread rapidly throughout the Islamic world.

One by one the Balkan rulers were reduced to submission, retaining their positions against payment of a yearly tribute. They formed part of the Ottoman empire, and had the duty of defending it against its enemies. Meanwhile the empire continued to expand in Anatolia at the expense of rival Turkish dynasties.

Under Bayezid, "The Thunderbolt", uprisings in the Balkans forced the elimination of many vassal states, and a centralized empire began to take shape. At the battle of Nicopolis in 1396, Bayezid crushed a coalition of European princes sent to oppose the expanding empire. The flower of European chivalry was left dead on the field, mostly French knights who charged straight into Bayezid's army of 60,000 men. Ten thousand prisoners were decapitated.

The growth of the Ottoman empire

- Ottoman Empire and vassals 1512
- conquests of Selim I, 1512–20
- conquests of Sulayman I, 1520–66
- Ottoman conquest, 1566–1639
- Austrian Habsburg possessions
- Spanish Habsburg possessions
- Venetian Republic and possessions
- - - - vassal border
- ---- frontiers 1600
- ••••• frontiers 1913
- Holy Roman Empire
- ⚔ 1538 battle, with date

The Ottoman empire expanded most rapidly in the course of the 15th and 16th centuries, notably under Selim I and Sulayman I (the "Magnificent").

The euphoria of victory was short-lived. A new, more formidable enemy had appeared on the eastern border of Ottoman dominions. Timur invaded Anatolia and defeated the Ottomans at the battle of Ankara in 1402. Bayezid was taken captive and committed suicide shortly afterwards. Ottoman lands were reduced to the nucleus from which they had started just a short time before.

Remarkably Bayezid's son Mehmed and his successor Murad II were able to piece the empire together again. By the time of the death of Murad in 1451, the empire had been restored to its former territorial extent.

In the interval between the suicide of Bayezid and the death of Murad, an event of enormous consequence had occurred. Efficient cannon and arquebuses had been developed in Europe. These revolutionized warfare, military architecture, battle formations and above all society.

Selim "the Grim" (1512-1520)
*conquered Mamluk Egypt, greatly
expanding Ottoman territory and
the tax-base of the empire. Much
of the new wealth was spent on
public buildings in Istanbul.*

THE CAPTURE OF CONSTANTINOPLE

The Ottomans were a military state and quick to borrow and improve new technology. By 1453, when Mehmed the Conqueror camped beneath the walls of Constantinople, artillery had been perfected, and his huge cannon were able to breach the walls that had withstood Muslim sieges since the 7th century.

With the conquest of Constantinople, Mehmed ruled a Muslim empire from the city of Constantine, the first Christian emperor. One of his first acts on entering the city was to transform Hagia Sophia into a mosque. Constantinople was now Istanbul, and would remain the Ottoman capital for the next 469 years.

The capture of Constantinople was a watershed of European history, marking the division between medieval and modern history. Greek scholars fleeing the Ottoman advance contributed to the rebirth of classical learning in Europe, and the rediscovery of Greek philosophical and political texts radically transformed European society and thought. At the same time, blocked to the east by the now vast Ottoman empire, Europe began to look west to the Atlantic.

Mehmed had learned the importance of sea power during the siege, and took steps to create an Ottoman navy, with shipyards at Gallipoli. Naval control of the eastern Mediterranean and the Black Sea was of vital strategic interest.

Mehmed died in 1481, and immediately dissatisfaction that had been hidden while he lived welled up into open revolt. The Janissaries were tired of continual war, and wanted to enjoy the fruits of their estates. The coinage had been repeatedly debased and Mehmed had alienated the 'ulama by confiscating property administered as pious endowments. His two sons, Jem and Bayezid, disputed the succession, and fought a bitter war, Jem ending his life an exile in Europe. Bayezid II consolidated the empire formed by his father, but in 1512, old and ill, he was deposed by his son Selim. A new wave of Ottoman conquest began, this time in the east.

In 1500, Shah Isma'il had come to the throne of Iran, the first ruler of the Safavid dynasty. He made Shi'ism the religion of the state, despite the fact that the majority of the population were sunni. Conflict with the Ottomans was inevitable, for they were the upholders of sunni Islam. At the battle of Çaldiran in 1514, Selim defeated the Safavids, but conflict between the two states continued.

Selim then turned his attention to the Mamluks. In 1516 he led his armies against Syria and Egypt. He confronted the Mamluk army outside Aleppo and defeated it, killing the sultan al-Ghawri. He then marched on to Egypt, and in 1517 won another victory outside Cairo. True to their chivalric traditions, the Mamluks refused to use firearms and were cut down by Selim's cannon. Selim received the submission of the Sharifs of Mecca and Medina, and was now protector of the Holy Cities. Control of the Red Sea and Aden, emporium of the Indian Ocean trade, greatly increased the revenues of the empire. In the 1530s, fleets were dispatched from Basra against the Portuguese. Muslims as far away as Indonesia and India looked on the Sultan as their protector. The Ottoman Sultanate was recognized by all but the Safavids of Iran as the successor to the caliphate.

The jade-handled ceremonial **dagger** *of Sulayman the Magnificent. Sulayman was known in the West as "The Magnificent", but to the Ottomans he was* Kanuni, *"The Law Giver".*

Selim was succeeded by Sulayman "The Magnificent". With the Middle East pacified, he turned once more towards Europe. The victory at Mohács in 1526 opened the way to Hungary, and 1529 found the Ottoman army camped beneath the walls of Vienna. The army retreated three weeks later, but the point was made: the Ottomans had become a world power.

The first major Ottoman defeat at Christian hands was at sea, the naval battle of Lepanto in 1571. The Ottoman fleet was demolished, but it was rebuilt within a year, to the consternation of Europe.

Many 16th-century European observers considered the Ottoman empire the model modern state: an efficient military machine ruled by an absolute monarch, with no hereditary aristocracy, a meritocracy in which any man of talent could rise.

Yet the cost of maintaining and employing such a huge military apparatus was one of the reasons for the decay of Ottoman power after the death of Sulayman in 1566. The practice of tax-farming to raise revenues, the increasing use of slave armies rather than the traditional backbone of the army, the cavalryman living on a land grant in return for military service, also contributed to the decline.

The economy was severely affected by inflation. Rural unrest spread and religious fanaticism increased. The Ottomans had always been very tolerant of Christian and Jewish communities and receptive of Western innovations in science and technology. However, in response to the worsening economic situation and to modernization, reactionary puritanism flourished. One populist religious movement rejected all innovations introduced since the time of the Prophet; they were opposed to the sufi orders, to music, dance, mathematics, science, philosophy, coffee and tobacco.

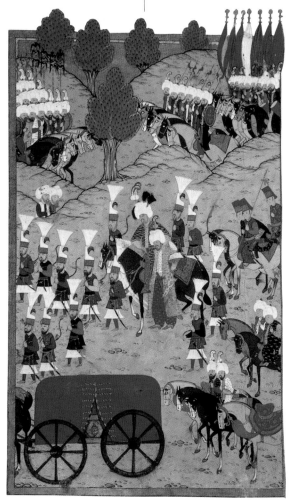

The highly organized Ottoman **army** *under the command of Sulayman the Magnificent marched on Vienna in 1529.*

SAFAVID PERSIA

The peoples of the steppe, Turks and Mongols, changed the demographic face of Iran as they did Anatolia. Concentrated particularly in the north, they formed some 25 percent of the population. These Turkish-speaking peoples were influenced by various heterodox religious brotherhoods as well as Shi'ism. The Safavid dynasty that ruled Persia from 1500 to 1722 originated in this milieu. It takes its name from the Safawiyya order, founded in the 14th century by Shaykh Safi al-Din. The centre of the order was Ardabil in Azerbijan. When the order declared jihad against the Christian populations of eastern Kurdistan and Georgia, its raids were carried out by the Qizil Bash, followers of the order. Their name means "red heads", so-called because of the red caps they wore.

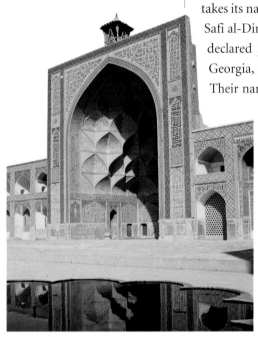

The Shah Mosque (now called the Imam Mosque) in Isfahan was begun by the greatest of the Safavid rulers, Shah Abbas, in 1611 and completed by his successor Safi in 1630.

The Safawiyya order had originally been sunni, but some time in the 15th century turned to an extreme form of Shi'ism. In 1500, the head of the order, Isma'il, embarked first on the conquest of neighbouring chieftaincies, then of Iran proper. In ten years, he brought the entire country under his rule. He declared shi'ism the national religion, but not the extreme form professed by his followers. Instead, he adopted *ithna 'ashari*, or "Twelver Shi'ism", a less radical variety. Shi'a 'ulama were imported from all over the Islamic world and organized into an administration, headed by a state-appointed official, the *sadr*. The 'ulama were given estates, and lived off the income, thus forming a religious aristocracy.

The Safavid shahs, for they used this old Iranian title, pursued just as radical a programme on the cultural front. They sponsored the revival of ancient Iranian traditions, harking back to the pre-Islamic Sasanid past in both literature and art. Their first capital was at Tabriz, close to the Ottoman border. This was occupied by the Ottomans after the Safavid defeat at Çaldiran in 1514, and the capital transferred first to Qazvin, then finally to Isfahan, which was transformed into one of the most glorious cities in the east. The long wars with the Ottomans continued with great savagery on both sides. Much of the hatred that divides sunni from shi'i dates from this time.

Safavid power reached its apogee under Shah Abbas (1587–1629). The Safavids had previously resisted the introduction of firearms, but Shah Abbas modernized his army, forming corps of artillerymen and musketeers. It was Shah Abbas who moved the capital to Isfahan, where he encouraged the establishment of an Armenian merchant colony. An alliance with the East India Company allowed the recapture of Hormuz from the Portuguese in 1622, providing Persia with a key port in the Indian Ocean trading network. Many of the institutions developed by the Safavid shahs persist in Iran to this day, but the dynasty declined after the death of Shah Abbas, and came to an end in 1722.

OPPOSITE

Shah Jahan ruled the Mughal empire from 1628 to 1658. In 1639-48 he built Shahjahanabad as his new seat of government in Delhi. The walls enclosed a population of 50,000, almost all engaged in supplying the needs of his fabulously opulent court.

The Babur Nama, *the memoirs of the founder of the Mughal dynasty, give an unusually detailed picture of every aspect of the author's life and times. In this illustration Babur demonstrates his love of gardens.*

THE MUGHAL EMPIRE

In 1496 a young descendant of Timur, Babur, set siege to Samarkand. He won the city, but soon lost it again. Only 13 years old, he was unable to handle the older and more ferocious warlords of the region. He was to gain and lose Samarkand again before his 18th birthday, but in 1504 managed to take the wealthy city of Kabul. Sometime in the 1510s he acquired guns and in the 1520s revived Timur's claim to northern India.

In 1526, Delhi and Agra were taken. After victory at the battle of Panipat against a coalition of Hindu princes, he took the title of *ghazi* – warrior of Islam. He was now in control of the heart of Hindustan. Babur's interest in his new domains was lively: he laid out gardens and introduced new plants, and carried out research into artillery techniques. However, his hard life, the Indian climate and indulgence in drugs and drink had undermined his constitution and he died in 1530.

Babur's son, Humayun, inherited a difficult situation. The Mughals – the word comes from the Persian for Mongol, although the family preferred to think of themselves as Turks – were the military occupiers of India and their position was based on Babur's personal reputation. Humayun did not have his father's personality and Afghan in-fighting followed him to India. He soon found himself at odds with one of the warlords, Sher Shah, as well as with his brothers. Defeated, Humayun fled to Persia.

Humayun eventually returned to Afghanistan where, after much fighting, he retook Kandahar and Herat. He re-entered Delhi in 1555, but died the following year. His son Akbar, aged 13, successfully claimed the throne. By the age of 19, he was firmly in control and began to put into practice the policies that were to mark his reign: religious tolerance and the attempt to find a path whereby the different groups within his empire could cooperate and coexist. Akbar's tolerance did not imply pacifism. His campaigns were ceaseless and he pushed back the boundaries of his empire in all directions. He made Agra rather than Delhi his capital. All the arts were encouraged, and at Akbar's sumptuous court everything from manuscripts to jewels were raised to their highest level in the imperial workshops.

Thanks largely to Sher Shah, India had a good infrastucture of roads and postal systems. Building on these foundations, Akbar also instituted reforms to increase the amount of land under cultivation and improve the lot of the peasant. He reigned for some 50 years and gave Hindustan prosperity and internal peace. However, the latter part of his reign was marked by uprisings and rebellions, not least by his sons.

The defensive walls *of Shah Jahan's Red Fort in Delhi enclosed his new capital, Shahjahanabad, built in 1639-48. The fort remains largely intact in the heart of Old Delhi.*

Akbar's eldest surviving son, Salim, came to the throne in 1605 and, lest he be confused with Selim, the Sultan of Turkey, took the throne name of Jahangir, "World Seizer". He proved less weak and disastrous than his father had feared. He shared his father's interest in the arts and manuscript production and painting reached new heights. Two figures dominate his reign; Jahangir's wife, the intelligent and politically astute Nur Jehan, whose father and brother were Jahangir's chief advisers, and Khurram (later Shah Jahan), his eldest son, who, following the usual Mughal pattern, rebelled against his father.

Like his father, Jahangir loved Kashmir, but in 1627 even its favourable climate could not restore his health, undermined by years of the family addiction to alcohol and opium, and he died in the autumn of the year.

When Shah Jahan succeeded to the throne, he showed a passionate interest in the arts and the luxury of the court was maintained in all its splendour. However, he never fully recovered from the death of his wife, Mumtaz Mahal in 1631. The empire meanwhile was stagnating. Campaigns to the south were a drain, but produced no new lands or spoils and most revenue came from ever more corrupt and oppressive tax-collectors.

There was tension too between his sons Dara Shikoh and Aurangzeb. The former, Shah Jahan's favourite, followed the family traditions of syncretic mysticism, tolerance, intellectual curiosity and sympathy for his non-Muslim subjects. Aurangzeb indulged in none of these things, which endeared him to the orthodox 'ulama. Fighting broke out between the brothers and in 1658 Aurangzeb defeated Dara Shikoh near Agra. Shah Jahan was captured and imprisoned (he was to die in jail). Declaring himself emperor, Aurangzeb hunted down and killed his brother. He placed India under a strict form of the shari'a and persecuted the "infidel" into accepting Islam. Laws against non-Muslims were implemented with full severity, music was banned and the writing of literature and history discouraged. Aurangzeb did not object to painting and portraits of him survive, usually dressed in the austere manner of a holy man. He attacked non-Muslim neighbours, such as the Rajputs, with politically disastrous results. Successful guerrilla campaigns proved to the Hindus that their Muslim overlords were by no means invincible and to throw them off was not an impossible dream.

After Aurangzeb, the Mughal dynasty declined rapidly. It came to an end in 1738, when Nadir Shah, a Turk from Central Asia, who had just displaced the Safavid dynasty in Iran, crossed the Indus, defeated the emperor and sacked Delhi.

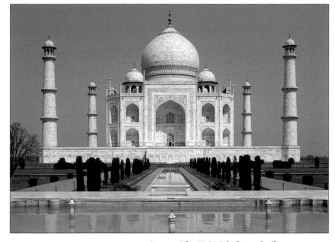

*The **Taj Mahal** was built between 1632 and 1643 by Shah Jahan as a tomb for his beloved wife, Mumtaz Mahal, who had died giving birth to their fourteenth child. It remains the consummate example of Mughal architecture in South Asia.*

THE LATER OTTOMAN EMPIRE

In the 17th century the Ottoman sultans ceased to wield absolute power, delegating authority to the Grand Vizier, while the wives and mothers of sultans often took informal charge of financial affairs. The modern army – large contingents of infantry armed with guns – was more expensive to maintain than the traditional cavalry, and tax-farming was introduced to raise the money to pay the troops. Already in the second half of the 16th century, the Janissaries had received the right to marry. By the 17th century membership in this elite corps had become first hereditary, then open to purchase, with an inevitable decline in fighting ability. They formed an increasingly unruly element, deposing sultans who did not meet their approval. Power shifted to civilian elites with private funds, while provincial authorities, military and civil, built up power bases through marriage and joint commercial ventures, founding local dynasties.

It was against this background that in 1683 Grand Vizier Kara Mustafa led the Ottoman armies once more to the walls of Vienna. They were put to flight after a siege of 60 days. This was the first major defeat of an Ottoman army, and the sultan was forced to accept humiliating terms by the Treaty of Karlowitz in 1699.

Between 1683 and 1718, the Ottomans fought three more wars against the Habsburgs, and lost them all.

In the 18th century Russia also expanded into Ottoman territory. In the course of three major wars the Ottomans lost the Crimea, Podolia and Bessarabia and the lucrative Black Sea trade passed into Russian control. The greater part of the Balkans having been lost to the Habsburgs, large Muslim populations now lived under non-Muslim rule.

Another threat to the territorial integrity of the empire came from an unexpected quarter. In the mid-18th century, Muhammad ibn 'Abd al-Wahhab launched an Islamic reform movement in Arabia, advocating the suppression of sufi orders and elimination of all practices not expressly sanctioned by the Qur'an and sunna. He forged an alliance with the Sa'ud dynasty, and despite eventual military defeat, the movement resurfaced in the 20th century and was instrumental in the founding of modern Saudi Arabia.

In 1798 Napoleon invaded Egypt, and made it clear to the Arabic-speaking provinces of the empire that Ottoman invincibility was a thing of the past. The ruling sultan, Selim III, was himself influenced by Enlightenment ideas. He fought against corruption and made sweeping reforms of the army, but in 1807 he was deposed by the Janissaries and put to death. His successor, Mahmud II,

In July 1799 Napoleon's army invaded Egypt, defeated an Ottoman army twice its size and captured Aboukir near Alexandria. This defeat convinced the Ottomans of the need for further military reforms.

broke the power of the Janissaries forever by massacring them in 1826. He set up a European-style cabinet and a state school system and actively promoted the study of medicine, science and technology. He also abolished traditional dress, replacing the turban by the fez, which became a symbol of reform.

The subject populations of Serbia and Greece fought wars for independence during the first three decades of the 19th century, and in 1830 France occupied Algeria, the first of a succession of French and English colonial adventures in Islamic lands.

The Ottoman governor of Egypt, Muhammad Ali Pasha, who effectively ruled the country from 1805 to 1848, severed his links with the Sultan, and took drastic steps to modernize the country. He turned Egypt into an autonomous secular principality, which his descendants continued to rule until the middle of the 20th century. He disestablished the 'ulama and confiscated for the state the pious endowments they controlled. He massacred the Mamluks, the conservative military elite that had ruled Egypt before the Ottomans, and trained a modern army, which fought with great success in the Sudan and against the Wahhabi movement in Arabia.

Muhammad Ali *made Egypt into an autonomous principality where the Ottomans had no authority. He even threatened to overthrow the Ottoman sultan. Here he entertains a British delegation sent to dissuade him from such action.*

The Ottoman sultan 'Abd al-Majid made yet another effort at institutional reform in 1839, reorganizing the army and establishing a legal system based on French models. These and other government-sponsored reforms were known as the *Tanzimat*, "reorganization". They were resisted on the one hand by the traditionalist 'ulama and on the other by the new technically trained elite, who thought them insufficient and called for more political participation.

England and France supported the Ottomans against the Russians during the Crimean War of 1854–56. The "Eastern Question" – which of the Great Powers would get what provinces of the weakening Ottoman empire – dominated European politics for the rest of century and was a contributory cause of the First World War. By 1875, the empire was virtually bankrupt. The following year 'Abd al-Hamid II promulgated a constitution which guaranteed freedom of the press and individual rights. The University of Istanbul was founded as well as schools for women. But in 1877, the sultan brought the Tanzimat reforms to an end and suspended parliament.

In 1908 a nationalist group called the Young Turks seized power, supported by the army. They re-established the constitution, re-convened parliament, deposed 'Abd al-Hamid and chose his brother, Mehmed V as sultan. In 1914 the Young Turks brought the empire into the war on the side of Germany, effectively sealing the fate of the Ottoman empire.

THE TWENTIETH CENTURY

The Ottomans entered the First World War on the German side, and at the end of the war her former provinces were distributed by the League of Nations to the Russians, French and British. The year following the end of the war, a young Turkish officer named Mustafa Kemal saved Anatolia, the heartland of the Ottoman Empire, from being divided among the victors. He first drove foreign forces from Anatolia, then repudiated the harsh peace treaty the sultan had been forced to sign.

Mustafa Kemal, later called Atatürk, set about the radical secularization and modernization of the new nation. In 1924 he abolished the sultanate. In 1926 he abolished the caliphate. The abolition of these two institutions, however shadowy they had become, deprived the Islamic world of potent symbols of unity. The end of the Ottoman empire and the division of its provinces among the colonial powers were blows to the widespread pan-Islamic movement. Atatürk led the first nationalist revolution in the Islamic world. He defied the Western powers and defeated European troops on the battlefield. This seemed to show that nationalism was the means to independence and freedom from foreign intervention. At the same time, the abolition of the Arabic alphabet and its replacement with the Latin, seemed to Muslims to renounce the Islamic past entirely and align Turkey with Europe.

In the years following the end of the Second World War, all the countries of the Arabic-speaking heartlands gained their independence from the colonial powers. The last to do so was Algeria in 1962. The colonial period transformed the Islamic world, even those countries like Turkey, Iran, Saudi Arabia and Yemen that had not been mandates, protectorates or colonies. The Muslim world now consists of independent nation states, many with secular governments and legal systems based on European models (see map, page 9).

Turkey has *absorbed many western influences in the last 100 years. This view of Istanbul c.1900 shows that Western fashions were already taking hold in the old Ottoman capital.*

Southwest Asia after the First World War

- British mandate
- French mandate
- Turkey after Treaty of Sèvres (1920)
- area annexed by Turkey 1921
- area restored to Turkey by Treaty of Lausanne (1923)
- — international border 1926

Relations with the West have dominated the recent history of many other Muslim countries, in particular the powerful oil exporting states of the Middle East and Indonesia. Originally developed by Western concessionary companies, these states now control their own resources. Saudi Arabia, Kuwait and the United Arab Emirates have modernized within traditional frameworks, while Saddam Hussein's Iraq had a socialist military regime based on a leadership cult. The savage 1980–88 Iran-Iraq war was an expression of ancient regional, religious and ethnic rivalries, exacerbated by territorial disputes. In 1990, Iraq invaded Kuwait, which was liberated by a coalition of the United States, Britain, Saudi Arabia and other Arab states. Subsequent sanctions against Iraq and continued bombing, as well as the presence of American troops on Saudi soil, now withdrawn, fuelled resentment among militants. The American and British invasion of Iraq in 2003 has put an end to the Iraqi regime, but the long-term future of the region remains problematic.

In oil-rich Iran, the Pahlavi dynasty, founded in 1925 by the radically secularizing Reza Khan, came to an end in 1979. The Islamic revolution that toppled the Shah had a profound effect throughout the Muslim world. This broad-based revolution took place not in the name of any socialist or nationalist ideology, but in the name of Islam. The initial excesses of the regime have given way to a successful attempt to govern through Islamic institutions and by Islamic law. Despite the fact that it took place within a particular shi'a context, the Iranian revolution has inspired Islamist movements everywhere in the Muslim world.

THE PALESTINIAN SITUATION

The Balfour Declaration of 1917 promised British support for a national home for the Jewish people in Palestine, provided nothing be done that might "prejudice the civil and religious rights of the existing non-Jewish communities". Muslim and Christian Arabs formed 92 percent of the population. When the state of Israel was formed on the British withdrawal in 1948, the war that followed ended with three quarters of a million Palestinians displaced from their homes. Most Palestinians have lived in refugee camps ever since, and subsequent wars in 1956, 1967 and 1973 have added to their numbers. Muslims regard uncritical Western support for Israel and indifference to the plight of the Palestinians and the essential justness of their cause as motivated by deep antipathy to Islam. Spiralling violence on both sides bodes ill for the future, and has driven many former moderates into the arms of militant Islamist groups.

Many Jewish immigrants *arrived in Palestine during the British mandate, some legally, some illegally. Even so, the Jewish population was still much smaller than that of the Palestinian Arabs. Israel's victory in the 1948 war drove about 725,000 Palestinians out of the country.*

ISLAMIC ART AND SCIENCE

Despite, or perhaps because of, a non-figurative tradition in the visual arts, Islamic architects, craftsmen and calligraphers have generated a rich and wholly distinctive tradition, one underpinned by a clarity of vision reflected in Islamic writing, education, and philosophical and scientific enquiry.

The Great Mosque (Mezquita) *in Córdoba is one of Islam's greatest architectural legacies to Europe. This part of the prayer hall, with its forest of red marble columns topped with a double arcade was built under al-Hakam II in 962–966.*

THE ARTS

ARCHITECTURE AND CALLIGRAPHY are the two great Islamic art forms and are often intimately linked, as in the brick and tile work of Iran and Central Asia, or the magnificent inscriptions, carved in wood and stone, or worked in mosaic, all across the Muslim world.

Architecture is the most visible mark of a culture, proclaiming its aspirations and identity. Islamic architecture is frequently pictured in terms of a fairly standard Irano-Indian style, rich in domes and slender minarets, with turquoise, green and gold predominating. This is, however, quite a recent development. Early Islamic architecture varied greatly according to local influences in the conquered lands. But certain unifying factors soon coalesced into a style that made it instantly recognizable.

Islam inherited the urban expectations of both the Byzantine world and Iran. Cities were therefore planned from an early date and, besides the mosque, certain basic elements of infrastructure were assumed: defensive walls, a citadel, bath houses, and hence systems for supplying the water, markets and caravanserais for merchants to stay and store their goods. The giving of alms led to the establishment of hospitals on the Byzantine-Iranian pattern, hospices, mental homes and orphanages. All these provided opportunities for architectural innovation and display.

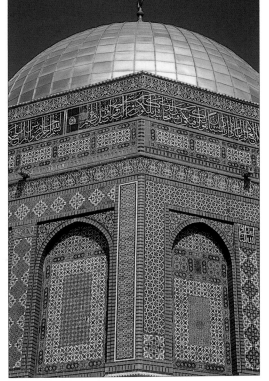

The Dome of the Rock *in Jerusalem is the oldest surviving Islamic building (see also p.51). Its architecture includes many Byzantine features and the use of calligraphy as one of the principal decorative elements marks it instantly as an Islamic building.*

THE FIRST MOSQUES

The earliest mosques were of great simplicity, but very soon, through contact with Byzantine architectural traditions, they began to change. The Dome of the Rock at Jerusalem, for example, or the Great Mosque at Damascus, once the Church of St John the Baptist, whose head was buried there, are still decorated with sumptuous Byzantine-style mosaics.

The first purpose-built mosques to have survived, however, such as the minaret at Samarra, echoed in the great 9th-century Mosque of Ibn Tulun in Cairo, have a bold simplicity which has survived in the architecture of North Africa. There, mosques, such as the Great Mosque at Kairouan, enormous in

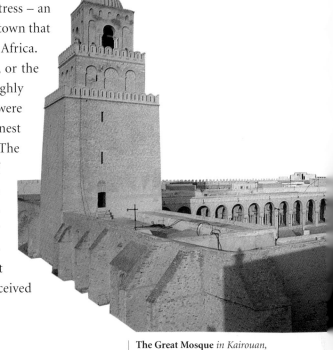

size, have a stark unadorned grandeur that suggests a fortress – an appropriate statement for a profoundly military faith in a town that was founded as a military base for the conquest of North Africa. The square minarets of the al-Zaytuna Mosque in Tunis, or the Kutubiyya in Marrakesh, follow the tendency to highly geometric forms, and these uncompromising patterns were carried by the Almohad invaders into Spain. The finest surviving example of this style is the Giralda at Seville. The tendency to bold simple shapes built up of cubes and half spheres has continued to the present in North Africa, in the tombs of holy men and even in domestic architecture.

This dramatic eschewing of unnecessary outer decoration reappears in another medium – mud brick – south of the Sahara, in such buildings as the mosque at Jenne, or the Yaana Mosque, which has recently received the Aga Khan Award.

PERSIAN INFLUENCES

As Islam penetrated Iran, another ancient culture with a magnificent architectural tradition, a new fusion occurred. Few of the early brick mosques have survived – the 8th-century one at Damghan being a rare example. Later mosques such as the 9th-century Fahraj Friday Mosque outside Yezd, show very clearly the simple and austere pattern of the early days. Many of the Seljuk buildings such as the Friday Mosque at Isfahan with its superb calligraphic brickwork were subsequently "modernized" in response to a growing taste for decoration or to repair damage caused by the frequent earthquakes in the region.

The rich architectural tradition of Iran ranges from this early simplicity, through the superb tile work of the Timurid mosque at Yezd to the 19th-century mosque at Shiraz, known familiarly as "the rose bowl" for the predominance of pink and the motif of roses in its decoration.

Many of the mosques did not stand alone, but formed part of a complex with madrasas, schools and libraries. There are also, as elsewhere in the Islamic world – for example the Mamluk tombs in Cairo – splendid examples of funerary architecture, most typically a square building surmounted by a dome. This basic shape became more elaborate with time and in India developed into perhaps the most famous example of Islamic architecture for the world at large: the Taj Mahal.

The Great Mosque in Kairouan, Tunisia, dates in its present form from the 9th century. The triple-towered minaret resembles a classical lighthouse.

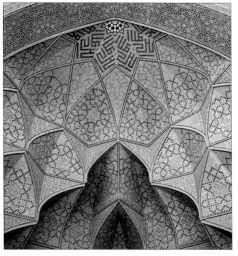

The Friday Mosque in Isfahan was built in the 11th century under the Seljuks. This detail shows the sophisticated blending of structural and decorative elements.

Islamic culture expected certain amenities of cities and city planning. From the Round City of al-Mansur's Baghdad, built in 763, to the great central maydans of Isfahan and Samarkand, city planning was an important art. Iran is particularly rich in practical examples of architecture from the numerous great caravanserais – for example the Seljuk Rebat Shaif between Nishapur and Merv – to the humble pigeon towers, where the birds provided both a source of food and natural fertilizer for the melon fields. The khans and caravanserais were vital for the protection of merchants and the continuance of external trade, but there are also superb examples of covered markets, hospitals and other public buildings.

Engineering joins with architecture in the question of water. Islam, born in the desert, was profoundly conscious of its importance and a great deal of thought and ingenuity went into developing the earlier Iranian and classical water technology in new ways. The *qanat* system of underground aqueducts to reduce evaporation is a spectacular example of this and came to influence agricultural techniques as far away as South America. Another example of experimentation with water is the Safavid development of the multi-storied bridge dam, such as the Khajo Bridge at Isfahan.

Water was needed, of course, not only for agriculture and to support a growing population, but also to fulfil the ritual obligation to wash before prayer.

Another area where engineering and architecture meet is military construction. This is a subject of great complexity, partly because fortifications were constantly updated and hence rarely survive in their original form, and partly because the constant borrowing of new military technology means that a mixture of elements is almost the norm.

The Khajo Bridge *at Isfahan, built in 1650, shows the ingenuity of Safavid architects. It serves not only as a bridge and a dam, but also as a recreation area and shopping centre.*

TURKISH ARCHITECTURE

The Turks also were great builders – and it is striking how many groups of nomads from the steppes, within a generation of settling, have produced the most magnificent and innovative architecture. As the Seljuk Turks penetrated the Byzantine empire from about the year 1000, they are generally credited with bringing west the Gothic arch, the first example of which is in the mosque at Van. Their style of building, plain and austere – moved across Anatolia with their conquests, Konya providing some especially fine examples, such as the Ince Minare.

The Turks were also moving east. By the end of the 14th century Timur, whom the west knew as Tamerlane, had set out to conquer the world, reaching the borders of Europe in the west and China in the east and penetrating northern India. After wreaking appalling devastation on many of the cities he conquered,

Timur decided that he needed a capital worthy of his power and set out to make Samarkand the most beautiful city in the world. Craftsmen were brought from countries he had conquered, the city was redesigned, and the finest examples of Central Asian architecture erected in a remarkable short space of time. Samarkand, largely inspired by Iran, is characterized by the Persian use of external tiles, predominantly blue and turquoise, with bold calligraphy as the dominant motif.

AESTHETIC ARCHITECTURE

The rise of the Ottoman dynasty and the fall of Constantinople, the old capital of the eastern Roman empire, Byzantium, brought the Turks into contact with the splendours of late classical architecture – hundreds of magnificent churches and monasteries, mosaics, statues and works of art. Unlike the Frankish crusaders, who sacked the city in 1204, Mehmet the Conqueror insisted that this artistic treasure house should be respected, converting many of the churches, including the Hagia Sofia, into mosques.

Soon, a new Ottoman style of architecture was flourishing, based on the Byzantine, characterized by its clusters of spreading domes and slender soaring minarets. The outsides were relatively undecorated, as a rule, but the inside was often tiled, particularly with the famous Iznik ceramics, with their patterns based on foliage and flowers, predominantly blue, turquoise and sealing-wax red.

The greatest Ottoman architect was Sinan (1491–1588). Originally an engineer, he solved difficult problems of road- and bridge-building with an originality and elegance that have survived to the present day. In his 97 years, he built 131 mosques and over 200 other buildings all over the empire, many commissioned by the sultan. They are all characterized by a particular architectural elegance and a skill at using any shaped piece of land to its greatest advantage. Perhaps his most famous work is the Sulaymaniye Mosque in Istanbul, where Sulayman the Magnificent is buried.

DOMESTIC ARCHITECTURE

Domestic architecture, traditionally had much more variety of styles than "official" architecture, which was designed to impress on the populace the glory of God, the power of the sovereign or the generosity of the donor and therefore needed to be in the latest fashion of the time. The classical model of the courtyard house, grand or humble, tends to predominate, but there are numerous

MINARETS AND DOMES

MINARETS, THE ELEGANT TOWERS attached to mosques can be square-based or round, plain or ornately decorated. Domes are a feature of most mosques and these too vary enormously in style and decoration, which may consist of tiling, gilding or carved stonework.

Brass crescent over a pear-shaped bulb.

A pavilion of eight columns supports a crown of stalactites.

Simple wooden railings and modest stalactite decoration were favoured by the Ottomans.

Pepperpot caps are found on many early square-based minarets.

This slender pencil minaret adorns the Ottoman Mosque of Sulayman Pasha (1528) in Cairo.

The three-tiered spire of the Qaitbey Mosque (1474) in Cairo features ornate Mamluk stonework.

The minaret of the Ibn Tulun Mosque in Cairo (879) was inspired by the Great Mosque at Samarra in Iraq.

The dome on the Mamluk Qaitbey Mosque combines geometric and floral designs.

The dome of the Great Mosque, Kairouan (c. 900) is classical in its simplicity.

Iranian-style mosques are famous for their rich external decoration.

other local models, from the farmhouses of the Balkans to the towers of Hadhramaut, the caves of Matmata or the yurts of the steppe.

Until the late 20th century, in areas where Islam was the minority religion, or shared its hegemony with another faith, mosques would generally be built in the style of the country – for example the ancient and beautiful Xian Mosque, several of the mosques of Beijing, those of Malacca, Sri Lanka and many other regions. The buildings were made in the local style and materials, in the first place because the builders did not have the skills or the option to work in the Indo-Persian tradition, but also for the safety of a minority group: it was not wise to be too conspicuous. Also Islam did not have to have a particular "look" – a Muslim could also be culturally African, Chinese or Bosnian. It was not necessary to renounce the culture for the faith. More recently, this has started to change. Traditional mosques in many areas are being replaced by a more standardized pattern, often funded from the Gulf, indicative of a narrowing of what the Muslim world considers aesthetically acceptable.

THE ISLAMIC STYLE

What, then, are the elements that make an Islamic building recognizable, even when it is not built in the Irano-Indian style? The lack of paintings and images, of course, is one factor, with the concomitant tendency for all decoration to be highly stylized, geometric, floral or calligraphic, and hypnotic rather than emotional. Domes, often flattened, following the Byzantine model, or in some areas ribbed, became characteristic of Islamic architecture. Doors, and such windows as there are, tend to be of great beauty, lovingly decorated and interesting in shape, whether in a palace or a simple house.

Buildings both public and private are turned inwards, with high defensive walls or heavily shuttered windows, to segregate the women, as Islam demands, and to protect the inmates in an unsettled world. Similarly, the ancient classical plan of building round a courtyard is preferred, the space enriched with water and flowers wherever possible.

It is hard to analyse what exactly marks out a building as Islamic – perhaps for many centuries it was the importance of basic structure and function rather than decoration. Where it existed, decoration was part of the function, as in the name of God worked into the brickwork of a mosque. Be that as it may, it is remarkable that within a century, a group that had no strong indigenous architectural tradition had managed to forge a "look" which is instantly recognizable and has lasted to the present.

The Sulaymaniye Mosque in Istanbul was built by Sinan, the great Ottoman imperial architect, in 1550–57. This view is from beneath the great central dome towards the mihrab.

LITERATURE

Classical Islamic culture was expressed in three unrelated languages, Arabic, Persian and Turkish. All three have enormously rich literatures. The primary document of Arabic literature is the Qur'an. It is the first Arabic book and the supreme and inimitable example of the Arabic language. Its concise, vigorous and allusive style deeply influenced later compositions in Arabic.

The other great source for the development of the Arabic literary language was pre-Islamic poetry, which was collected from the oral tradition by the scholars of Basra and Kufa in the 9th century. At the Umayyad court in Damascus a genre of prose literature developed called *adab*. The most famous exponent of the genre was the genial al-Jahiz (d.868), whose *Book of Animals*, the earliest Arabic treatise on zoology, aside from fascinating discussions of things like animal mimicry, contains jokes, satirical anecdotes and learned etymologies.

World, dynastic and local history were assiduously cultivated throughout the classical period. These histories ranged from the huge compilation of historical hadith by the 'Abbasid historian al-Tabari, to the one-volume overviews of world history by Ibn Qutayba and al-Dinawari, both produced in the 9th century. The most original of Muslim historians was Ibn Khaldun, whose *Muqaddima* (Introduction to History) is the first attempt to discern the underlying laws governing history and society.

Arabic popular literature includes the *1001 Nights*, familiar to everyone, as well as tales of adventure and romance less familiar in the west, like the Arabic *Romance of Alexander the Great*, the *Romance of Sayf ibn Dhi Yazan* and most popular of all, the *Romance of 'Antar*. These are similar to the medieval European chivalric romances.

In the 10th century the New Persian language, based on the court language of the Sasanids enriched with large numbers of loan words from Arabic, became a vehicle of literary expression at the wealthy Samanid court in Khurasan. The earliest examples that have survived are the poems of Rudaki, but the cornerstone of New Persian literature is the national epic of Iran, the *Shahnama* of Firdowsi, who died in 1020. This heroic epic of the shahs of Persia and their perennial wars with the Turanians contains 60,000 lines. The subject is the pre-Islamic past of Iran but the metre is based on Arabic metrics and the language is New Persian.

Perhaps because of the influence of the *Shahnama*, Persian literature is one of poetry and verse romances. Nizami lived in the 12th century and is perhaps the most profound and difficult of Persian poets. His *Khamsa* is a collection of five verse romances totalling 30,000 couplets. Omar Khayyam, Hafiz and Sa'di

ADAB

'Abd al-Hamid ibn Yahya al-Katib, an Umayyad official credited with the creation of this genre, defined its aims as follows: "Cultivate the Arabic language so that you may speak correctly; develop a handsome script which will add lustre to your writings; learn the poetry of the Arabs by heart; familiarize yourself with unusual ideas and expressions; read the history of the Arabs and Persians and remember their great deeds."

wrote shorter lyrics that are considered the finest in any of the three Islamic languages. Jalal al-Din al-Rumi's *Mathnawi* is one of the most profound mystical poems in any language.

Like Arabic, Persian has a very rich historical literature. The 12th-century historian Rashid al-Din wrote a history of the Mongols, using Mongolian and Chinese sources, which is one of our main sources for the history of their conquests. Because Persian became the court language of Mughal India, there is a rich Indo-Persian historical and literary tradition as well.

The earliest Ottoman Turkish literatures are written in simple language, without the rhetorical flourishes and flowery style that later came into vogue. The *Mewlid* of Süleyman Çelebi, a poem on the life of the Prophet, including a description of the Night Journey and Ascent to Heaven *(mi'raj)* was very popular.

During the 14th and 15th centuries, an intensive effort was made to translate into Turkish the principal works of Arabic and Persian literature. Murad II in particular sponsored and encouraged this effort. Throughout the Ottoman period, educated men read the three languages of Islamic culture, and some could write in all three. Many of the early Ottoman sultans were poets, often writing under pen-names. Murad II wrote under the name Muradi, while Mehmed II, conqueror of Constantinople, wrote verses under the name 'Awni.

The two most famous Ottoman poets were Fuduli, who died in 1556 and Baqi, who died in 1600. Baqi attained technical perfection in the handling of complex metrical forms, and his work is still read. He was the court poet of Sulayman the Magnificent. Fuduli came from Baghdad, and unusually, wrote all his poetry in Azeri Turkish.

The Ottomans produced a long line of official historians. Perhaps the most famous is Mustafa 'Ali, who died in 1599. He was the first to introduce critical methods into Ottoman historiography. The objectivity and honesty of Ottoman historians, and the freedom with which they criticized the bad decisions of the great and powerful, including the sultan, are notable.

CALLIGRAPHY

Arabic calligraphy is used not only for documents and books, but also as decoration on porcelain and metalware, for carpets and textiles, on coins and, above all, as architectural ornament.

MAQAMAT

In the 10th century a new literary genre was created by al-Hamdhani, called "The Wonder of the Age". His *Maqamat* ("Sessions"), written in rhymed prose, recounts the adventures of a confidence trickster who takes on different personalities in each "session" and always succeeds in bilking his victim. He was imitated by al-Hariri a hundred years later, and this genre had many imitators, in Hebrew as well as Arabic. This genre may well have influenced the development of the Spanish picaresque novel.

This beautiful illustrated manuscript *of the Persian epic, the* Shahnama, *is written in the* nasta'liq *script. Legend says that the scribe who created this style of writing based it on a flying bird that appeared to him in a dream.*

THE ARABIC ALPHABET

The Arabic alphabet has 28 letters. Each may have up to four forms, depending upon its position in the word. All the letters are, strictly speaking, consonants. There are three vowel sounds in Arabic, a, i and u. Each exists in a short and long form. The long form can be indicated in the script, but not the short. A system of indicating the short vowels was developed in the 8th century, and is used for texts, such as the Qur'an, but not ordinarily in everyday writing.

This page of the Qur'an *is written in the flowing* naskhi *script. Scribes made it their duty to convey the words of God as perfectly as possible.*

At the start of the Islamic era two types of script seem to have been in use: one was square and angular and was called *kufic* (after the town of Kufa in Iraq). It was used for the earliest copies of the Qur'an, and for architectural decoration in the first period of the Islamic empire. The other, called *naskhi*, developed by the famous scribe Ibn al-Bawwab, was rounded and cursive and was used for letters and business documents. By the 12th century, kufic was no longer used for ordinary purposes. In conservative North Africa, however, it developed into the handsome *maghribi* style of writing still used today.

In the first half of the 10th century, the calligrapher Ibn Muqla established the rules of shape and proportion that have been followed by calligraphers since his time. He developed the traditional classification of Arabic writing into the "six styles" of cursive writing: *naskhi* (from which most present-day printing types are derived), *thuluth* (a more cursive outgrowth of naskhi), *rayhani* (a more ornate version of thuluth), *muhaqqaq* (a bold script with sweeping diagonal flourishes), *tawqi* (a somewhat compressed variety of thuluth) and *ruq'a* (the style commonly used today for handwriting in most of the Arab world). From these six, and from kufic, later calligraphers developed and elaborated a range of new scripts. A particularly graceful and delicate script called *ta'liq* came into use in Iran. The horizontal strokes of the letters are elongated, and the words often written at an angle across the page. Another script called *nasta'liq* combines the Arabic naskhi and the Persian ta'liq into a beautifully light, legible script.

Once the early creative flowering had faded elsewhere in the Middle East, the Ottomans took up the art with passion. A popular saying was that "The Qur'an was revealed in Mecca, recited in Egypt and written in Istanbul." Ottoman styles include *diwani*, so called from the word diwan (state council or government office). It was at first used primarily for documents issued by the Ottoman Council of State. It is an extremely graceful and very decorative script, with strong diagonal flourishes, though less easy to read than some other styles.

Calligraphy is still very much alive wherever the Arabic alphabet is used. Advertisements, newspaper headlines, book jackets, wall posters and shop signs all display fine examples of the various styles.

THE DECORATIVE ARTS

Because Islam spread into areas with highly developed traditions in many different crafts, it is impossible to do full justice to the richness and variety of the decorative arts across the whole Muslim world. Traditionally Islam has excelled in woodworking, ceramics, textiles and metalwork and a few of the most important examples of work in these fields will be discussed here.

Many of the areas where Islam spread were poor in forests, with the result that wood tended to be treated as a precious material, skilfully carved and fretted – and also because it helps to prevent warping in extreme climates, Islamic woodwork is often made in small panels, fitted together with consummate art.

Some of the earliest examples are carved wood panels dated to the 7th century from Egypt, which show Coptic influence, with designs of vines and fruit. The oldest large-scale example is the minbar of the Great Mosque at Kairouan (863), made of teak, indicating the breadth of commercial contacts. Other splendid examples are the 11th-century Kairouan *maqsura* and the Mamluk minbar (late 13th century) in the Mosque of Ibn Tulun in Cairo and the Fatimid palaces provide secular examples. Fine wood carving occurs all across the Islamic world and is characterized by its geometric and stylized floral patterns and by the frequent use of calligraphy. Wood was also used for a particularly Muslim item of interior decoration: the *mashrabiyya* or elaborate screens used to cover the windows to guard the privacy of the women, while allowing them a glimpse of the outer world.

Inlay work, particularly associated with Egypt and later Syria, is again typical of Islamic use of small quantities of wood. The marquetry may be done with other woods, or with tortoiseshell or mother-of-pearl, both very popular in the later period. Western Islam also made considerable use of painted woodwork, both in architecture and furnishings. A word should perhaps be said here about ivory carving, of which some fine examples survive, generally in the form of small panels or caskets, or occasionally boards for games such as *mankala*, many of them from Muslim Spain.

The Islamic world has produced a wealth of ceramics of every kind of the highest quality, and for everyday use. Early examples include the faience excavated at Susa and the yellowish-gold wares of Fustat and Samarra. The blue-green and deep green wares of Iraq also appear at an early date and sherds are found at numerous points on the eastern coasts of Arabia, as are sherds of Iranian wares: clear evidence of trade.

Iran and Central Asia in particular produced the widest range of styles – often influenced by Chinese styles – from the supremely elegant 10th-century plates and bowls with cream grounds and black kufic inscriptions to the exuberant 13th-century Rayy ware often with figurative decoration or the 14th-century Sultanabad wares with their delicate shades of blue and grey.

This fine 14th-century Mamluk mosque lamp *is enameled with the name of the ruler and a phrase from the Qur'an.*

Tile-making reached the highest level of skill, becoming an intrinsic part of the internal and external architecture of many mosques – for example whole walls covered in gigantic calligraphy – and also palaces. One of the places particularly known for its tiles was Kashan in Iran.

This 16th-century Iznik plate, *with its splendid decoration of Mediterranean ships, represents a new departure for Islamic art.*

Perhaps because of the Muslim prohibition on the use of gold vessels, potters experimented with ways to produce glazes that looked like gold. The Hispano-Mauresque ware of al-Andalus is a well-known example of such experiments.

One of the last great flowerings of Islamic ceramic art was in Turkey, where Iznik produced plates, bowls, and jugs as well as tile revetments with beautifully clear and dramatic floral designs which decorate some of the finest Ottoman mosques.

Less Islamic glass than pottery has survived, but there are, in particular, exquisite mosque lamps of enameled glass from Egypt and Syria, in a style that was copied in Muslim Spain.

Islamic textiles, carpets and furnishings are important for several reasons. Firstly, the areas where Islam first spread had long been famous for their textiles – the linen of Egypt, for example, and the brocaded silks and carpets of Iran. The historian al-Mas'udi tells the story of the army of the Conquest dividing the magnificent "carpet of the spring of Chosroes", too unsophisticated to appreciate the treasure they were destroying. This soon changed. The Islamic world became a major textile producer, and clothes and textiles then, as now, were of the greatest importance to the economy.

Textiles were important as raw materials, woven cloth and finished goods. All three were traded and probably caused more money to change hands on the international market than anything except metals and arms. Skilled weavers were highly prized and were generally men, but much embroidery was done by women, a way of supplementing the family income, working in leisure moments at home, as Palestinian refugees do to the present day. For wealthier women, it was one of the few means of self-expression for the illiterate, and some of the most charming Islamic embroidery was produced in the Ottoman harems.

The Iznik potters *were at first influenced by Chinese blue and white ceramics, then experimented with colours such as tomato red and sage green. This tankard reflects the Ottoman love of flowers.*

Textiles were not only of economic importance, they were also social indicators. In the past, decoration normally had purpose: to indicate a person's wealth, rank, place of origin, job or religious affiliation. Robes were bestowed as a mark of favour in the Muslim, Christian and Far Eastern worlds alike. Muslim rulers formalized this practice by setting up workshops producing official textiles – *tiraz* – normally worked with the ruler's name, or auspicious or pious phrases, which were bestowed as a mark of honour on foreign ambassadors and those in favour about the court. Such highly prized pieces found their way into the treasuries of churches and monasteries around Europe, and often feature in medieval European paintings.

A way of judging the impact of one culture on another is the number of loan words. In the field of textiles (as in that of basic foods), the West owes Islam a considerable debt: damask from Damascus, muslin from Mosul, tabby (as in tabby cats) from the at-Tabiyya quarter of Cairo, seersucker from the Persian "milk and sugar" and, of course, cashmere from Kashmir, to name but a few.

For the West, the art form most associated with the Islamic world is the carpet. These seem to have been exported in quantity rather later than silks, probably because of their weight. From the 15th century, however, they were everywhere, but like the silks have often survived only in paintings.

There are several reasons for this emphasis on textiles within the Islamic world. In the case of carpets, since it was required that a person should have a clean place to pray, it was natural that the prayer rug should develop early and also that fine carpets should be made to adorn mosques – although strictly for both purposes a reed mat is adequate. The oldest surviving Islamic carpets have come to light beneath layers of floor coverings donated over the centuries to mosques. These carpets are knotted, of silk or wool, but there is another type – the kelim. Kelims are woven carpets, normally of wool, and are particularly associated with nomads in various parts of the Islamic world. The simplest looms are stretched out on the sand and, as well as for kelims, the woven cloth is used for tents, bags, tent dividers, cushions and bedding, men's cloaks and sometimes women's clothes. Where there are so few possessions, textiles take on enormous importance, making up the bulk of a family's material goods and also being one of the few ways for women of the household to show off their skills.

Men naturally lavished great care on possessions on which their life might depend, so metalwork is primarily seen in weapons and armour, such as the splendid Irano-Indian sets of etched steel from the 17th and 18th centuries. Another important form of metalwork is jewellery. Under Islamic law a woman's possessions were unalienably her own (unlike in the Christian West) and she kept much of her wealth in gold or silver about her person. However, since styles change, old pieces are frequently melted down by succeeding generations so relatively few pieces from the past have survived. Styles range from enormous archaic silver brooches and great necklaces of amber and coral worn for "good luck" by the Berber women of Morocco to exquisite pieces of enamel, filigree and gold rich with gems worked for the Mughal courts of northern India.

The third area of metalworking is probably the one with which the West is most familiar: domestic vessels, for cooking and serving food, ewers for water or scent and decorative objects of various kinds.

Early Islamic textiles, *such as this 11th-century silk cloth, are sometimes found in Christian churches in Spain. This example, decorated with harpies and griffins, was found in the tomb of San Pedro de Osma in Burgo de Osma cathedral.*

SCIENCE

THE PRESERVATION, ELABORATION AND TRANSMISSION of the scientific tradition of late antiquity is one of the great achievements of classical Islamic civilization. The essential process of translation into Arabic and assimilation to an Islamic cultural context took place in Baghdad between the 8th and the 10th century.

This 9th-century brass astrolabe *was made in what is now Iraq by the instrument-maker 'Ahmad Ibn Khalaf.*

These translations established the framework for original speculation, generating debate about the relationship between reason and revelation that persists to this day. These texts, embedded in their Arabic commentaries, were ultimately transmitted to Europe, beginning in the 11th century, and formed the basis for pre-modern Western science and philosophy.

There were three scientific traditions in late antiquity, the Greek, the Indian and the Chinese. The conquests gave Muslim scholars access to the first two of these, but Chinese science remained beyond the ken of the Islamic world, although some Chinese technologies percolated into Islamic lands along the Silk Road and in the wake of the Mongol conquests.

The first concerted efforts to incorporate the body of Greek scientific thought into an Islamic context are conventionally supposed to have begun with the establishment of the 'Abbasid dynasty. Yet even in Umayyad times there is evidence of interest in both Greek and Indian learning. The little Umayyad audience hall and bath of Qasr 'Amra, built in 711, the year Muslim armies invaded Spain, contains a painted representation of the zodiac on the inside of the dome. It is made on what appears to be a stereographic projection, as described by Ptolemy. The same room contains paintings of personifications of History, Philosophy and Poetry. Each figure is labelled in Greek. The interest in Greek science hinted at in the frescoes of Qasr 'Amra is confirmed by references in the early historians to alchemical experiments made by Khalid ibn al-Yazid, the grandson of the first Umayyad Caliph, Mu'awiya. Astronomy, astrology and alchemy were thus the first sciences to preoccupy Muslim scholars. Towards the end of the Umayyad period, the first literary work in Arabic appeared. This was *Kalila wa Dimna*, an Arabic translation of a Pahlavi version of a lost Sanskrit original done by a Zoroastrian convert to Islam, Ibn al-Muqaffa'. This serpentine line of transmission is typical. This little work is not a slavish translation of the original, a version of the well-known mirror for princes in the form of animal fables called the Panchatantra, but an elegant recreation for a Muslim audience in a language that had never before been used for secular prose literature. So already in Umayyad times influences from Greece and India were beginning to be felt. These increased exponentially with the founding of the new capital, Baghdad, in 763.

The position of Baghdad at the crossroads of Asia and its multiethnic population made it the ideal clearing house for ideas as well as merchandise. It was located very near the town of Gondeshapur, in the Ahwaz, where a school of medicine had flourished since Sasanid times, staffed largely by Nestorian Christians who had sought refuge in Persia from persecution by the Byzantines after the Council of Ephesus in 431 excommunicated Nestorius. The Nestorians brought with them a knowledge of two sciences later to be intensively cultivated by Muslim scholars: medicine and astronomy. A physician from the academy at Gondeshapur named Jirjis ibn Bakhtishu cured the caliph al-Ma'mun of an ailment, and became court physician. For almost five generations, members of this Christian family practised as physicians and produced medical works, melding the Indian and Hellenic traditions.

The Nestorians, like much of the population of Iraq and Syria, spoke Aramaic and the more learned had Greek as a second language. The written form of Aramaic used by the Christian communities of Iraq and Syria was Syriac. Greek science reached the Arabic-speaking world largely through translations into Syriac, although there are notable cases of Arabic-speakers learning Greek in order to read the sources in the original.

The two rabbinical academies of Sura and Pumbedita were very near Baghdad, and indeed, the Gaons of these academies were confirmed in office by the caliphs. Jewish scholars played an important role, particularly in the fields of medicine and pharmacy.

There was yet another source of specialized knowledge in the region of the Islamic heartland. This was in Harran, ancient Carrhae, where the last pagan community to survive in a sea of monotheism still held out. They were star worshippers, and had inherited not only Hellenistic traditions but preserved some of the mathematical legacy of ancient Babylonia.

The constellation of Andromeda *is one of many attractive illustrations in* The Book of the Fixed Stars *compiled by Abd al-Rahman ibn Umar al-Sufi in the 10th century. The individual stars forming the constellation are shown in red.*

Aristotle teaching *in an illustration from* Choice Wise Sayings and Fine Statements *by 11th-century Egyptian writer Mubashshir ibn Fatik.*

This community produced a number of scholars, including the famous Thabit ibn Qurra, who made significant contributions to mathematics and astronomy.

Al-Mansur, the founder of Baghdad, sent embassies to the Byzantine emperor asking for Greek mathematical texts, in particular the *Elements* of Euclid. His son Harun al-Rashid acquired a number of other Greek texts as booty in raids on Byzantine territory. The fact that the Arabic annals often mention diplomatic embassies sent to find specific works is an indication of how rare they were.

Al-Ma'mun created the Bayt al-Hikma, "House of Wisdom" and staffed it with Christian and Muslim scholars. Remarkably like a modern research institute, it was dedicated to the systematic translation of Greek scientific works into Arabic. Some 57 scholars were associated with the House of Wisdom, and its running costs ran to 500 gold dinars a month. These original versions underwent continual revision, as new texts were translated. In the process, all the procedures of modern scholarship were developed, such as collating a number of manuscripts to establish a critical text, glossaries, marginal commentaries and the compilation of dictionaries of technical terms. Scholars working in the House of Wisdom encountered Arabic numerals in translations of Indian astronomical works, as well as the place-value system that allowed all numbers to be expressed by means of nine figures plus zero (Arabic *sifr*).

Muslim scholars loved to quote the legend Aristotle inscribed above the door to his house: "Let no one enter who does not have a knowledge of mathematics", and it was in mathematics and logic – considered the basis for all other sciences – that Muslim scientists made their most lasting contributions.

The copy of Euclid brought back from Constantinople was translated twice, once for Harun al-Rashid and once for al-Ma'mun. These translations were used to prepare a critical edition by Ishaq ibn Hunayn and Thabit ibn Qurra. A commentary on Euclid by Hero of Alexandria was also translated. In the 13th century, the standard commentary was written by Nasir al-Din al-Tusi. This was one of the earliest Arabic texts to be printed in 16th-century Europe, using Arabic type designed especially for the Vatican Press. Many other works by Euclid or attributed to him were translated, along with at least eleven works by Archimedes, as well as later Greek authors including Nichomachus of Gerasa, Theodosius of Tripoli, Menelaus and Apollonius of Perga.

These, together with a number of translations of Indian mathematical works inspired al-Khwarizmi's *Addition and Subtraction in Indian Arithmetic,* translated into Latin in Toledo in the 11th century under the title

Nasir al-Din al-Tusi's *observatory at Maragha in Iran was the most advanced in the Islamic world in the 13th century.*

Algorismi de numero indorum, introducing Arabic numerals to the west and giving us the word algorithm, the Latin version of the author's name. His other fundamental work was the *Kitab al-Jabr wa l-Muqabala*, the first book on algebra. The Latin translation of this work was the standard text on the subject in some European universities well into the 16th century.

Translations of Ptolemy's *Almagest* laid the foundations of mathematical astronomy, and well into the 18th century Islamic observatories like the famous Jantar Mantar in Delhi were engaged in revising and perfecting his stellar co-ordinates.

Several Arabic translations of Ptolemy's *Geography* were done, including one by al-Khwarizmi. As with the *Almagest*, this generated an enormous interest in mathematical geography. The length of a terrestrial degree was accurately measured and used to correct Ptolemy. The study of Ptolemy culminated in the work of al-Idrisi, whose maps and accompanying description of the known world were produced at the request of the 12th-century Norman ruler of Sicily, Roger II.

Not all major translation efforts were government sponsored. The famous Banu Musa (The Sons of Musa) not only commissioned translations from the Greek but wrote a number of impressive original contributions to science. Muhammad ibn Musa wrote on celestial mechanics, the origin of the earth, the atom, and an essay on the Ptolemaic universe. His brother Ahmad wrote an important treatise on mechanics while another brother, al-Hasan, studied the geometrical properties of the ellipse. Sometimes the Banu Musa collaborated, and several of their joint productions, translated into Latin by Gerard of Cremona in the 11th century, influenced Fibonacci.

Two other men who played a key role in the transmission of Greek learning were Hunayn ibn Ishaq and Qusta ibn Luqa. Hunayn, a Jacobite Christian, was known in Europe in the Middle Ages as Joanitius. He was the son of an apothecary, whose father sent him to Baghdad. He was financially supported by the Banu Musa, who urged him to learn Greek. He set about translating almost the entire corpus of Greek medical works into Arabic, including all of Galen and Hippocrates. Many of the works of these two authors now only exist thanks to Hunayn's translations.

Hunayn also translated the famous Hippocratic oath, which became obligatory for Muslim physicians. He also wrote 29 original works on medical subjects. The most important of these is a collection of ten essays on opthalmology which cover in systematic fashion the anatomy and physiology of the eye and the treatment of various eye diseases. It is the first Arabic medical

A doctor cups a patient *in front of a crowd of curious onlookers in an illustration from a 13th-century Arabic manuscript.*

Al-Idrisi *(c.1099–1165) wrote a comprehensive world geography illustrated with maps for Roger II of Sicily. This world map based on his work is oriented to the south, in keeping with Islamic cartographic tradition.*

THE HOUSE OF WISDOM

When the Byzantine emperors conquered Syria, the scientific works of the Greeks were still in existence… as time went on, and the Muslim dynasty flourished, the Muslims developed an urban culture which surpassed that of any other nation. They began to wish to study the various branches of philosophy, of whose existence they knew from their contact with bishops and priests among their Christian subjects. The Caliph al-Mansur therefore sent an embassy to the Byzantine emperor, asking him to send him translations of books on mathematics. Muslim scholars studied these books, and their desire to obtain others was whetted. When al-Ma'mun, who had some scientific knowledge, assumed the caliphate, he wished to do something to further the progress of science. For that purpose, he sent ambassadors and translators to the Byzantine empire, in order to search out works on the Greek sciences and have them translated into Arabic.

Ibn Khaldun, 14th-century North African historian

work to include anatomical drawings. It was translated into Latin and for centuries remained the most authoritative work on the subject.

Qusta ibn Luqa wrote 40 original works on the most varied subjects: medicine, politics, insomnia, "burning mirrors" (convex mirrors used to focus the sun's rays and set fire to things), hair diseases, fans, anecdotes from the lives of the Greek philosophers, a study of dyes, a little essay on nutrition and a study of paralysis.

The greatest of the 9th-century physicians was al-Razi. He wrote more than 184 works, 56 of them on medical topics. Deeply versed in Greek medicine, his originality lay in his open advocacy of experimental observation. Many of the works of Plato and Aristotle were also translated, along with the commentaries that had grown up around their works. The late classical philosophers had tried to reconcile the two, and this neo-Platonic tradition was inherited by the Muslim world through the commentaries that accompanied their texts.

In the 12th century, Ibn Rushd (Averröes) and al-Ghazali embodied the conflict between reason and revelation. The rationalism of Ibn Rushd, his separation of philosophy from theology was violently antipathetic to al-Ghazali, whose intuitive and mystical sense of the Divine rejected scholasticism. Normative Islam follows al-Ghazali, and Ibn Rushd found no following in Islamic lands, but his commentaries on Aristotle, translated into Latin, had a profound effect on European thought.

Many of the scientific works produced by the House of Wisdom and the succeeding generations of Muslim thinkers were translated into Latin and gave birth to European science and philosophy. The Christian conquest of Toledo in 1085 allowed first-hand contact between European and Muslim scholars. Avid for learning, men from all over Europe flocked to Toledo, where another great movement of translation occurred. Arabic works were translated into Hebrew and thence into Latin. Some Christian scholars even learned Arabic, as Hunayn ibn Ishaq had set about learning Greek long before. After the conquest Seville in 1248, another intense period of translation and adaptation ensued. Works by Muslim agronomists like Ibn al-Awwam were translated and were still being used in one form or another in the 16th century.

The task performed by the scholars associated with the House of Wisdom involved nothing less than the transfer of the philosophical and scientific legacy of the ancient world, first into the Arabic language, then into the conceptual framework of Islam. For one of the few times in human history, a culture with its own language, religion and customs embarked upon the extraordinary task of fitting an alien intellectual tradition into its own language and conceptual framework. In the process the experimental method, the basis of all scientific progress, was clearly enunciated.

MODERNITY & TRADITION

The Islamic world was profoundly affected by the economic, political and social changes that swept the world in the 19th century, responding to European expansion and economic and military dominance in a variety of ways. Now all Muslim countries are politically independent, but still seeking a balance between tradition and modernity that will allow them to develop on their own terms.

Modernity is not incompatible *with tradition, as this photograph shows. Oil-producing countries like Saudi Arabia have created modern infrastructures and educational systems within a traditional social framework.*

MODERNITY

I T IS EASIER TO LIST THE ELEMENTS that make up the condition of modernity than it is to define the term. The condition itself is relatively new in historical terms, dating back a mere 200 years. It was the outcome of two European revolutions, the Industrial Revolution and the French Revolution. The complex of techniques and ideas they generated are loosely grouped under the label "modernity".

Industrialization created the need for an educated work force, and this led to mass education and consequent social and economic mobility and new social groupings, such as labour unions and political parties. Representative government was found to be the most efficient form of government. The accumulation of capital led to reinvestment and the ability to replicate resources. The need for new markets and new sources of raw materials spurred colonial expansion. Industrial expansion was based on scientific advances, which gave rise to the idea of progress and in time seriously undermined accepted religious beliefs. Secular nation states with constitutional and democratic governments were formed. As the colonial period ended following the Second World War, the present global system of sovereign national states, often cutting across former ethnic and tribal divisions, was in place.

The very concept of the nation state was alien to Islam, for Muslim identity is not based on nationality, but faith. Nor, traditionally, do Muslims link ethnicity to territory. The ideal of a single Muslim community, defined in spiritual rather than territorial terms and guided by a caliph, persisted as an ideal even after the formal abolition of the Caliphate by Atatürk in 1926 and the formation of sovereign nation states in Islamic lands.

EAST AND WEST

Throughout the European Middle Ages, Islamic lands were the home of technological innovation and intellectual creativity, particularly in the sciences and philosophy. The movement of ideas, like the movement of spices, was from east to west. Highly developed agricultural production, urban crafts and commerce created great wealth and permitted the growth of large and splendid cities. The position of Islamic lands astride the great Eurasian trade routes, their overland and maritime commerce with India, the Indonesian archipelago, China,

Throughout the Middle Ages *and well into modern times, textiles were the major trade goods of the Islamic world and silk, cotton and linen were introduced wherever climatic conditions allowed. These modern silks from India continue an ancient tradition of craftsmanship.*

Africa south of the Sahara and East Africa, gave the great cities of the Middle East access to the silks, spices, and other luxury goods in such demand in Europe. Muslim merchants controlled the land routes, as well as the maritime commerce in the Indian Ocean.

The commercial expansion of Europe beginning in the 13th century eventually led, in the 15th, to economic and technological parity with Islamic lands. The combination of political power and private finance generated European expansion, as it did the growing capitalist economies of Europe.

When the Portuguese reached India in 1498, the technological gap between the newcomers and the civilization they found was narrow. Aside from having better guns – and no inhibitions about using them on unarmed shipping – the Portuguese were not obviously more technologically advanced than the cultures they encountered. The Samorin of Calicut was appalled at the cheap trade goods Vasco da Gama offered to exchange for pepper, and advised him that if he wanted to participate in the Indian Ocean trading network to bring gold on his next voyage.

The Portuguese plan of dominating Indian Ocean trade by force was countered by local Muslim principalities, which quickly adopted new-model European firearms and were able to withstand them. The Portuguese survived by becoming one among many such trading principalities and gradually being absorbed into the preexisting network. By the time the Dutch reached the Indian Ocean a century

A complex interlocking system of overland and sea routes linked Islamic lands with northern Europe, China, and Africa. Ideas, technologies, and luxury goods flowed along these routes, whose maintenance a primary responsibility of Muslim rulers.

Trade in Medieval Eurasia

— Arab trade route
— Silk Road   } routes opened during the
--- other route   } 'Mongol Peace' c.1250–1350
— Chinese trade route
— Genoese trade route
— Venetian trade route
— main Hanseatic trade routes
— other trade route

later, Europe was already in its pre-Industrial stage. The Dutch were able, by main force, to gain control of all the sources of supply of the spices, and by the middle of the 17th century established a monopoly over all the goods of Asia exported to European markets. Maritime Southeast Asia was thus the first region to experience pre-modern European commercial practices. The network of Muslim shipping that had plied the waters of the Indian Ocean since the 8th century was severely disrupted.

Over the next three centuries, Islamic lands increasingly bore the brunt of European colonialism. Between 1798 and 1814, the British occupied almost all of India, by 1850 they controlled the entire subcontinent. In 1830, France occupied Algeria. In 1839, the British occupied Aden. France took Tunisia in 1881, Britain Egypt the following year. The Sudan was occupied in 1889. The Italians occupied Libya in 1912, the same year the French marched into Morocco. Following the First World War, and the defeat of the Ottomans, the former Ottoman provinces of Syria, Lebanon, Palestine, Iraq and Transjordan were all placed under French or British mandates or protectorates, while Muslim populations in Central Asia were absorbed into the Soviet Union.

The arrogance *of European colonialism is unwittingly captured in this painting of a Moroccan shaykh humbling himself before a French colonel.*

Reform

The Ottoman defeat before the walls of Vienna in 1683, and the humiliating terms of the Treaty of Karlovitz had made the necessity of reform obvious.

In 1726, a young reformer in Constantinople, Ibrahim Muteferrika, received permission from the religious authorities to establish the first printing press in the Ottoman empire. Among the books he issued was a history of the discovery and conquest of the New World. More importantly, he published a work called the *Nizam al-Umam*, "The Ordering of the Nations", intended to convince the sultan of the necessity of introducing European tactics and organizational methods into the Ottoman army. European advisors were hired and a school of geometry opened soon afterwards. These reforms met resistance from the corps of Janissaries, as did later attempts to form a new style army.

Another, different sort of reform movement also occurred in the 18th century, this time in Arabia. A reformer named Muhammad ibn 'Abd al-Wahhab set forth a programme to renew and purify Islam, cleansing the faith of non-Qur'anic accretions. The rulers of central Arabia, the Al Sa'ud, embraced this movement, and although defeated by the Ottoman army, this Unitarian puritanical movement continued to flourish.

In 1798 Napoleon invaded Egypt. The ease with which the French army occupied the country, the printing press that produced propaganda broadsheets

On Technology

"It is vital for the Muslims, formerly in advance of the West in the sciences, not to let themselves be eclipsed by them."

From Ibrahim Muteferrika's application to start a printing press, Constantinople 1726.

and newspapers in Arabic, his claim to be a Muslim, his entourage of indefatigable savants who carried out a meticulous description of the country, the artists who drew everything from the pyramids to pairs of sandals, his scientific laboratory which was demonstrated to the 'ulama – all this amazed and astonished the inhabitants, as it was designed to.

As well as soldiers, Napoleon's ships carried ideas. Nationalism, representative government, patriotism, liberty and equality – including sexual equality – were incendiary concepts. Even more than the Ottoman defeat outside the walls of Vienna, the brief Napoleonic occupation of Egypt caused men to reflect on the reasons for European military and technological superiority.

In 1826, the Sultan abolished the Janissaries and reorganized the army. This reorganization involved various political and institutional reforms as well, but these were not far-reaching enough to halt the decline of Ottoman power. The introduction of a code of civil liberties in 1839 was another important break with the past.

The Ottoman governor of Egypt from 1805 to 1848, Muhammad Ali, made a brutal concerted effort to modernize the administration, the economy and the army, using European advisors and officers. His successful campaigns in Arabia against the puritan movement launched by Muhammad ibn 'Abd al-Wahhab, his conquest of the Sudan and victories against the Ottomans in Syria, appeared to justify his military reforms. He made himself the *de facto* independent ruler of Egypt. His massacre of the Mamluks, the hereditary military elite which – like the Janissaries in Istanbul – resisted all attempts at military reform, is his most symbolic act, a drastic removal of a survival from the past.

Napoleon set up French and Arabic printing presses in Egypt in 1798, first in Alexandria, then in Cairo. This attractively printed broadsheet gives the text of a speech by Napoleon on the eve of war with Austria.

He confiscated the lands and property administered as pious endowments (*awqaf*), control and administration of which had traditionally been in the hands of the 'ulama. This was a major blow at the Islamic infrastructure of the country and was followed by another. The 'ulama were divested of what remaining power they had, a radical assault on tradition which confirmed many in the belief that modernization was incompatible with Islam. Muhammad Ali authorized the establishment of a printing press, which played an important role in the spread of learning. Muhammad Ali's grandson Ismail was even more extreme in his attempts to transform Egypt into a modern state, building the Suez Canal and setting up an ambitious educational programme. But in doing so Egypt was bankrupted and in 1882 the British took over the financial administration of the country.

But the most far-reaching transformation of a Muslim country was in Turkey itself, at the hands of Mustafa Kemal, "Atatürk". The Arabic alphabet, with all its religious associations, was abolished and replaced by the Latin script. This was an act of tremendous symbolic significance. It was followed by the closing of Islamic schools and legal institutions. The 'ulama were disestablished. The mystical Sufi orders, to which most adult males belonged, were suppressed. In 1926 the institution of the caliphate itself was abolished. Turkey is today officially a secular state, although the population is overwhelmingly Muslim in faith.

The Suez Canal, opened in 1869, was one of the greatest engineering feats of the 19th century. It reduced the length of the sea route to India by 9,700 miles (15,600 km), but bankrupted Egypt. Britain bought a controlling interest in the canal in 1875.

The most extreme attempt at secularization, accompanied by great brutality, occurred in Iran, under Reza Shah. A civil law code was introduced and the administration of the pious endowments taken from the hands of the 'ulama, as they had been in Egypt and Turkey. Islamic schools were closed, Islamic dress, even the veil, forbidden. The pilgrimage to Mecca, one of the "Five Pillars of Islam" was prohibited. Reza Shah's successor, Muhammad Reza Shah, continued the anti-Islamic policies of his father, and the result was the Islamic Revolution under Ayatollah Khomeini.

The establishment of secular regimes led to the loss of status and power by traditional elites. Almost everywhere the shari'a was replaced by law codes imported from the west, although the shari'a typically continued to rule family law. The disestablishment of the 'ulama by Muhammad Ali, Atatürk, Reza Shah, and more recent leaders, created a crisis of authority. Traditionalist scholars, represented by the 'ulama, were the custodians of Divine Law and its interpretation. They formed the elite from which high ranking government officials, muftis, qadis and administrators had always been drawn. Their removal from positions of authority affected the stability of society and one of the traditional checks on power. The spread of literacy, without the safeguard of supervised study and certificates of qualification *(ijaza)*, democratized access to religious learning. The consequences of this, both positive and negative, resonate throughout the Muslim world.

The Turkish Republic was founded by Mustafa Kemal, later known as Atatürk ("Father of the Turks"), who drove foreign armies from Anatolia and established a modern secular state.

RESPONSES TO MODERNITY

Beginning in the 19th century, generations of Muslim intellectuals responded to the challenges posed by modernity and secularizing regimes, articulating a wide spectrum of analyses and programmes that are roughly grouped under the headings of reformists and modernists. 19th-century modernists held that the only way for Muslims to regain control of their destinies was through the modernization of institutions, particularly education. This was normally a position taken by elites, military or civil, who had had direct contact with Western civilization. Many of these men were enthusiastic about certain aspects of modernity, although all warned against the superficial adoption of Western practices. Many modernists thought religion should be a private matter. If properly understood, they maintained, there was no conflict between Islam and modern science. The modernist suggestion that social change should be reflected by changes in the interpretation of Divine Law was a new departure and attracted controversy.

Tehran in the 1950s, following the reforms of Reza Shah, began to resemble a European city. All forms of traditional dress were banned under the Shah's unpopular modernization programme.

The reformists assumed a traditional posture and argued that Islam must be renovated from within to withstand modernity from without. The purification of Islam by the elimination of practices not sanctioned by the Qur'an and sunna would lead to unity and triumph over their adversaries. Although they vigorously opposed Westernization, reformists recognized the need for institutional reform and the value of education, science and technology. Reformist movements like the Muslim Brotherhood, founded by Hasan al-Banna in 1928, actively tried to improve the lot of the people by building schools, clinics and factories. The Muslim Brotherhood and similar reform movements have broad popular support throughout the Islamic world and many adherents among the professional classes.

Islamism was born out of opposition to corrupt secular regimes, particularly that of the late Shah in Iran, but its emphasis on return to the sources of Islam, the Qur'an and sunna and rejection of all other authority harks back to reformers like Muhammad ibn 'Abd al-Wahhab. It represents the radical militant wing of Islam and has had notable success in the burgeoning cities

Rule by secularizing military elites has been a feature of a number of modern Islamic states. This poster vividly illustrates the leadership cult fostered by Saddam Hussein in Iraq.

of the Islamic world, providing networks of social services to the urban poor in return for militant support. Islamists emphasize the simplicity of Islam, which must inform every aspect of personal life and society. Only rule by Divine Law can guarantee a just society. Like Christian fundamentalists, they reject modernist metaphorical interpretations of the Qur'an. Modernity is rejected, although not technology, which has greatly aided the spread of Islamist ideas. Western civilization is the enemy, and America is identified with the Qur'anic Satan, who tries to seduce humanity from the straight path to salvation.

Ayatollah Khomeini *was able to reverse decades of secularization in Iranian society when he came to power through the 1979 revolution that ousted the shah.*

GLOBALIZATION

The process of modernization that began in the early 19th century and in the 20th century culminated in the creation of a system of nation states locked into an international economy has evolved into a global system marked by extreme mobility which has already transcended the structure from which it grew. Muslim communities now exist in almost every country in the world, and the border between the "Abode of Islam" and the "Abode of War" can no longer be mapped.

The classical shari'a, elaborated in the wake of the triumphal expansion of Islam, did not contemplate the possibility of permanent Muslim communities dwelling in non-Muslim lands. These communities are challenged by difficult questions. Can a practising Muslim fully comply with civil laws that conflict with the shari'a? Can he or she participate fully in political processes? Does loyalty to Islam transcend loyalty to the state? Should Muslims assimilate to the dominant society or remain separate? What are the limits of tolerance of the host community? Many of these are questions first posed with the rise of secular regimes within the Muslim world itself, but they have been given added urgency for European and American Muslims by the events of September 11 and their aftermath. The Muslim extremists who hijacked four airliners, crashing two of them into the World Trade Center in New York and one into the Pentagon, had been living in the United States for a long time in order to plan this symbolic terrorist assault on the West and its values.

Just as territorial borders have been transcended, the revolution in information technology is eliminating internal barriers. It is no longer possible for states or elites to control access to information. Educational systems established during the period of modernization have created widespread literacy, and Muslim men and women have direct access to the foundation texts of their faith as well as to secular literature. This has displaced traditional elites, and created, on the one hand, reform and revivalist movements and, on the other, increased secularization. It has led to productive and dynamic dialogues with the past that have already resulted in reassessments of the nature of the shari'a, the relationship between religion and politics, and the traditional role of women in Islamic society. Militant Islamism, with its narrow and literal reading of Qur'an and *hadith*, bypassing the complexity of classical interpretations, is oddly enough also a product of the spread of literacy and the loss of traditional *'ulama*. The richness and flexibility of classical Islam, which could accommodate within the *umma* not only the "peoples of the book", but such variant social systems as the matriarchy of Minangkabau in Sumatra, is still a fruitful model for the future. Muslims throughout the world will continue to formulate responses to the challenge of globalization from within the tradition that has proved so creative and dynamic in the past.

OPPOSITE

All over the Islamic world *children learn to read the Qur'an in the original Arabic. These Indonesian boys are reading from large, legible copies of the Qur'an.*

COUNTRY PROFILES

THIS DIRECTORY IS INTENDED to provide a range of up-to-date reference material covering the leading Muslim nations of the world today. The criterion for inclusion was quite simply any nation with a majority (i.e. more than 50%) of the population professing Islam as their religion. It is recognized that this criterion excludes India, which is the country with the second largest Muslim population today, and China with its unreported and unrecorded Islamic peoples. The selection of data is intended to provide a general portrait of each nation through its social, political, economic and cultural characteristics. One of the key features is comparability – the data has been assembled to allow direct comparison of any one nation with any other. Naturally, every attempt has been made to ensure accuracy and validity at the time of going to press (June 2003). For more detailed analyses of the Islamic nations, the *DK Financial Times World Desk Reference* is recommended.

 Date of independence or formation

 Date when current borders were established

 National day

 Vehicle identification code

 Time zone: hours plus or minus from GMT

 International telephone dialling code

 Internet country identifying code

POLITICS

 Dates of last and next legislative elections

 Name of head of state. In many cases this is a nominal position and does not indicate that this is the country's most powerful person

 System of government

WORLD AFFAIRS

 Membership of international organizations. A selection of principal organisations; countries may have membership status within numerous other organizations

 Date of entry into the United Nations

PEOPLE & SOCIETY

 Population density: people per square mile

 Percentage of population living in urban/rural areas

 Religious affiliation

 Use of death penalty

ECONOMICS

 World Gross National Product ranking

 Balance of payments

 Gross National Product per capita

 Annual rate of inflation

MEDIA

 Level of political censorship

 Television ownership

 Main national newspapers/ total daily circulation

 TV/Radio stations State-owned/independent

SPENDING

 Vehicle ownership: vehicles per thousand people

 Defence spending: percentage of annual GDP

 Education spending: percentage of annual GDP

 Health spending: percentage of annual GDP

RESOURCES

 Total electric power capacity

 Electricity generation by energy source

 Estimated livestock resources

 Oil production: barrels per day/total oil reserves barrels

EDUCATION

 Literacy rate: percentage of total population

 Students in tertiary education

 School leaving age

 Percentage of each age group enrolled in each education sector

DEFENCE

 Annual defence budget

 Requirement for compulsory military service

 Nuclear capability

 Total combined forces personnel

HEALTH

 People per doctor

 Average life expectancy

Birth rate: births per thousand people

Infant mortality: deaths per thousand live births

Sources of statistical data

Cambridge International Reference on Current Affairs (CIRCA)
Europa World Yearbook
European Bank for Reconstruction and Development (EBRD)
Food and Agriculture Organization (FAO)
International Atomic Energy Agency (IAEA)
International Institute for Strategic Studies (IISS)
International Labor Organization (ILO)
International Monetary Fund (IMF) World Economic Outlook
International Union for Conservation of Nature (IUCN)
Organization for Economic Cooperation Development (OECD)
OECD Development Assistance Committee (DAC)
Organization of Petroleum Exporting Countries (OPEC)
United Nations: *Demographic Yearbook, Energy Statistics Yearbook, Industrial Commodity Statistics Yearbook, International Trade Statistics Yearbook, Statistical Yearbook,* Children's Fund (UNICEF), Development Program (UNDP)
United States Central Intelligence Agency (CIA)
World Bank: *World Development Indicators, World Development Report, World Bank Atlas*
World Conservation Monitoring Center (WCMC)
World Economic Forum
World Health Organization (WHO)

ALBANIA

OFFICIAL NAME **Republic of Albania** CAPITAL **Tirana**
POPULATION **3.2m** CURRENCY **Lek** OFF. LANG. **Albanian**

LYING AT THE south-eastern end of the Adriatic Sea, opposite the heel of Italy, Albania is a poverty-stricken, mountainous country which became a one-party Communist state in 1944. The "land of the eagles", as it is known locally, first held multi-party elections in 1991. Economic collapse provoked uprisings and virtual anarchy in 1997, and the country was only stabilized by the intervention of OSCE troops.

POLITICS

 2001/2005   President Alfred Moisiu   Multi-party republic

AT THE LAST ELECTION

People's Assembly 140 seats

4% **DP**   8% **Other**

52% **PSS**   33% **BF**   3% **PDS**

PSS = Socialist Party of Albania   **BF** = Union for Victory (led by the Democratic Party – **PD**)   **DP** = Democrat Party (splinter from PD)   **PDS** = Social Democratic Party

Albania was dominated for more than 40 years by communist ruler Enver Hoxha, who died in 1985. An exodus of Albanians in 1991 finally persuaded the regime to call multi-party elections. The resulting center-right coalition failed, however, to create a Western-style liberal state.

Many people were ruined by investing in "pyramid" savings schemes which collapsed in 1997, prompting a rebellion in the south and forcing the government to resign. A coalition led by the socialist PSS won elections held that year. In 2002 the PSS was wracked by internal disputes, and by July, party leader Fatos Nano had won through to become prime minister.

WORLD AFFAIRS

  CE, PfP, WTO, OSCE, OIC   1955

Foreign policy in the 1990s was dominated by the fate of Kosovo, the predominately ethnic Albanian region in neighbouring Yugoslavia. Separatism also erupted in Macedonia in 2001, although Albania's own influence is small. Membership of NATO and the EU is a long-term goal.

PEOPLE & SOCIETY

 302 people per sq mile   43% urban 57% rural

 Sunni Muslim 70% Greek Orthodox 20% Roman Catholic 10%   Death penalty not used

Official statistics admitted the existence of ethnic minorities in Albania only in 1989. The Greek minority strongly contests these statistics, which state that 98% of the population are Albanian. Located mainly in the south, the Greeks claim to make up 10% of the population. They suffer considerable discrimination.

Map

Total Land Area :
27 400 sq. km (10 579 sq. miles)

POPULATION
◉ over 100 000
○ over 50 000
• over 10 000
• under 10 000

LAND HEIGHT
2000m/6562ft
1000m/3281ft
500m/1640ft
200m/656ft
Sea Level

Maja e Jezercës 2693m
NORTH ALBANIAN ALPS
S E R B. & M O N. (YUGOSLAVIA)
Lake Scutari
Koplik
Bajram Curri
Shkodër
Pukë
Kukës
Gjiri i Drinit
Lezhë
Rrëshen
Gjiri i Rodonit
Peshkopi
Burrel
Shijak
Kruje
M A C E D O N I A
Durrës
TIRANË
Kavajë
Elbasan
Librazhd
Rrogozhinë
Shkubinit
Perrenjas
Lake Ohrid
Lushnjë
Cërrik
Kuçovë
Lake Prespa
Fier
Devollit
Berat
Korçë
Bilisht
Vlorë
Corovodë
Orikum
Këlcyrë
Ersekë
Tepelenë
Gjirokastër
G R E E C E
I O N I A N   S E A
Sarandë
Konispol
A D R I A T I C   S E A
Strait of Otranto

0   40 km
0   40 miles

MOROCCO

| 1956 | 1956 | July 30 | MA | 0 | +212 | .ma |

OFFICIAL NAME **Kingdom of Morocco**   CAPITAL **Rabat**
POPULATION **31m**   CURRENCY **Moroccan dirham**   OFF. LANG. **Arabic**

MOROCCO IS SITUATED IN northern Africa, but at its northernmost point lies only 12 km (8 miles) from mainland Europe, across the Strait of Gibraltar. The late King Hassan's international prestige gave Morocco status out of proportion to its wealth. The main issues the country faces are the internal threat of Islamic militancy and the unresolved fate of Western Sahara, occupied by Morocco since 1975.

POLITICS

 L. House 2002/2007 U. House 2000/2003   HM King Mohammed VI   Constitutional monarchy

Morocco is a constitutional monarchy with a bicameral legislature. King Mohammed VI is seen as a less dominating figure than his late father, Hassan II. His accession has raised hopes for change. The king's marriage in 2002 to computer engineer Salma Bennani was presented as evidence of a more modern and open outlook. The queen is expected to provide a role model for Moroccan women.

AT THE LAST ELECTION

House of Representatives 325 seats
5% UC
15% USFP | 15% PI | 13% PJD | 13% RNI | 8% MP | 6% MNP | 25% Others
USFP = Socialist Union of Popular Forces
PI = Istiqlal (independence) Party   PJD = Justice and Development Party   RNI = National Rally of Independents
MP = Popular Movement   MNP = National Popular Movement
UC = Constitutional Union

House of Councillors 270 seats

An indirectly elected House of Councillors was formed in December 1997

Mohammed VI and his government have ushered in a more liberal stance towards Islamic activists. In 2000, Abdessalam Yassine, spiritual leader of the banned Islamic movement Justice and Good Deeds, was released after ten years' imprisonment without trial. Popular support for Islamic fundamentalism is fuelled by the fear that Morocco is losing its Islamic identity. Pro-Islamist rallies have far outnumbered those by supporters of greater rights for women.

The majority party in parliament chooses the government, but the king reserves the right to appoint or dismiss the prime minister. The formation of a socialist-led government, after elections in 1997, was seen as a breakthrough for the increasing role of the party system. Although the ruling parties maintained their strength in the 2002 elections, support for Islamists rose dramatically.

WORLD AFFAIRS

 NAM, OIC, AL, AMU, IBRD   1956

Morocco's important role in the quest for lasting peace in the Middle East was underlined by Israeli prime minister Yitzhak Rabin's visit to Rabat following the signing in Washington of the 1993 peace accord with the Palestine Liberation Organization. King Hassan's foreign policy was ambiguous, for while he negotiated with Israel he also headed the Jerusalem Committee of the Islamic Conference Organization (OIC). Generally more pro-Western than other Arab states, Morocco has also earned respect by protecting its Jewish minority.

International disapproval has focused on Morocco's occupation since 1975 of the former Spanish colony of Western Sahara. Resistance by Polisario Front guerrillas, who are fighting for an independent Western Sahara, commenced in 1983 and has continued, despite a UN-brokered peace plan in 1991. Since then, UN proposals have

---

ECONOMICS

 56th $-501m

 $1,180 $ 0.6%

Morocco is seeking to make itself attractive to foreign investment, though the arid climate and illicit drug-trafficking hinder its progress. There is an abundant labour force, but high unemployment.

RESOURCES

 13.8bn kwh   Comb. 87% Hydro 13% Nuclear 0%

 Sheep 17.3m Goats 5.2m Cattle 2.7m   241 b/d (reserves 659m bbl)

Morocco possesses 75% of the world's phosphate reserves. The discovery of large oil and gas deposits in the northeastern desert in mid-2000 could yield an annual revenue of $400 million.

DEFENCE

 $1.32bn   Compulsory

 None   196,300

Morocco's long struggle in Western Sahara against Polisario Front guerrillas has given the kingdom's forces a formidable reputation. Moroccans have also fought as mercenaries in the Gulf.

MEDIA

 Some censorship   Medium

 15 daily 27 per 1,000 people   TV: 1/1 Radio: 1/2

The succession of Mohammed VI fuelled hopes of a more liberal climate, but the media remain strictly controlled. State-owned TV began transmissions in Arabic and French in 1962.

EDUCATION

 49%   311,743 students

 14 years   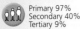 Primary 97% Secondary 40% Tertiary 9%

Literacy rates are lowest in rural areas and girls are particularly affected. The literacy level and elementary school enrolment rates are well below average for countries with similar living standards.

HEALTH

 1 per 2,000 people   68 years

 24 per 1,000 people   47 per 1,000 live births

High infant mortality and poor nutritional standards remain a problem for the poorest Moroccans. Outside the cities, primary health care is virtually non-existent; people depend on traditional remedies.

SPENDING

 41 per 1,000 people   4.2%

5%   1.2%

Income per head is considerably lower than in the neighbouring countries of Algeria and Tunisia. Almost one in five Moroccans live below the poverty line, and the rural–urban gap in wealth is considerable.

included a referendum on self-determination and autonomy for Western Sahara under Moroccan sovereignty. The process remained stalled in 2003, with the UN extending its mandate repeatedly.

Relations with the EU were strengthened with the signing of an association agreement in late 1995, envisaging free trade in industrial goods within 12 years. However, sovereignty disputes with Spain over rocky islets in the Mediterranean were at the heart of a high-profile confrontation in 2002.

PEOPLE & SOCIETY

 180 people per sq mile

 56% urban 44% rural

 Muslim 99% Christian & others 1%

Death penalty used

Morocco, the westernmost of the Maghreb states, is the main refuge for descendants of the original Berber inhabitants of northwest Africa. About 35% of Moroccans are Berber-speaking. They live mainly in mountain villages, while the Arab majority inhabit the lowlands. Before independence from France, 450,000 Europeans lived in Morocco; numbers have since greatly diminished. Some 45,000 Jews enjoy religious freedom and full civil rights – a position in society unique among Arab countries. Most people speak Arabic, and French is also spoken in urban areas. Sunni Islam is the religion of most of the population. The king is the spiritual leader through his position as Commander of the Faithful. Female emancipation has been slow to take root in Morocco, but women are starting to take a more prominent role in society.

ECONOMIC FOCUS

EXPORTS

USA 5%, Germany 6%, UK 7%, Spain 8%, Other 42%, France 32%

IMPORTS

UK 5%, Italy 6%, Germany 6%, Spain 10%, Other 45%, France 28%

STRENGTHS
Morocco's pro-business policies and abundant labour force are helpful in attracting foreign investment. The country has low rates of inflation. The tourist industry (already of importance to the economy), phosphate mining and agriculture all have great potential for future exploitation.

WEAKNESSES
Morocco suffers from high unemployment rates coupled with a rising population growth. Recent droughts have hit the agricultural sector hard. The illicit production of cannabis (Morocco is Europe's main source of resin) complicates closer links with the EU.

PROFILE
The government's large-scale privatization programme, which began in 1992, was designed to attract foreign investment, particularly from Europe. A severe drought in 1995 made austerity measures necessary. The new socialist-led government has given social policy a higher priority. The expected revenue to be gained from the exploitation of Morocco's oil reserves will be channelled into the development of rural areas.

The town of Boumaine-Dadès lies in the southern foothills of the Atlas Mountains. The region's outstanding scenery makes it one of Morocco's major tourist attractions.

MAURITANIA

OFFICIAL NAME **Islamic Republic of Mauritania** CAPITAL **Nouakchott**
POPULATION **2.8m** CURRENCY **Ouguiya** OFF. LANG. **Arabic**

LOCATED IN NORTHWEST AFRICA, Mauritania is a member of both the AU and the Arab League. Formerly a French colony, the country has taken a strongly Arab direction since 1964; today, it is the Maures who control political life and dominate the minority black population. The Sahara extends across two-thirds of Mauritania's territory; the only productive land is that drained by the Senegal river in the south and south-west.

ECONOMICS

 155th $90m

 $370   4.7%

Largest gypsum deposits in the world. Offshore fishing among the best in West Africa. Significant debt cancellations in 2002. Affected by drought, locust attacks and fluctuating commodity prices.

RESOURCES

 155m kwh   Comb. 81%
Hydro 19%
Nuclear 0%

 Sheep 7.6m
Goats 5.1m
Cattle 1.5m   Not an oil
producer

Iron continues to be exploited, despite low world prices. There are some gold and diamond deposits. Mining and fisheries represent 99.7% of exports. Offshore oil exploration yielded finds in May 2001.

DEFENCE

 $25m   Compulsory

 None   15,750

The 15,000-strong army is a strain on Mauritania's budget. Troops are used increasingly in public works projects. France is the main arms supplier. Conscription is authorized for 2 years.

MEDIA

 Censorship   Medium

 1 daily
0.5 per 1,000
people   TV:1/0
Radio: 1/0

The press is heavily censored, and the broadcast media are state-owned. *Chaab*, the government newspaper, is also published in French (*Horizons*).

EDUCATION

 42%   12,912

 16 years   Primary 83%
Secondary 18%
Tertiary 6%

Although over half the population is still illiterate, primary school enrolment rates have increased from 49% in 1987 to 88% in 2000.

HEALTH

 1 per 10,000
people   52 years

173 per 1,000 live births

people

Historic regional inequalities persist and the best facilities are in the capital. The overall level of care is on a par with neighbouring states.

SPENDING

 8 per 1,000
people   2.9%

4.3%   1.4%

The small ruling Maures elite form the richest sector. Wealthy Maures travel to Mecca, Saudi Arabia, to perform the *hajj* (Muslim pilgrimage).

POLITICS

 L. House 2001/2006
U. House 2002/2004   President Maaouya ould
Sid Ahmed Taya   Multi-party
republic

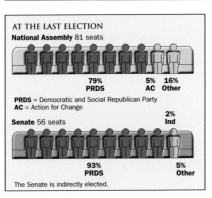

AT THE LAST ELECTION
National Assembly 81 seats

79% PRDS   5% AC   16% Other

PRDS = Democratic and Social Republican Party
AC = Action for Change

Senate 56 seats   2% Ind

93% PRDS   5% Other

The Senate is indirectly elected.

Mauritania officially adopted multi-party democracy in 1991. However, the 1992 and 1997 presidential elections simply returned to power the incumbent military ruler, President Maaouya ould Sid Ahmed Taya, with around 90% of the vote. Opposition parties have accused the government of electoral fraud; initially boycotting legislative elections, they increased their representation in the 2001 poll, but the AC party was subsequently banned.

WORLD AFFAIRS

 OIC, AL, OIF,
AU, CILSS   1961

Mauritania seeks to maintain a balance between sub-Saharan Africa and the Arab world, but has had political tensions with all its neighbours. It has now effectively withdrawn from the Western Sahara dispute. Relations with Senegal have improved since the conflicts of 1989.

PEOPLE & SOCIETY

 7 people per
sq mile   59% urban
41% rural

Muslim 100%   Death penalty
used

The politically dominant Maures make up the majority of the population. Ethnic tension centres on the oppression of blacks by Maures. The old black bourgeoisie has now been superseded by a Maurish class; tens of thousands of blacks are estimated to be in slavery.

Total Land Area : 1 025 520 sq. km (395 953 sq. miles)

LAND HEIGHT
500m/1640ft
200m/656ft
Sea Level

POPULATION
over 500 000
over 10 000
under 10 000

SENEGAL

 1960   1960   April 4   SN   0   +221   .sn

 114th $-310m

 $490   3.1%

OFFICIAL NAME **Republic of Senegal** CAPITAL **Dakar**
POPULATION **9.9m** CURRENCY **CFA franc** OFF. LANG. **French**

S ENEGAL'S CAPITAL, DAKAR, lies on the westernmost cape of Africa. The country is mostly low, with open savannah and semi-desert in the north and thicker savannah in the south. After independence from France in 1960, Senegal was ruled until 1981 by President Léopold Senghor. He was succeeded by his prime minister, Abdou Diouf, who held power for almost 20 years until his election defeat in March 2000.

ECONOMICS

Good infrastructure. Relatively strong industrial sector. Few natural resources exploited, other than fish, phosphates and groundnuts. Access to oil potential hampered by rebellion and poor transport links.

POLITICS

 2001/2006   President Abdoulaye Wade   Presidential democracy

 1.3bn kwh   Comb. 100% Hydro 0% Nuclear 0%

Sheep 4.82m Goats 4m Cattle 3.23 m   Not an oil producer

RESOURCES

Senegal's electricity capacity is largely dependent on imported fuel; cheaper supplies are expected to become available soon. Initial explorations suggest that oil reserves may exist off Casamance.

Senegal has been a multi-party democracy since 1981 when, under the then new president Abdou Diouf, the constitution was amended to allow more than four political parties. However, the PS held power from the 1950s until 2000, and its influence has been pervasive. Presidential elections in 2000 marked a political watershed. Diouf was defeated by Abdoulaye Wade of the liberal democratic PDS, the dominant party in the "Sopi" (Change) coalition which went on to win a landslide victory in the 2001 legislative elections. A new constitution, approved in 2001 by referendum, abolished the Senate and restricts the president to two terms.

AT THE LAST ELECTION
National Assembly 120 seats — 8% PS — 2% AJ–PADS — 74% SC — 9% AFP — 3% URD — 4% Other
SC = Sopi Coalition (led by the Senegalese Democratic Party – PDS) AFP = Alliance of Progressive Forces PS = Senegalese Socialist Party URD = Union for Democratic Renewal AJ–PADS = And Jëf – African Party for Democracy and Socialism

DEFENCE

 $61m   Compulsory

 None   9,400

Senegalese troops took part in Operation Desert Storm in 1991, and intervened in conflicts in Liberia, Rwanda and the Central African Republic. They also helped to quell revolts in Gambia and Guinea-Bissau.

MEDIA

 No censorship   Low

 16 daily 5 per 1,000 people   TV: 1/2 Radio: 1/7

The independent media flourished with multi-partyism. Senegal had the first satirical journal in Africa with the founding of *Le Politicien* in 1978.

WORLD AFFAIRS

 OIC, ECOWAS, CILSS OMVG, FZ   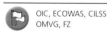 1960

Maintaining good relations with its former ruler France, which is also Senegal's main ally and aid donor, is the major foreign affairs concern. Senegal's relations with neighbouring Gambia, Mauritania and Guinea-Bissau continue to be a constant preoccupation.

EDUCATION

 37%   29,303 students

 13 years   Primary 70% Secondary 20% Tertiary 4%

Illiteracy is Senegal's major educational challenge, especially for women, of whom only 23% can read. There are universities at Dakar and St.-Louis.

Total Land Area : 192 530 sq. km
(74 336 sq. miles)

POPULATION
over 1 000 000
over 100 000
over 50 000
over 10 000
under 10 000

MAURITANIA
Richard Toll
Dagana
Saint-Louis
Lac de Guier
Louga
Dara Linguère Matam
Mékhé
Pikine Thiès Mbaké
DAKAR Diourbel
Mbour
Joal-Fadiout Kaolack Kaffrine Koungheul
Nioro du Rip
GAMBIA Tambacounda
Bignona Vélingara Kolda
Sédhiou Médina Gounas
Cap Roxo Ziguinchor
GUINEA-BISSAU GUINEA
ATLANTIC OCEAN
CASAMANCE
Saloum
Vallée du Ferlo
Senegal
MALI
Bakel
Kédougou 581m
Falémé
Gambia

N

0   100 km
0   100 miles

LAND HEIGHT
200m/656ft
Sea Level

PEOPLE & SOCIETY

 133 people per sq mile   48% urban 52% rural

 Sunni Muslim 90% Christian 5% Traditional beliefs 5%   Death penalty not used

HEALTH

 1 per 10,000 people   53 years

 37 per 1,000 people   60 per 1,000 live births

The state health system is very rudimentary. A successful education campaign has helped to contain the incidence of HIV/AIDS.

Senegal has a fairly well-developed sense of nationhood, and intermarriage between groups has reduced ethnic tensions. Many groups can still be identified regionally, however. A French-influenced class system, inherited from colonial days, is still prevalent. The 2001 constitution gave women property rights for the first time.

SPENDING

 10 per 1,000 people   1.4%

 3.5%   2.6%

Wealth disparities are considerable, and poverty is widespread. Members of the former ruling Senegalese Socialist Party are the wealthiest group.

GAMBIA

| 1965 | 1965 | Feb 18 | WAG | 0 | +220 | .gm |

ECONOMICS

 172nd $-48m

$340   4%

Low tariffs make the Gambia a focus of regional trade. Its well-managed economy is favourably viewed by donors. Smuggling deprives government of significant revenues. Major crop failure in 2002.

RESOURCES

77m kwh   Comb. 100%
Hydro 0%
Nuclear 0%

Sheep 106,000
Goats 145,000
Cattle 265,000   Not an oil producer

The Gambia river is one of Africa's few good waterways, but it is underused owing to its separation from its natural hinterland by the Gambia–Senegal border. Oil deposits are believed to exist offshore.

DEFENCE

$3m   Not compulsory

None   870

Most arms are bought from the UK, although supplies are now increasingly coming from Nigeria too. A defence pact with Senegal collapsed along with the federation in 1989.

MEDIA

Some censorship   Low

2 daily
2 per 1,000 people   TV: 1/0
Radio: 1/8

The independent media are restricted. Radio news broadcasts are dominated by state-controlled Radio Gambia, and the government runs the only national television station.

EDUCATION

37%   1,702 students

Schooling is not compulsory   Primary 81%
Secondary 31%
Tertiary 2%

Efforts to increase enrolment have been successful. Levels are now over 80% for primary and 30% for secondary. A university was established in 1998.

HEALTH

1 per 20,000 people   46 years

41 per 1,000 people   73 per 1,000 live births

Most people have access to basic medicines, but these are no longer free. Advanced medical care in the public sector is limited. A nationwide HIV/AIDS awareness campaign was launched in 2002.

SPENDING

8 per 1,000 people   0.7%

4.8%   2.3%

Public service and the professions have created wealth and some people are comfortably off, but great wealth is not a feature of Gambian life. Unemployed young men in Banjul are regarded as the underclass.

OFFICIAL NAME Republic of the Gambia   CAPITAL **Banjul**
POPULATION 1.4m   CURRENCY **Dalasi**   OFF. LANG. **English**

A NARROW COUNTRY on the western coast of Africa, the Gambia was renowned as a stable democracy until an army coup in 1994. Agriculture accounts for 65% of GDP, yet many Gambians are leaving rural areas for the towns, where average incomes are four times higher. Its position as an enclave within Senegal seems likely to endure, following the failure of an experiment in federation in the 1980s.

POLITICS

 2002/2007   President Yahya Jammeh   Multi-party republic

AT THE LAST ELECTION

National Assembly 53 seats

85% APRC   4% PDOIS   9% Nom   2% NRP

APRC = Alliance for Patriotic Reorientation and Construction
Nom = Nominated   **NRP** = National Reconciliation Party
PDOIS = People's Democratic Organization for Independence and Socialism

The People's Progressive Party (PPP) was in government from 1962 until 1994, for most of which time the Gambia was one of Africa's few democracies. Military leader Yahya Jammeh was elected president in controversial elections in September 1996, and the following January his APRC won the majority of seats in a parliamentary election. Jammeh and the APRC were re-elected in 2001–02.

WORLD AFFAIRS

 OIC, AU, ECOWAS, CILSS, Comm   1965

Commonwealth and Western criticism of the 1994 coup which brought President Jammeh to power has softened over recent years, but international concern was reawoken by an apparent crackdown on opponents following Jammeh's re-election in 2001. Relations with Senegal have been troublesome since the end of federation in 1999.

PEOPLE & SOCIETY

 363 people per sq mile   31% urban 69% rural

 Sunni Muslim 90%
Christian 9%
Traditional beliefs 1%   Death penalty not used

About 90% of Gambians follow Islam, although there is no official state religion. There is a yearly influx of migrants, who come from Senegal, Guinea and Mali to trade in groundnuts. The Gambia is still a very poor country, with 80% of the labour force engaged in agriculture. Women are active as traders and merchants in an otherwise male-dominated society.

Total Land Area : 10 000 sq. km (3861 sq. miles)

LAND HEIGHT
100m/328ft
Sea Level

POPULATION
over 10 000
under 10 000

1958 · 1958 · Apr 3 · RG · 0 · +224 · .gn

OFFICIAL NAME **Republic of Guinea** CAPITAL **Conakry**
POPULATION **8.4 million** CURRENCY **Guinea franc** OFF. LANG. **French**

GUINEA LIES ON the western coast of Africa. Central highlands slope down to coastal plains and swamps; the north is semi-desert. Military rule, established in 1984, ended with disputed elections in 1985. Civil wars in neighbouring states have spilled over into domestic conflict in Guinea.

POLITICS

 2002/2007   President Lansana Conté   Multi-party republic

The death in 1984 of Sekou Touré, who headed the Marxist single-party regime of the Guinea Democratic Party (PDG) from 1958, opened the way for the military to intervene, with promises of multi-party elections. In 1990, a referendum overwhelmingly approved democratic changes, but the military appointed a Transitional Committee, delaying elections until 1993. Incumbent leader General Lansana Conté heavily defeated the Malinke leader, Alpha Condé, who had been exiled until 1992. A controversial constitutional referendum in 2001 allowed Conté to stand for a possible third term. Legislative polls, postponed in December 2001 but eventually held in July 2002, increased the PUP majority.

AT THE LAST ELECTION

National Assembly 114 seats

17% UPR   3% PDG

74% PUP   3% UPG   3% Others

PUP = Party of Unity and Progress   **UPR** = Union for Progress and Renewal   **UPG** = Union for the Progress of Guinea   **PDG** = Democratic Party of Guinea

WORLD AFFAIRS

 OMVG, OIF, OIC, ECOWAS, AU   1958

Balancing the interests of the major aid donors, France and the US, is a growing concern. Relations with neighbouring states, badly affected by conflicts in border regions, were symbolically patched up in 2002.

PEOPLE & SOCIETY

 88 people per sq mile   28% urban / 72% rural

 Muslim 65% / Traditional beliefs 33% / Christian 2%   Death penalty used

The two largest ethnic groups are the Fulani, based in the highland region of Fouta Djallon, and the Malinke, who lost the power they had held under Touré, and have suffered reprisals. Today, the coastal peoples, including the Soussou, are dominant, benefiting from renewed rivalry between the Malinke and Fulani. Women acquired influence within Touré's Marxist party, but a Muslim revival since 1984 has reversed this trend.

POPULATION   LAND HEIGHT

over 500 000
over 50 000
over 10 000
under 10 000

1000m/3281ft
500m/1640ft
200m/656ft
Sea Level

Total Land Area: 245 860 sq. km (94 926 sq. miles)

[Map of Guinea with surrounding countries: SENEGAL, GUINEA-BISSAU, MALI, SIERRA LEONE, LIBERIA, IVORY COAST (CÔTE D'IVOIRE); ATLANTIC OCEAN. Cities: CONAKRY, Koundara, Gaoual, Niagassola, Doko, Touge, Tikinsso, Siguiri, Niantanina, Lélouma, Labé, Sélouma, Koundian, Kouroussa, Mandiana, Boke, Télimélé, Dabola, Kankan, Kamsar, Fria, Mamou, Faranah, Kindia, Coyah, Forécariah, Kissidougou, Kérouane, Koumandou, Konsankoro, Guékédou, Beyla, Macenta, Lola, Nzérékoré, Monts Nimba 1752m. Rivers: Gambia, Konkouré, Kogon, Bafing, Niger, Milo. 100 km / 100 miles scale]

  128th $-165m

 $450   6%

ECONOMICS

Natural resources including bauxite, gold and diamonds. Good soil and climate give high cash-crop yields. Relatively low inflation. Legacy of maladministration from Touré years.

 542m kwh   Comb. 65% / Hydro 35% / Nuclear 0%

 Sheep 892,161 / Goats 1.01m / Cattle 2.68m   Not an oil producer

RESOURCES

Bauxite provides the majority of export earnings. Guinea, with 30% of known world reserves, is the world's largest producer after Australia. Demand for electricity for bauxite processing is high.

 $45m   Compulsory

 None   9,700

DEFENCE

Defence forces consist of an army and a militia, a gendarmerie, and a tiny navy and airforce. Communist states used to be the main arms procurement markets. Weaponry is now supplied by France and the US.

 Some censorship   Low

 1 daily / 2 per 1,000 people   TV: 1/0 / Radio: 1/0

MEDIA

Guinea's limited broadcast media are state-owned. The main newspaper, *Horoya*, is a weekly. There has been a slight relaxation in censorship.

 41%   8,151 students

 13 years   Primary 59% / Secondary 15% / Tertiary 1%

EDUCATION

French was readopted as the main teaching language in 1984, after Sekou Touré's Marxist-inspired experiments with traditional languages.

 1 per 10,000 people   48 years

 39 per 1,000 people   95 per 1,000 live births

HEALTH

Health provision is very poor, reflected in Guinea's high infant mortality rate and low average life expectancy. Private health care was legalized in 1984.

 2 per 1,000 people   1.5%

 1.8%   2.3%

SPENDING

Private enterprise has brought with it a new business class and Guinea now has some wealthy exiles, but much of the country remains poor and underdeveloped; GNP is below $500 per capita.

ALGERIA

1962   1962   Nov 1   DZ   +1   +213   .dz

OFFICIAL NAME **People's Democratic Republic of Algeria**   CAPITAL **Algiers**
POPULATION **31.4m**   CURRENCY **Algerian dinar**   OFF. LANG. **Arabic & Tamazight**

A FRICA'S SECOND-LARGEST COUNTRY, Algeria, which extends from a densely populated Mediterranean coastline to the empty north Sahara, won independence from France in 1962. The military blocked Islamist militants from taking power after winning general elections in 1991, setting up a new civilian regime and fighting a bloody terrorist conflict ever since. Algeria has one of the youngest populations, and highest birth rates, in the region.

POLITICS

 L.House 2002/2007 U.House 2000/2003   President Abdelaziz Bouteflika   Military regime

Until 1988, Algeria was a single-party socialist-style regime. The aging ruling elite adopted privatization policies which were strongly opposed by Islamist militants. The Islamic Salvation Front (FIS) won elections in 1991, but was prevented from taking power by the army. Since 1992 the country has been scarred by appalling violence and tens of thousands of people have been killed in a terrorist campaign and by ruthless state counter-terrorism. Hopes for peace rose when Abdelaziz Bouteflika became president in 1999, although the election was marred by the withdrawal of all other candidates. Parliamentary elections in 2002, won by the FLN, also suffered from a low turnout and a partial opposition boycott. Violence continues, with an annual death toll still in the thousands.

AT THE LAST ELECTION

National People's Assembly 380 seats

| | 8% Ind | 6% Other |

51% FLN   12% RND   11% MRN   10% MSP   5% PT

FLN = National Liberation Front
RND = National Democratic Rally
MRN = Movement for National Reform
MSP = Movement for a Peaceful Society
Ind = Independent   PT = Workers' Party
Other = Progressive Republican Party, Union for Democracy and Liberty, Social Liberal Party

Council of the Nation 144 seats

3% FFS

53% RND   33% App   9% FLN   2% MSP

96 seats are elected, 48 are appointed by the president

Islamist militants want Algeria to become a theocracy. The imposition of military rule to prevent the militants taking office in 1992 unleashed violence spearheaded by the extremist Armed Islamic Group (GIA).

The FIS's 1991 election victory was in part due to popular reaction against economic reforms. After a brief suspension following the army takeover in 1992, the liberalization programme was revived under pressure from the IMF and the World Bank.

WORLD AFFAIRS

 AMU, OPEC, OIC, NAM, AL   1962

Algeria's struggle for independence from France lasted from 1954 until 1962. Throughout the 1960s and 1970s, Algeria's success in rejecting a colonial power made it a champion for the developing world. It had a leading voice within the UN, the Arab League and the Organization of African Unity. However, relations with the West remained essentially stable. Algeria was increasingly seen by the diplomatic community as a useful bridge between the West and Iran. In 1981, Algerian diplomats helped to secure the release of US hostages being held in Tehran. Algeria also attempted to act in a mediating role during the 1980–1988 Iran–Iraq War.

Algeria's influence overseas has diminished as the country has become increasingly unstable politically. A victory for the fundamentalist FIS in Algeria would greatly encourage Islamist militants in neighbouring Morocco and Tunisia, and further undermine Egypt's embattled government.

France fears the spill-over of terrorism and has been shocked by the killings, especially those of seven French priests and of the French Roman Catholic bishop of Oran. Many European governments are anxious to help stabilize the regime to avoid refugees seeking entry into France, Spain and Italy.

PEOPLE & SOCIETY

 34 people per sq mile

 58% urban 42% rural

 Sunni Muslim 99% Christian & Jewish 1%

 Death penalty used

Algeria's population is predominantly Arab, under 30 years of age, and urban; around a quarter are Berber. More than 85% speak Arabic, the official language, and 99% are Sunni Muslim. Mosques also provide social and medical services. Of the million or so French who settled in Algeria before independence, only about 6,000 remain. Most Berbers consider the mountainous Kabylia region their homeland. Demonstrations there have met with violent police crackdowns, particularly in the Berber Spring of 1980, and on its anniversary in 2001. The Berber language, Tamazight, was recognized as an official language in 2002.

Total Land Area : 2 381 740 sq. km (919 590 sq. miles)

ECONOMIC FOCUS

EXPORTS

Netherlands 8%
Spain 11%
Other 32%
France 12%
USA 15%
Italy 22%

IMPORTS

USA 5%
Spain 6%
Germany 7%
Other 43%
Italy 9%
France 30%

STRENGTHS

Oil and gas. Recent collaboration with Western oil companies should see improvements in productivity. Natural gas is supplied to Europe, with plans in hand for the construction of a third undersea pipeline.

WEAKNESSES

Political turmoil threatens many new projects and has led to an exodus of European and other expatriate workers important to the economy. Lack of skilled labour coupled with high unemployment. Limited agriculture. Shortages of basic foodstuffs. A thriving black market.

PROFILE

Under the pro-Soviet National Liberation Front, centralized socialist planning dominated the Algerian economy. In the late 1980s, the economic collapse of the Soviet Union led to a change in policy, and Algeria began moving towards a market economy. The majority of the economy's most productive sectors remain under state control, although private investment is encouraged in the oil industry and, since early 2001, in telecommunications. Western investment levels are likely to remain small as long as the political situation is unstable.

Saharan town, *showing the range of Algeria's scenery, from lush, irrigated gardens near water sources to barren sand dunes beyond. 80% of Algeria is desert.*

MALI

1960 | 1960 | Sept 22 | RMM | 0 | +223 | .ml

ECONOMICS

132nd		$-178m	
$240		5.2%	

Mali is a producer of high-quality cotton. There is irrigation potential from the Niger and Senegal rivers. Mali's vast size and landlocked status present considerable communications problems.

RESOURCES

398m kwh	Comb. 42% Hydro 58% Nuclear 0%
Sheep 6.4m Goats 9.9m Cattle 6.82m	Not an oil producer

Gold deposits are now being mined, and prospecting is under way for tungsten, diamonds, and oil. The exploitation of other natural resources is hampered by Mali's poor infrastructure and landlocked situation.

DEFENSE

$63m	Compulsory
None	7,800

Mali's 7,800-strong armed forces are presently keeping a low profile, and have stayed out of politics since the overthrow of President Traoré in 1991.

MEDIA

Constitution guarantees free press	Low
5 daily 1 per 1,000 people	TV: 1/2 Radio: 1/100+

Even before the 1991 coup, previously rigid controls were being relaxed. The 1992 constitution guarantees the freedom of the press, and Mali's broadcast and print media are now among the freest in Africa.

EDUCATION

41%	18,662 students
13 years	Primary 53% Secondary 14% Tertiary 2%

Only half of children go to primary school and just 14% to secondary school. A 10-year program to raise education levels for girls was launched in 2001.

HEALTH

1 per 10,000 people	52 years
48 per 1,000 people	120 per 1,000 live births

A health program began in 1998, with the aim of higher immunization rates for children and more widespread health care access.

SPENDING

3 per 1,000 people	2.5%
3%	2.1%

Poverty is widespread, and wealth is limited to a very small group; Malians disapprove of flaunted wealth and public ostentation is rare.

OFFICIAL NAME **Republic of Mali**   CAPITAL **Bamako**
POPULATION **12m**   CURRENCY **CFA franc**   OFF. LANG. **French**

MALI IS LANDLOCKED in the heart of west Africa. Its mostly flat terrain comprises virtually uninhabited Saharan plains in the north and more fertile savanna land in the south. The Niger River irrigates the central and southwestern regions. Mali achieved independence from France in 1960. Multiparty democratic elections under a new constitution, in 1992 and then in 1997, provoked accusations of severe irregularities.

POLITICS

2002/2007 | President Amadou Toumani Touré | Multi-party republic

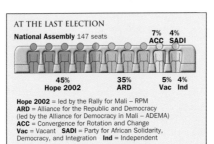

AT THE LAST ELECTION

National Assembly 147 seats

7% ACC   4% SADI
45% Hope 2002   35% ARD   5% Vac   4% Ind

Hope 2002 = led by the Rally for Mali – RPM
ARD = Alliance for the Republic and Democracy (led by the Alliance for Democracy in Mali – ADEMA)
ACC = Convergence for Rotation and Change
Vac = Vacant   **SADI** = Party for African Solidarity, Democracy, and Integration   **Ind** = Independent

The successful transition to multiparty politics in 1992 followed the overthrow in the previous year of Moussa Traoré, Mali's dictator for 23 years. The army's role was crucial in leading the coup, while Colonel Touré, who acted as interim president, was responsible for the swift return to civilian rule in less than a year. For a decade President Alpha Oumar Konaré's ADEMA government attempted to alleviate poverty while placating the opposition. Touré was returned to power in the 2002 presidential elections with the support of all main opposition parties, and in the legislative polls ADEMA saw its majority disappear.

WORLD AFFAIRS

 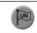

OIF, FZ, OIC, AU, ECOWAS | 1960

Mali concentrates on maintaining good relations with the ECOWAS countries and its northern neighbors. Relations with Libya, which is suspected of fomenting Tuareg revolt, are tense. There are good relations with the US, and other Western aid providers.

PEOPLE & SOCIETY

25 people per sq mile	31% urban 69% rural
Muslim 80% Traditional beliefs 18% Christian & others 2%	Death penalty not used

Mali's most significant ethnic group, the Bambara, is also politically dominant. The relationship between the Bambara–Malinke majority and the Tuareg nomads of the Saharan north is tense and sometimes violent. The extended family is a vital social security system and link between the urban and rural poor. There are a few powerful women in Mali but, in general, women have little status.

Total Land Area : 1 220 190 sq. km (471 115 sq. miles)

LAND HEIGHT
500m/1640ft
200m/656ft
over 100m/328ft

0   200 km
0   200 miles

POPULATION
over 100 000
over 50 000
over 10 000
under 10 000

NIGER

  139th $-168m

 $180   4%

OFFICIAL NAME **Republic of Niger** CAPITAL **Niamey**
POPULATION **11.6m** CURRENCY **CFA franc** OFF. LANG. **French**

L ANDLOCKED IN THE WEST of Africa, Niger is linked to the sea by the Niger River. Saharan conditions prevail in the northern regions, in the area around the Aïr mountains, and, particularly, in the vast uninhabited northeast. Niger was ruled by one-party or military regimes until 1992. A much-troubled democratic process was then disrupted by military coups in 1996 and 1999. It is one of the poorest countries in Africa.

ECONOMICS

Niger has vast uranium deposits. Discoveries of gold and oil in the late 1990s revived hopes for economic viability. The collapse of uranium prices in the 1980s created a large debt burden.

RESOURCES

  234m kwh   Comb. 100% Hydro 0% Nuclear 0%

Sheep 4.5m Goats 6.9m Cattle 2.26m   Not an oil producer

Mining is small-scale and oil reserves, discovered in the Lake Chad area, are not yet commercially viable. Salt is a traditionally exploited resource, as are such plant resources as the doum and palmyra palms.

POLITICS

 1999/2004   President Mamadou Tandja   Multi-party republic

AT THE LAST ELECTION

National Assembly 83 seats

5% ANDP

46% MNSD   20% CDS   19% PNDS   10% RDP

MNSD = National Movement for the Development of Society
CDS = Democratic and Social Convention PNDS = Niger Party for Democracy and Socialism RDP = Rally for Democracy and Progress ANDP = Niger Alliance for Democracy and Progress

The death in 1987 of the military dictator, President Seyni Kountché, paved the way for prodemocracy demonstrations and eventually led to multiparty elections in 1993. An ensuing power struggle between President Mahamane Ousmane and his political opponents provoked a military coup in 1996. General Ibrahim Barre Mainassara promulgated a new constitution and won a presidential election condemned as fraudulent by the opposition. Mainassara was assassinated by his presidential guard in early 1999. The new military leadership drew up yet another constitution. MNSD leader Mamadou Tandja won the presidential poll later that year.

DEFENSE

  $29   Compulsory

None   5,300

Niger's armed forces and paramilitary elements total 10,700 personnel. Niger politics have been dominated by the military since 1974.

WORLD AFFAIRS

 OIC, CILSS, AU, ECOWAS, FZ   1960

Relations have improved with Libya and Algeria since the end of the Tuareg rebellion in 1995. ECOWAS members and the OAU condemned the 1999 coup, as did all key donors.

MEDIA

   Some censorship   Low

1 daily 0.2 per 1,000 people   TV: 1/1 Radio: 1/2

The government controls most broadcasting, though the BBC World Service's Hausa-based programming is an influential medium.

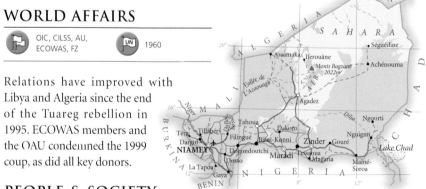

Total Land Area : 1 266 700 sq. km (489 073 sq. miles)

POPULATION
over 100 000
over 50 000
over 10 000
under 10 000

LAND HEIGHT
1000m/3281ft
500m/1640ft
200m/656ft
150m/492ft

EDUCATION

   16%   4,513 students

12 years   Primary 31% Secondary 7% Tertiary 1%

The various local languages are emphasized more strongly than in most francophone states. School attendance only accounts for 30% of children.

PEOPLE & SOCIETY

  24 people per sq mile   21% urban 79% rural

 Muslim 85% Traditional beliefs 14% Christian & others 1%   Death penalty not used

HEALTH

  1 per 20,000 people   45 years

50 per 1,000 people   114 per 1,000 live births

In spite of the progress made in rural health care, immunization, malaria control, and child nutrition are still unavailable to much of the population.

Considerable tensions exist in Niger between the Tuaregs in the north and the southern groups. A five-year rebellion by northern Tuaregs ended in 1995 with a peace agreement. In eastern Niger, Toubou and Arab groups have also been in revolt. A more subtle antagonism exists between the Djerma and Hausa groups. The Djerma elite dominated politics for many years until 1993, when control passed to the Hausa majority. Niger is an overwhelmingly Islamic society. Women have only limited rights and restricted access to education.

SPENDING

   4 per 1,000 people   1.8%

2.7%   1.2%

A small circle of secretive trading families controls much of Niger's wealth and tend to evade taxation. More than 870,000 people live in slavery.

NIGERIA

ECONOMICS

 57th $6.98bn

$260   16.5%

One of world's top oil producers. Vast reserves of natural gas, only partly exploited. Almost self-sufficient in food. Strong entrepreneurial class. Large domestic market. Overdependence since the 1970s on oil.

RESOURCES

 15.5bn kwh   Comb. 65%
Hydro 35%
Nuclear 0%

 Sheep 20.5m
Goats 24.3m
Cattle 19.8m   2.15m b/d
(reserves of
22,500m bbl)

Nigeria's sizable iron ore deposits are not yet utilized in the state-run steel industry; imported ore is used instead. There are plans for establishing an aluminium industry. Nigeria also has deposits of coal and tin.

DEFENCE

$516m   Not compulsory

None   78,500

Since 2001 the armed forces have been deployed to restore internal control after outbreaks of religious unrest in northern and central states, in which hundreds of civilians have been killed.

MEDIA

 Some censorship   Medium

 22 daily
27 per 1,000
people   TV: 1/many
Radio: 2/3

The Nigerian press is traditionally one of Africa's liveliest. Media freedom has improved since the return to civilian government. The state-run Nigerian Television Authority runs 67 channels.

EDUCATION

 64%   207,982 students

 15 years   Primary 98%
Secondary 33%
Tertiary 4%

Education has suffered from the government's massive debt repayment burden. During the oil-boom years, Nigeria concentrated on creating 31 universities, but standards in primary education have fallen since 1970.

HEALTH

 1 per 5,000 people   52 years

 39 per 1,000 people   84 per 1,000 live births

The health service is mainly concentrated in urban areas, and only 49% of the population had access to water and health services. More than 3.5 million Nigerians were living with HIV/AIDS as at end-2001.

SPENDING

 8 per 1,000 people   1.3%

 0.5%   0.8%

Nigerians with access to the rich pickings of political office spent on a massive scale during the country's oil boom. Habits have not changed with the fall in oil revenues: borrowing has simply grown.

OFFICIAL NAME **Federal Republic of Nigeria**   CAPITAL **Abuja**
POPULATION **120m**   CURRENCY **Naira**   OFF. LANG. **English**

A FRICA'S MOST POPULOUS STATE, Nigeria gained its independence from Britain in 1960. Its terrain varies from tropical rainforest and swamps in the south to savannah in the north. Nigeria has been dominated by military governments since 1966. After many delays, a promised return to civilian rule came about in 1999, with the election as president of Olusegun Obasanjo, a former general who had been head of state from 1976 to 1979.

POLITICS

 L. House 2003/2007
U. House 2003/2007   President Olusegun Obasanjo   Multi-party republic

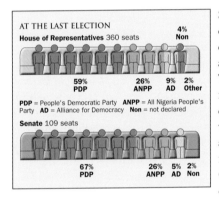

AT THE LAST ELECTION
House of Representatives 360 seats

59% PDP   26% ANPP   9% AD   2% Other   4% Non

PDP = People's Democratic Party   **ANPP** = All Nigeria People's Party   **AD** = Alliance for Democracy   **Non** = not declared

Senate 109 seats

67% PDP   26% ANPP   5% AD   2% Non

Since May 1999 Nigeria has had a civilian constitution, after 16 years of military dictatorships. President Olusegun Obasanjo and his PDP promise national reconciliation. The Obasanjo regime faces difficulties in reversing ethnic rivalries. The situation deteriorated from early 2000, with ethnic violence involving Yoruba separatists. The adoption of *shari'a* (Islamic law) by many northern states has provoked rioting between Christians and the majority Muslims. Major clashes in 2002 left 700 people dead.

WORLD AFFAIRS

 OPEC, ECOWAS, AU, Comm, OIC   1960

Nigeria is a keen sponsor of ECOWAS and of the AU, and has been the main contributor to ECOWAS intervention forces. An implacable opponent of apartheid, its relations with South Africa were restored after democratic elections there in 1994.

PEOPLE & SOCIETY

 341 people per sq mile   45% urban
55% rural

Muslim 50%
Christian 40%
Traditional beliefs 10%   Death penalty used

Total Land Area : 910 770 sq. km (351 648 sq. miles)

LAND HEIGHT
2000m/6562ft
1000m/3281ft
500m/1640ft
200m/656ft
Sea Level

POPULATION
over 1 000 000
over 500 000
over 100 000
over 50 000
over 10 000
under 10 000

Until fighting erupted in the south-west in mid-1999, Nigeria had enjoyed some success in containing tensions caused by ethnic, religious and linguistic diversity. Traditionally, except in the Islamic north, women have possessed independent economic status. In recent years they have, however, been subjected to some prejudice in professional circles.

CHAD

OFFICIAL NAME: **Republic of Chad** CAPITAL **N'Djamena**
POPULATION **8.4m** CURRENCY **CFA franc** OFF. LANG. **Arabic and French**

L ANDLOCKED IN NORTH CENTRAL Africa, Chad has had a turbulent history since independence from France in 1960. Intermittent periods of civil war, involving French and Libyan troops, followed a military coup in 1975. Following a coup in 1990, an interim government commenced the transition to multi-partyism, now enshrined in a new constitution. The discovery of large oil reserves could eventually have a dramatic impact on the economy. The tropical, cotton-producing south is the most populous region.

POLITICS

 2002/2006 President Idriss Déby Presidential democracy

AT THE LAST ELECTION
National Assembly 155 seats

72% MPS
6% FAR
7% RDP
15% Other

MPS = Patriotic Salvation Movement
RDP = Rally for Democracy and Progress
FAR = Front of Action Forces for the Republic

Idriss Déby overthrew President Hissène Habré in 1990 after an armed invasion from Sudan. He promised multi-partyism, and in 1992 legalized political parties for the first time since the early 1960s. After many delays, the transitional process led to a successful referendum in 1996 on a new constitution based on the French model. President Déby was confirmed in office in elections in 1996 and again in 2001. His ruling MPS just achieved an overall majority in the 1997 elections, and expanded its share of seats further in 2002. A shaky Libyan-brokered peace deal in 2002 failed to end the rebellion in the north which had begun in 1999.

WORLD AFFAIRS

 OIC, CILSS, FZ, LCBC, AU 1960

Chad's most important relationship is with France. Relations with the CAR are strained by cross-border skirmishes.

PEOPLE & SOCIETY

  17 people per sq mile   24% urban 76% rural

Muslim 50%
Traditional beliefs 43%
Christian 7%
Death penalty used

About half the population, mainly the Sara-speaking and related peoples, is concentrated in the south in one-fifth of the national territory. Most of the rest are located in the central sultanates. The northern third of Chad has a population of only 100,000 people, mainly nomadic Muslim Toubou.

Total Land Area : 1 259 200 sq. km (486 177 sq. miles)

POPULATION

- ⊙ over 500 000
- ◉ over 100 000
- ○ over 50 000
- ● over 10 000
- • under 10 000

LAND HEIGHT

- 3000m/9843ft
- 2000m/6562ft
- 1000m/3281ft
- 500m/1640ft
- 200m/656ft
- 100m/328ft

 143rd $-158m

 $200 12.4%

Recent discovery of large oil deposits could transform Chad's poor financial situation. Cotton industry; potential for other agriculture in south. Lack of transportation infrastructure. Political instability.

 91m kwh Comb. 100% Hydro 0% Nuclear 0%

 Sheep 2.4m Goats 5.25m Cattle 5.9m No production Reserves unexploited

The opening of a pipeline in 2003 taking oil from newly found reserves in the southern Doba region to the Cameroonian coast is set to make Chad a net oil exporter. There is uranium in the Aozou strip.

 $13m Compulsory

 None   25,350

On seizing power, Déby swelled the existing army with irregulars. The policy has now been reversed and the army reduced to 25,000, including former rebels. France provides military aid and personnel.

 Some censorship Low

 2 daily 0.2 per 1,000 people TV: 1/0 Radio: 1/7

Broadcasting is controlled by the government, which sometimes allows the airing of opposition views. There are a few independent publications, of which the best known is the weekly *N'Djamena-Hebdo*.

 43% 5,901 students

12 years Primary 67% Secondary 11% Tertiary 1%

All schools suffer from a lack of trained teachers. Chad has the lowest ratio of female enrolment in schools in Africa. Only 55% of children attend classes and barely a third of them are girls.

1 per 20,000 people 46 years

48 per 1,000 people 101 per 1,000 live births

Chad has very few city hospitals and under 300 smaller health centres in rural areas. One in five children die before the age of five.

 2 per 1,000 people 0.8%

 1.7% 2.3%

Poverty is almost universal in Chad; the middle class is very small. There are very few wealthy individuals. Habré looted the treasury when he was overthrown in 1990.

TUNISIA

1956 | 1956 | March 20 | TN | +1 | +216 | .tn

OFFICIAL NAME **Republic of Tunisia** CAPITAL **Tunis**
POPULATION **9.7m** CURRENCY **Tunisian dinar** OFF. LANG. **Arabic**

NORTH AFRICA'S SMALLEST COUNTRY, Tunisia lies sandwiched between Libya and Algeria. The populous north is mountainous, fertile in places, and has a long Mediterranean coastline. The south is largely desert. Habib Bourguiba ruled the country from independence in 1956 until a bloodless coup in 1987. Under President Ben Ali, the government has slowly moved toward multi-party democracy, but is challenged by Islamic fundamentalists. Closer ties with the EU, whose members include Tunisia's main trading partners, were strengthened through the first Euro-Mediterranean conference held in 1995. Manufacturing and tourism are expanding.

POLITICS

 1999/2004   President Zine al-Abidine Ben Ali   Presidential democracy

Formally a multi-party democracy since 1988, Tunisia is still dominated by the RCD and President Ben Ali. The RCD has clamped down on Islamic fundamentalists, particularly the outlawed Al-Nahda, or Renewal Party. In 1991, 500 Al-Nahda members were arrested following a failed coup, thought to be inspired by fundamentalists. Its leader, Rachid Ghannouchi, is in exile.

The RCD has been under increasing attack over its human rights record. The Tunisia League of Human Rights was suspended in January 2001. The RCD is committed to promoting women's rights.

President Ben Ali has made some effort to liberalize the political system. The life presidency has been abolished, and political parties and press freedom are encouraged. While allowing for a degree of political plurality, a complex proportional representation system ensured that there was an overwhelming victory for the RCD in the 1994 and 1999 elections. Since then there has been evidence of a renewed crackdown against the left-wing opposition. Measures to further democratization and promote human rights were overshadowed in 2002 when a referendum on constitutional change gave Ben Ali a mandate to stand for a further two terms.

AT THE LAST ELECTION

Chamber of Deputies 182 seats

4% PUP   3% MR

81% RCD   7% MDS   4% UDU   1% SLP

RCD = Constitutional Democratic Rally MDS = Movement of Social Democrats PUP = Popular Unity Party
UDU = Unionist Democratic Union MR = Movement for Renewal SLP = Social Liberal Party

WORLD AFFAIRS

 AL, OIC, NAM, OIF, AMU   1956

A foreign policy priority is to strengthen contacts with the West, which have generally been good because of Tunisia's liberal economic and social policies. Attention is focused on the EU, Tunisia's main export market. Tunisia played an important role in the run-up to the first Euro-Mediterranean conference, which was held in 1995.

Tunis was host to the Palestine Liberation Organization after it was expelled from Lebanon. Relations with other Arab states, particularly Kuwait and Saudi Arabia, were soured by Tunisia's support for Iraq in the 1991 Gulf War. The government regards the political impact of Islamic fundamentalism in neighbouring Algeria with concern. Relations with Libya are improving, helped by the fact that Tunisia turned a blind eye to sanctions busters operating through its territory.

ECONOMICS

 62nd $-821m

 $2,100   1.9%

A healthy economy is sustained with the help of Tunisia's main trading partners, the member states of the EU. Tourism from Europe is also high. The agricultural sector is hampered by droughts.

RESOURCES

 8.97bn kwh   Comb. 99% Hydro 1% Nuclear 0%

Sheep 6.6m Goats 1.45m Turkeys 2.9m   73,000 b/d (reserves of 300m bbl)

Tunisia is one of the world's leading producers of phosphates for fertilizers. Oil and gas are important exports, but growing domestic energy demands mean that Tunisia is now a net energy importer.

DEFENSE

 $377m   Compulsory

None   35,000

Despite its small size, the military is an important political force, armed mainly with US weapons. Officer training is carried out in the US and France, as well as in Tunisia.

MEDIA

 Censorship   Medium

 8 daily 31 per 1,000 people   TV: 2/0 Radio: 1/0

Reforms since the late 1980s have in theory increased press freedom in Tunisia, traditionally considered a source of liberal ideas in the Arab world. In practice, government restrictions remain.

EDUCATION

 71%   180,044 students

16 years   Primary 100% Secondary 73% Tertiary 17%

Education is compulsory for nine years between the ages of six and 16. Arabic is the first language in schools, but French is also taught, and is used almost exclusively in higher education.

HEALTH

 1 per 1,429 people   70 years

 17 per 1,000 people   26 per 1,000 live births

Well-developed family planning facilities have almost halved Tunisia's birth rate over the past 30 years. Primary care facilities cover all but the most isolated rural communities.

SPENDING

 54 per 1,000 people   1.9%

 7.6%   2.2%

Around 10% of Tunisians are estimated to live below the UN poverty line. Social security covers sickness, old age, disability and maternity, but not unemployment.

PEOPLE & SOCIETY

 162 people per sq mile

 66% urban 34% rural

 Sunni Muslim 98% Christian 1% Jewish 1%

 Death penalty used

The population of Tunisia is almost entirely Muslim, of Arab and Berber descent, although there are Jewish and Christian minorities. Many Tunisians still live in extended family groups, in which three or four generations are represented.

Tunisia has traditionally been one of the most liberal Arab states. The 1956 Personal Statutes Code of President Bourguiba gave women fuller rights than in any other Arab country. Further legislation has since given women the right to custody of children in divorce cases, made family violence against women punishable by law and helped divorced women to get alimony. Family planning and contraception have been freely available since the early 1960s. Tunisia's population growth rate has halved since the 1980s. Women make up 31% of the total work force and 35% of the industrial work force. Company ownership by women is steadily increasing; politics, however, remains an exclusively male preserve.

These freedoms are threatened by the growth in recent years of Islamic fundamentalism, which also worries the mainly French-speaking political and business elite who wish to strengthen links with Europe.

The Ben Ali regime has been criticized for its actions against Islamic activists. Despite continuing condemnation of its human rights record, the government's efforts to foster democracy were praised in 2002 when it received the "Mediterranean Award," given by European human rights leagues.

Total Land Area : 155 360 sq. km (59 984 sq. miles)

POPULATION

- ⊙ over 500 000
- ◎ over 100 000
- ○ over 50 000
- ● over 10 000
- · under 10 000

LAND HEIGHT

- 1000m/3281ft
- 500m/1640ft
- 200m/656ft
- Sea Level

0   100 km
0   100 miles

ECONOMIC FOCUS

EXPORTS

Spain 5%, Belgium 5%, Other 24%, Germany 20%, France 23%, Italy 23%

IMPORTS

USA 4%, Spain 4%, Other 31%, Germany 17%, France 24%, Italy 20%

STRENGTHS

A well-diversified economy, despite limited resources. Oil and gas exports, also agricultural exports: olive oil, olives, citrus fruit, dates. Expanding manufacturing sector; important sectors are textiles, construction materials, machinery, chemicals. European investment. Ranked as the most competitive economy in Africa by the World Economic Forum in 2000.

WEAKNESSES

Dependence on growth of drought-prone agricultural sector. Growing domestic energy demand on oil and gas resources.

PROFILE

Since Tunisia began a process of structural adjustment in 1988, supported by the IMF and the World Bank, it has had an increasingly open, market-oriented economy. Annual inflation remained stable, despite higher food and energy prices. Prices have been freed, most state companies privatized, and import barriers reduced. The balance of payments relies on fluctuating tourism receipts to offset a trade deficit. The government must also balance growth with better social provisions. Members of the EU are Tunisia's main trading partners; trade has increased significantly since 1999.

Roman remains in the western Tozeur region. Diverse archaeological remains can be found throughout Tunisia.

LIBYA

ECONOMICS

 59th $1.98bn

$5,220   13.6%

Reliance on production of oil, gas, aluminium and petrochemicals. Sanctions in protest to the harbouring of terrorists recently lifted. The Great Man-Made River project has proved unsuccessful.

RESOURCES

 19bn kwh   Comb. 100% Hydro 0% Nuclear 0%

Sheep 5.1m Goats 1.95m Cattle 220,000   1.43m b/d (reserves of 29.5bn bbl)

Libya's economy depends almost entirely on petroleum and natural gas resources. Libya also has reserves of iron ore, potassium, sulphur, magnesium and gypsum. Animal husbandry is the basis of farming.

DEFENCE

   $546m   Compulsory

None   76,000

In 1989 the armed forces were replaced by "the Armed People". Conscription is selective, and can last up to two years. In addition, there is a People's Militia numbering 40,000.

MEDIA

  Censorship   Medium

3 daily 14 per 1,000 people   TV: 1/0 Radio: 1/1

Libya's press and TV are a mouthpiece for the leadership. Satellite TV and the Internet are heavily censored. The main daily newspaper is published in Arabic and has a circulation of 40,000 readers.

EDUCATION

 80%   126,348 students

15 years   Primary 100% Secondary 77% Tertiary 57%

Some 1.5 million Libyans are in formal education. It is compulsory between the ages of six and 15, and rates of attendance are very high. There are 13 universities, and institutes for vocational training.

HEALTH

   1 per 769 people   71 years

28 per 1,000 people   26 per 1,000 live births

An adequate system of free primary health care exists except in remote areas, and there are two big hospitals. Sanctions have led to a lack of equipment and a shortage of medical supplies.

SPENDING

   159 per 1,000 people   4.1%

7.1%   3.4%

There is widespread poverty after years of import constraints; UN sanctions worsened the situation. Gaddafi refuses to use oil revenues for basic expenses, such as salaries – teachers earn about $1,200 a year.

OFFICIAL NAME Great Socialist People's Libyan Arab Jamahiriyah
CAPITAL Tripoli   **POPULATION** 5.5m   **CURRENCY** Libyan dinar   **OFF. LANG.** Arabic

LIBYA IS SITUATED between Egypt and Algeria on the Mediterranean coast of north Africa, with Chad and Niger on its southern borders. Apart from the coastal strip and the mountains in the south, it is desert or semi-desert. Libya's strategic position in north Africa and its abundant oil and gas resources made it an important trading partner for the European states. It has for many years been politically marginalized by the West for its links with terrorist groups, but UN sanctions were suspended in 1999, when it handed over the two men suspected of the 1988 Lockerbie bombing.

POLITICS

 Not applicable   Colonel Muammar al-Gaddafi   One-party state

Executive power is exercised by the General People's Committee. The General People's Congress elects the head of state, the Leader of the Revolution. Political dissidents, including Islamist militants, are violently suppressed. Libyan dissidents have been murdered abroad, allegedly by government agents. Political parties were banned in 1971, but opposition groups are active in Egypt and Sudan. In the past few years, the regime has made an effort to improve its image. Measures have included the freeing of some political prisoners and permitting foreign travel.

AT THE LAST ELECTION

General People's Congress 750 seats

The constitution makes no provision for direct elections. Last renewal May 2000

In 1977, a new form of direct democracy was promulgated, through which some 2000 People's Congresses sought to involve every adult in policy-making. In theory, their wishes are carried out by popular committees. In practice, ultimate control rests with Colonel Gaddafi and his collaborators, many of whom date from the 1969 revolution. In recent years some are thought to have been alienated from Gaddafi, including his deputy, Major Abdessalem Jalloud, who in 1994 was reportedly marginalized after expressing differences with him. In 1995, another of Gaddafi's close associates, Khoueldi Hamidi, a defence commander, was also said to have become disillusioned with Gaddafi. In 2000, Gaddafi embraced African unity – an unpopular concept among most Libyans, increasing Gaddafi's alienation from his former associates. He is now believed to rely on members of his own clan, particularly his five sons.

WORLD AFFAIRS

 AL, NAM, OIC, OPEC, AMU   1955

Gaddafi has attempted to style himself as the champion of African integration and regional stability. He was a chief architect of the African Union and has played host to various peace negotiations in the trans-Saharan area. This transformation has also involved a less confrontational stance toward the West, dropping key policies which had left Libya internationally isolated in the past – support for various terrorist groups and strong opposition to Israel – and pursuing a crackdown on internal corruption. UN sanctions imposed in 1992 were eased, and relations with the UK were resumed in 1999. Gaddafi gave tacit approval to the US-led "war on terrorism" in 2001. However, the US still added Libya to the "axis of evil" in 2002.

PEOPLE & SOCIETY

 8 people per sq mile

 88% urban 12% rural

 Sunni Muslim 97% Others 3%

 Death penalty used

Arabs and Berbers, split into many tribal groupings, form 95% of the population. They were artificially brought together when Libya was created in 1951 by the unification of three historic Ottoman provinces. The pro-Western monarchy then set up perpetuated the dominance of Cyrenaican tribes and the Sanusi religious order.

The 1969 revolution brought to the fore Arab nationalist Colonel Gaddafi, who embodied the character and aspirations of the rural Sirtica tribes from Fazzan: fierce independence, deep Islamic convictions, belief in a communal lifestyle and hatred for the urban rich. His revolution wiped out private enterprise and the middle class, banished European settlers and Jews, undermined the religious Muslim establishment, and imposed a form of popular democracy through the *jamahiriyah* (state of the masses). However, resentment of the regime grew as it became clear that power now lay mainly with the Sirtica tribes, especially Gaddafi's own clan, the Qadhadhfa.

Since the revolution, Libya has become a society where most are city-dwellers. Jews have been invited to return as investors, and immigrants from sub-Saharan Africa have been drawn in to provide low-cost labour. However, clashes in 2000, in which 100 died, highlighted unresolved social issues.

Total Land Area :
1 759 540 sq. km (679 358 sq. miles)

LAND HEIGHT

- 2000m/6562ft
- 1000m/3281ft
- 500m/1640ft
- 200m/656ft
- Sea Level
- -200m/-656ft

POPULATION

- ⊙ over 500 000
- ◎ over 100 000
- ○ over 50 000
- ● over 10 000
- • under 10 000

N

0   200 km

0   200 miles

ECONOMIC FOCUS

EXPORTS

- France 5%
- Turkey 6%
- Spain 12%
- Italy 38%
- Other 17%
- Germany 22%

IMPORTS

- UK 7%
- South Korea 7%
- Tunisia 7%
- Other 42%
- Germany 13%
- Italy 24%

STRENGTHS

Oil and gas production. High investment in downstream industries – petrochemicals, refineries, fertilizers, and aluminium smelting.

WEAKNESSES

Single-resource economy subject to oil-market fluctuations. Most food is imported. Reliance on foreign labour. History of international unreliability. Lack of water for agriculture.

PROFILE

Western oil companies had close business ties with Libya until the imposition in 1992 of UN sanctions over the Lockerbie affair. In 1993, Colonel Gaddafi called for the programme of privatization, authorized by the General People's Congress in late 1992, to be revived, but there have been few tangible results. An ambitious programme of industrialization was launched in the 1970s. Gaddafi's most controversial economic project has been the Great Man-Made River. Started in 1984 and engineered jointly by European and Korean companies, this programme was designed to bring underground water from the deserts of the Sahara to the coast, but the pipes are already corroding, with thousands of gallons of water leaking into the sand.

Roman amphitheatre, Sabratah. *Libya's impressive classical heritage testifies to its importance in ancient times.*

EGYPT

| 1936 | 1982 | July 23 | ET | +2 | +20 | .eg |

OFFICIAL NAME Arab Republic of Egypt   CAPITAL Cairo
POPULATION 70.3m   CURRENCY Egyptian pound   OFF. LANG. Arabic

O CCUPYING THE NORTH-EAST CORNER of Africa, Egypt is bisected by the highly fertile Nile valley separating the arid western desert from the smaller semi-arid eastern desert. Egypt's 1979 peace treaty with Israel brought security, the return of the Sinai and large injections of US aid. Its essentially pro-Western military-backed regime is now being challenged by an increasingly influential Islamic fundamentalist movement.

POLITICS

| 2000/2005 | President Mohammed Hosni Mubarak | Presidential democracy |

Egypt has been politically stable since the Second World War, with just three leaders since 1954 when Nasser came to power. Anwar Sadat was assassinated in 1981, but was immediately replaced by Hosni Mubarak, a man in the same mould. The NDP retains its grip on the political process by means of the state of emergency, and has close links with the military. Elections in 2000 were more transparent, and the Islamic opposition fared slightly better than before, but many candidates elected as independents then joined the NDP.

AT THE LAST ELECTION

People's Assembly 454 seats

86% NDP   8% Ind   2% App   1% NPU   2% NWP   1% Others

NDP = National Democratic Party   Ind = Independents
App = Appointed   NWP = New Wafd Party   NPU = National Progressive Unionist Party

444 members of the Assembly are elected and 10 appointed by the head of state

Egypt is a multi-party system in theory. In practice, the ruling NDP, backed by the military, runs a one-party state. The NDP government is engaged in a struggle against Islamist terrorist groups seeking to turn Egypt into a Muslim theocracy along Iranian lines. Extremists have been responsible for numerous attacks on police and tourists. The fundamentalist message, with promises of improved conditions, has proved attractive to both urban and rural poor. Although the government uses draconian measures to counter the terrorist threat, and banned the only legal Islamic party, the Labour Party, in May 2000, it continues to allow religious organizations to pursue their social programmes. The ruling NDP have repeatedly extended the national state of emergency in force since the assassination of President Sadat by Islamic terrorists in 1981. The most recent extension was in February 2002 for a further three years. Emergency laws have been invoked to justify the ban on religious parties, especially the Muslim Brotherhood. Human rights groups claim that emergency powers are routinely applied to silence the NDP's political opponents.

WORLD AFFAIRS

| Damasc, OIC, AU, OAPEC, AL | 1945 |

Egypt has close relations with the West, particularly the US and its allies. The support of Egypt for the alliance against Iraq in the 1991 Gulf War was crucial, and Egypt received a massive economic reward from Saudi Arabia. It is also one of only two Arab countries to be technically at peace with Israel, for which it faces criticism from hard-line Islamic states in the region. However, the Israeli military action in 2002 has weakened Egypt's support for the country, and it continues to lobby for the creation of an autonomous Palestinian state.

Relations with Iran are particularly tense, as Iran actively supports many of the Islamist groups operating against the incumbent NDP government, and characterizes Egypt as a corrupt state under the influence of the US. Egypt has, however, expressed concern over the international treatment of Iraq; President Mubarak advocated a diplomatic, rather than military, solution. He has urged restraint in the "war on terrorism" and against Iraq in 2003.

PEOPLE & SOCIETY

 183 people per sq mile

 43% urban 57% rural

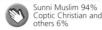 Sunni Muslim 94% Coptic Christian and others 6%

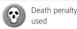 Death penalty used

Egypt has a long tradition of ethnic and religious tolerance, though the rise in Islamic fundamentalism has sparked sectarian clashes between Muslims and Coptic Christians. Most Egyptians speak Arabic, though many also have French or English as a second language. There are Berber-speaking communities in the western oases. Small colonies of Greeks and Armenians live in the larger towns. Islam is the dominant religion, followed by Coptic Christianity. Although many Jews left Egypt for Israel after 1948, a small community remains in Cairo.

Cairo is the second-most populous city in Africa, and a key social question in Egypt is the high birth rate. In 1985 the government set up the National Population Council, which made birth control readily available. Since then, the birth rate has dropped from 39 to fewer than 25 per 1,000 people, but population growth is still high. The population is predicted to reach almost 100 million by 2025. The growing influence of Islamic fundamentalists, who oppose contraception, could see the rate accelerate once more.

Egyptian women have been among the most liberated in the Arab world, and under a law passed in 2000 they now have the right to initiate divorce proceedings. The steady rise of Islamic fundamentalism, however, threatens their position, particularly in rural areas.

ECONOMIC FOCUS

EXPORTS

India 4% | Israel 5% | Netherlands 7% | Italy 10% | USA 12% | Other 62%

IMPORTS

Saudi Arabia 4% | France 5% | Italy 7% | Germany 9% | USA 14% | Other 61%

STRENGTHS

Oil and gas revenues. Well-developed tourist infrastructure. Remittances from Egyptians working overseas. Suez Canal tolls. Agricultural produce, especially cotton. Light industry and manufacturing.

WEAKNESSES

Tourism revenues hit by "war on terrorism". Dependence on imported technology. High birth rate.

PROFILE

Under President Nasser, Egypt followed an economic policy inspired by the Soviet model. Rigid and highly centralized, it gave Egypt one of the largest public sectors of all developing countries. Economic restrictions were first relaxed in 1974. President Sadat's open-door policy allowed joint ventures with foreign partners for the first time, although the business classes were the only ones to profit. Most Egyptians suffered from new austerity measures. Under President Mubarak, economic reform has quickened and there is more awareness of poverty and high unemployment. Priorities now are to encourage manufacturing, sustain economic growth, and reduce the gap between rich and poor.

Total Land Area : 995 450 sq. km (384 343 sq. miles)

LAND HEIGHT

2000m/6562ft
1000m/3281ft
500m/1640ft
200m/656ft
Sea Level
-200m/-656ft

POPULATION

over 5 000 000
over 1 000 000
over 500 000
over 100 000
over 50 000
over 10 000
under 10 000

18th-Dynasty Temple of Queen Hatshepsut *dating from the Middle Kingdom, c.1480 BCE. It is at Deir el-Bahri on the west bank of the Nile opposite Thebes, the capital at the time.*

SUDAN

ECONOMICS

84th	$-618m
$310	6.4%

Sudan produces oil, gas, cotton, gum arabic, sesame and sugar. Low levels of industrialization. Lack of foreign exchange for importing energy and spare parts for industry. Drought. Huge distances between towns.

RESOURCES

1.3bn kwh	Comb. 29% Hydro 71% Nuclear 0%
Sheep 47m Goats 39m Cattle 38.3m	200,000 b/d (reserves of 300m bbl)

Large oil and gas reserves were found in the south in the 1980s; oil exports started in 1999. The half-thermal, half hydro-electric generating capacity is insufficient, and week-long power cuts are frequent.

DEFENCE

$588m	Compulsory
None	122,500

The NC controls the military and police and has its own paramilitary militia. Sudan's 122,500-strong army was for many years engaged in fighting the two southern factions, the SPLA and SPDF.

MEDIA

Some censorship	High
8 daily 27 per 1,000 people	TV: 1/0 Radio: 1/1

The press and broadcasting industries are state-controlled and subject to censorship. Opposition radio stations broadcast dissenting views.

EDUCATION

58%	200,538 students
14 years	Primary 56% Secondary 29% Tertiary 7%

Primary school children must have two years of Islamic religious instruction, and men wishing to enter university must first serve for a year in the People's Militia.

HEALTH

1 per 10,000 people	56 years
37 per 1,000 people	81 per 1,000 live births

As most health funds are tied to urban hospitals, health service standards in rural areas are basic. The civil war has led to an increase in communicable diseases, especially the parasitic infection leishmaniasis.

SPENDING

10 per 1,000 people	4.3%
3.7%	0.7%

Wealth is limited to the NC and southern rebel elites, while the rest of the population struggles to survive from day to day.

OFFICIAL NAME **Republic of the Sudan** CAPITAL **Khartoum**
POPULATION **32.6m** CURRENCY **Sudanese pound or dinar** OFF. LANG. **Arabic**

BORDERED BY THE RED SEA, Sudan is the largest country in Africa. Its landscape changes from desert in the north to lush tropical in the south, with grassy plains and swamps in the centre. Tensions between the Arab north and African south have led to two civil wars since independence in 1956. The second of these conflicts remains unresolved. In 1989, an army coup installed a military Islamic fundamentalist regime.

POLITICS

2000/2004 — President Omar Hassan Ahmad al-Bashir — Presidential regime

AT THE LAST ELECTION
National Assembly 400 seats
89% NC — 10% Vac — 1% Ind
NC = National Congress supporters Vac = Vacant Ind = Independents

Elections in 2000, boycotted by the opposition, returned General Omar al-Bashir and his NC bloc to power. The 1999 constitution allowed "political associations", and parties in existence in 1989 were unbanned in 2002. There has been nearly 20 years of civil conflict between Muslim north and Christian south. Despite peace talks involving the Sudan People's Liberation Army (SPLA) and its former rival, the Sudan People's Defence Force (SPDF), hostilities in the oil-rich Upper Nile region in 2002 put the peace process at risk.

WORLD AFFAIRS

AU, OIC, AL, IGAD, COMESA — 1956

Sudan's support for Iraq in the 1991 Gulf War and suspicion that it sponsors terrorism have led to its increasing isolation from the West and the Arab world. Only Iran, Yemen, and Libya maintain friendly relations.

Total Land Area : 2 376 000 sq. km (917 374 sq. miles)

PEOPLE & SOCIETY

34 people per sq mile — 37% urban 63% rural
Sunni Muslim 70% Traditional beliefs 20% Christian & other 10% — Death penalty used

Sudan has a large number of ethnic and linguistic groups. About two million Sudanese are nomads. The major social division, however, is between the Arabized Muslims in the north and the mostly African, largely animist or Christian population in the south. Attempts to impose Arab and Islamic values throughout Sudan have been the root cause of the civil war that has ravaged the south since 1983.

SOMALIA

OFFICIAL NAME Somalia CAPITAL Mogadishu
POPULATION 9.6m CURRENCY Somali shilling OFF. LANG. Somali & Arabic

OCCUPYING THE HORN OF AFRICA, Italian Somaliland and British Somaliland were united in 1960 to form an independent Somalia. Except in the more fertile south, the land is semi-arid. Years of clan-based civil war have resulted in the collapse of central government, the frustration of US and UN intervention initiatives aimed at easing a huge refugee crisis, and mass starvation.

POLITICS

 1984/Uncertain No internationally recognized head of state Transitional regime

Somalia has remained in anarchy since the former dictator President Siad Barre fled in 1991. The unified state dissolved amid conflict in the south and separatism in the north.

AT THE LAST ELECTION

National Assembly (suspended)

There has been no prospect of organizing new elections since the overthrow of Siad Barre. A transitional assembly was formed in 2000 on a non-party basis.

The US led a UN peacekeeping force to the south in 1992, but failed to loosen the grip of the warring factions. Throughout the 1990s rival warlords contended for supreme power.

A conference of businessmen and influential figures, held in neighbouring Djibouti in 2000, established a transitional assembly and appointed former Barre minister Abdulkassim Salat Hassan as president. The new government, although warmly received in Mogadishu, was immediately rejected by most of the warlords and by the northern separatist authorities in "Somaliland" and "Puntland".

WORLD AFFAIRS

 OIC, IGAD, AL, NAM, AU 1960

The UN force withdrew in 1995, after which the international community appeared to abandon Somalia until giving support to the transitional government from 2000. The US belief in the existence of terrorist training camps in Somalia has eroded relations since September 11, 2001.

PEOPLE & SOCIETY

 40 people per sq mile 28% urban 72% rural

 Sunni Muslim 98% Christian 2%   Death penalty used

The clan system is fundamental to Somalia. Shifting allegiances characterize its structure – a tendency stifled by Siad Barre's dictatorship but revived after his fall in 1991. His undermining of the traditional brokers of justice, the elders, contributed to the power vacuum that resulted in civil war, and his persecution of the Issaqs led to Somaliland's declaration of secession in 1991. However, national identity remains strong, shown by widespread opposition to the UN peacekeeping force.

ECONOMICS

 157th $-157m

 $100 Over 100%

Every commodity, except arms, is in extremely short supply, with a growing market in stolen food aid. The south has little economic potential. Export of livestock to the Arabian peninsula has resumed in the north.

RESOURCES

 278m kwh   Comb. 100% Hydro 0% Nuclear 0%

 Sheep 13.2m Goats 12.5m Camels 6.2m Not an oil producer

Commercially exploitable minerals remain untapped. An oil exploration agreement was signed with a French oil group in February 2001.

DEFENCE

 $39m Not compulsory

 None No formal data, estimated to be 75,000 militia

Former soldiers have been urged to re-enlist. Efforts to demobilize Somalia's estimated 75,000 militia began in 2000.

MEDIA

 Censorship Low

 5 daily 1 per 1,000 people TV: 0/2 Radio: 0/11

Mogadishu has a number of faction-run radio stations. Somali Television Network, an independent multi-channel, multilingual service, began broadcasting in 1999.

EDUCATION

 24% 10,400 students

14 years Primary 14% Secondary 8% Tertiary 2%

The system collapsed during the civil war. There were reports of improvised open-air schools starting up again in urban areas in 1993. Somali has been a written language only since 1972.

HEALTH

 1 per 20,000 people   48 years

47 per 1,000 people 117 per 1,000 live births

The state-run health system has collapsed entirely. A few very rudimentary facilities are run by foreign relief workers.

SPENDING

   1 per 1,000 people 4.4%

   0.4% 0.6%

Bandits and warlords gained rich pickings in the aid-stealing racket. Money sent by relatives living overseas is the main income for some people.

Map

Gulf of Aden
Bereeda Raas Caseyr
Shimbiris 2407m
Boosaaso
Saylac Berbera
DJIBOUTI
Ceerigaabo Jiceel Raas Xaafuun
Hargeysa Burco Qardho Laas Dawaco
Bender Beyla
Nugaal
Garoowe
Eyl
Jirriiban
Gaalkacyo
Dhuusa Marreeb Hobyo
Beledweyne
Luuq Buulobarde
Mareeq
Baardheere Baydhabo Jawhar
Buurhakaba
Bu'aale MOGADISHU
Jamaame Marka
Baraawe
Kismaayo Jilib

ETHIOPIA
KENYA
INDIAN OCEAN
Equator

Total Land Area: 627 340 sq. km (242 216 sq. miles)

POPULATION
over 1 000 000
over 100 000
over 50 000
over 10 000
under 10 000

LAND HEIGHT
2000m/6562ft
1000m/3281ft
500m/1640ft
200m/656ft
Sea Level

0 200 km
0 200 miles

DJIBOUTI

 1977 1977 June 27 DJI +3 +253 .dj

OFFICIAL NAME **Republic of Djibouti** CAPITAL **Djibouti**
POPULATION **652,000** CURRENCY **Djibouti franc** OFF. LANG. **Arabic & French**

A CITY STATE WITH a desert hinterland, Djibouti lies in north-east Africa on the strait linking the Red Sea and the Indian Ocean. Known from 1967 as the French Territory of the Afars and Issas, Djibouti became independent in 1977. Its economy relies on the main port, the railway to Addis Ababa and French aid. A guerrilla war which erupted in 1991 as a result of tension between the Issas in the south and the Afars in the north has largely been resolved.

ECONOMICS

 169th $-14m

 $880   2%

Free port in key Red Sea location. Continuing development of Djibouti and Tadjoura port facilities. Dependence on French aid and garrison. Other ports on Red Sea now providing stiff competition.

RESOURCES

 187m kwh   Comb. 100%
Hydro 0%
Nuclear 0%

 Sheep 465,000
Goats 513,000
Cattle 269,000   Not an oil producer

The few mineral resources are scarcely exploited. Geothermal energy is being developed and natural gas has been found. The guerrilla war delayed attempts to develop underground water supplies for agriculture.

DEFENCE

 $22m   Not compulsory

 None   8,450

The size of the armed forces is a state secret, but is estimated at 8,400 personnel; former FRUD guerrillas were integrated into the army. There is a 3,200-strong French garrison.

MEDIA

 Some censorship   Low

 No daily papers   TV: 1/0
Radio: 1/0

Djibouti is a member of the Arab Satellite Communications Organization. The media are largely state-controlled, but there is one opposition newspaper.

EDUCATION

 65%   478 students

 12 years   Primary 39%
Secondary 16%
Tertiary 0%

Schooling is mostly in French, although there is a growing emphasis on Islamic teaching. Higher education was reorganized in 2000–01 with the creation of the core of a future University of Djibouti.

HEALTH

1 per 7,143 people   43 years

40 per 1,000 people   115 per 1,000 live births

AIDS is a growing problem in Djibouti port, with its large prostitute population. 1999 estimates suggested that there were some 37,000 AIDS and HIV sufferers. French-financed hospitals cater for the urban elite.

SPENDING

 15 per 1,000 people   3.9%

 2.9%   5.4%

The wealth in Djibouti tends to be concentrated among those closest to government. Djiboutians working in the ports also do well. The nomads of the interior are the poorest group.

POLITICS

 2003/2008   President Ismael Omar Guelleh   Presidential democracy

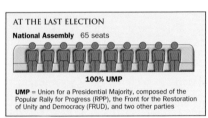

AT THE LAST ELECTION

National Assembly   65 seats

100% UMP

UMP = Union for a Presidential Majority, composed of the Popular Rally for Progress (RPP), the Front for the Restoration of Unity and Democracy (FRUD), and two other parties

President Hassan Gouled Aptidon, an Issa, backed by France, dominated politics from independence in 1977 until his retirement in 1999. The Afar guerrilla group FRUD took control of much of the country in 1991. The French intervened militarily, but forced Gouled to hold multi-party elections in 1992. FRUD became a legal party after a 1994 peace deal. An alliance of the ruling RPP and FRUD won all seats in elections in 1997, and again within the UMP coalition in 2002, despite competition from recently unbanned opposition parties. Presidential elections in 1999 had been won by Ismael Omar Guelleh amid opposition claims of electoral fraud.

WORLD AFFAIRS

 OIC, OIF, IGAD, AU, AL   1977

France, with a key military presence, presses for greater democratization. Djibouti and its neighbours Ethiopia and Eritrea all seek to contain Afar secessionism. In 2000 the southern town of Arta hosted the Somali reconciliation conference.

PEOPLE & SOCIETY

 73 people per sq mile   84% urban
16% rural

Sunni Muslim 94%
Christian 6%   Death penalty not used

The main ethnic groups are the Afars and Issas, who make up 35% and 60% of the population respectively. Tensions between these groups developed into a guerrilla war in 1991. The population was swelled in 1992 by 20,000 Somali refugees fleeing civil war in their own country. The rural people are mostly nomadic.

Total Land Area : 23 180 sq. km (8950 sq. miles)

POPULATION
over 100 000
under 10 000

LAND HEIGHT
1000m/3281ft
500m/1640ft
200m/656ft
Sea Level
-200m/656ft

0   30 km
0   30 miles

AZERBAIJAN

OFFICIAL NAME: **Republic of Azerbaijan**   CAPITAL: **Baku**
POPULATION: **8.1 million**   CURRENCY: **Manat**   OFFICIAL LANGUAGE: **Azerbaijani**

SITUATED ON THE WESTERN coast of the Caspian Sea, Azerbaijan was the first Soviet republic to declare independence. The issue of the disputed enclave of Nagorno Karabakh, whose Armenian population seeks secession, led to full-scale war between 1988 and 1994 and is still a dominant concern. Over 200,000 refugees, and more than twice as many internally displaced, added to the problems of the troubled economy. Azerbaijan's oil wealth, however, gives it long-term potential.

POLITICS

 2000/2005   President Heydar Aliyev   Multi-party republic

The determination of the Nagorno Karabakh enclave to secede from Azerbaijan led to war until 1994, with Armenian forces gaining control of over 20% of Azeri territory. Peace talks have yet to reach an accord.

New Azerbaijan (NA) replaced the Communists in power in 1995 and again dominated elections in 2000, which observers criticized as seriously flawed. NA supports the septuagenarian President Heydar Aliyev, first elected in 1993 and re-elected in 1998.

AT THE LAST ELECTION

National Assembly 125 seats

2% CSP   1% Vacant
61% NA   22% Ind   5% APF   9% Others

NA = New Azerbaijan   Ind = Independents   APF = Azerbaijan Popular Front   CSP = Civic Solidarity Party   Vacant = Seat reserved for member from Nagorno Karabakh

WORLD AFFAIRS

 ŁAPC, OIC, CIS, CE, OSCE   1992

Relations with Armenia remain the central issue in foreign policy. The West, as well as neighbouring Iran (with its large Azeri population) and Russia, are interested in Azeri oilfields in the Caspian Sea. Turkey – with its common history and culture – is a natural ally.

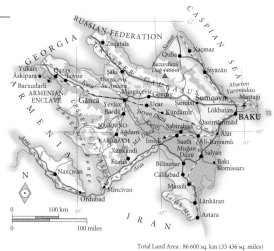

Total Land Area : 86 600 sq. km (33 436 sq. miles)

POPULATION
over 1 000 000
over 100 000
over 50 000
over 10 000
under 10 000

LAND HEIGHT
4000m/13 124ft
3000m/9843ft
2000m/6562ft
1000m/3281ft
500m/1640ft
200m/656ft
Sea Level

PEOPLE & SOCIETY

 242 people per sq mile   52% urban 48% rural

 Shi'aithna Muslim 61% Sunni Muslim 26% Other 13%   Death penalty not used

Thousands of Armenians, Jews and Russians have left as a result of rising Azeri nationalism. Racial hostility against those who remain is increasing. Women, once prominent in the ruling party, have lost their political status. The once effective social security system is under great strain.

ECONOMICS

 113rd $-52m

 $600   1.5%

Extensive oil and natural gas reserves. Antiquated Soviet-era industry. Poor infrastructure and corruption threaten development. Fallout from war in Nagorno Karabakh still drains state resources.

RESOURCES

 18bn kwh   Comb. 89% Hydro 11% Nuclear 0%

Sheep 5.56m Goats 416,000 Cattle 2m   300,000 b/d (reserves of 7bn bbl)

Azerbaijan's Caspian Sea oil fields have attracted international interest. The shallow-water Guneshli field alone has over four million barrels of reserves. Offshore natural gas is also plentiful.

DEFENCE

 $833m   Compulsory

None   72,100

Azerbaijan has been a member of NATO's Partnership for Peace programme since 1994. Its naval forces operate under CIS control.

MEDIA

 Some censorship   High

6 daily 10 per 1,000 people   TV: 1/1 Radio: 1/0

A 1998 decree abolished censorship, but media freedom is limited by newsprint controls, license restrictions, and intimidation.

EDUCATION

 96%   165,800 students

17 years   Primary 100% Secondary 84% Tertiary 22%

When it came to power in the mid-1990s NA began to reverse communist control over education policy, especially history teaching. Baku State is the largest of an increasing number of universities.

HEALTH

1 per 278 people   72 years

19 per 1,000 people   13 per 1,000 live births

The already poor health care system effectively collapsed as a result of war and the transition to a market economy.

SPENDING

 41 per 1,000 people   3.7%

3.4%   1%

New oil revenues are threatening to create a nouveau riche elite without reaching the 60% of Azerbaijan's population currently living in poverty.

TURKEY

1923 · 1939 · Oct 29 · TR · +2 · +90 · .tr

OFFICIAL NAME **Republic of Turkey** CAPITAL **Ankara**
POPULATION **68.6m** CURRENCY **Turkish lira** OFF. LANG. **Turkish**

TURKEY, MAINLY IN WESTERN ASIA, also includes the region of Eastern Thrace in Europe. It thus controls the entrance to the Black Sea, which is straddled by Turkey's largest city, Istanbul. Most Turks live in the western half of the country. The eastern and south-eastern reaches of the Anatolia Plateau are Kurdish regions. Turkey's location gives it great strategic significance in the Black Sea, the Mediterranean and the Middle East. Lying on a major earthquake fault line, many Turkish towns are vulnerable to earthquakes such as the one which devastated Izmit in 1999.

ECONOMICS

 23rd $3.4bn

 $3,100 54.4%

Advanced market economy, but with persistently high inflation. Self-sufficient in agriculture. Government bureaucracy hampers growth, but structural reforms are underway.

RESOURCES

 111bn kwh Comb. 62%
Hydro 38%
Nuclear 0%

 Sheep 29.4m
Goats 8.06m
Cattle 10.8m 64,621 b/d
(reserves of 260m bbl)

Under the controversial South-eastern Anatolian Project, Turkey is building 22 dams on the Euphrates and Tigris rivers. East provinces are rich in chromium, of which Turkey is the world's largest producer.

DEFENCE

 $7.22bn Compulsory

 None 514,850

Turkey's armed forces are the second-largest in NATO. The great majority of its personnel are conscripts; 18 months' service is compulsory for all males at the age of 20.

MEDIA

 Some censorship High

 35 daily
64 per
1,000 people TV: 1/5
Radio: 1/>50

The Turkish press is diverse, vigorous and largely privately owned. Censorship laws have been amended to ease restrictions on non-Turkish-language broadcasting.

EDUCATION

 85% 1.43m students

 14 years Primary 100%
Secondary 70%
Tertiary 14%

In 1997, compulsory education was extended from five to eight years. State schools are co-educational and free. Engineering is usually the strongest faculty in Turkey's many universities.

HEALTH

 1 per 833 people 70 years

 1 per 1,000 people 34 per 1,000 live births

Turkey possesses an adequate national system of primary health care. By Western standards, however, hospitals are underequipped. There are fewer doctors per head than in any western European country.

SPENDING

 68 per 1,000 people 5%

 2.2% 3.3%

The economic expansion of the 1980s has created a new class of wealthy entrepreneurs. Many Turks take jobs as *Gastarbeiter* (guest workers) in Germany and the Netherlands.

POLITICS

 2002/2007 President Ahmet Necdet Sezer Parliamentary democracy

Bulent Ecevit became prime minister in 1999 in a right-wing coalition. Fresh elections in November 2002 produced a stunning victory for the Islamist-dominated AK, while Ecevit's own party, and many others, failed even to gain representation in the legislature. AK leader Recep Tayyip Erdogan, having been banned from the 2002 election for previous militant remarks, succeeded his deputy as prime minister in March 2003.

AT THE LAST ELECTION

Turkish Grand National Assembly 550 seats

66% AKP   32% CHP   1% Ind

AKP = Justice and Development Party
CHP = Republican People's Party
Ind = Independents

The popularity of Islamist parties has challenged Turkey's cherished identity as a secular state. In 1995 the Welfare Party (RP) became the largest parliamentary party and ascended to government in 1996. Ousted in mid-1997, it was banned in 1998. Many of its members took refuge in its successor, the Virtue Party, which in turn was banned in 2001. The AK scored a comprehensive victory in 2002. It has assured that it does not wish to impose a theocracy.

From 1984 a bitter civil war was fought in south-east Turkey, killing thousands over the next two decades. In 1999 Abdullah Ocalan, leader of the secessionist Kurdistan Workers' Party (PKK) was sentenced to death. However, he remained in prison as, in April 2002, the PKK disbanded and regrouped as a political organization committed to seeking equal rights for Kurds within Turkey. EU pressure has led to constitutional amendments which lifted the harsh ban on broadcasting and education in Kurdish.

Turkey's human rights record has been subject to intense international criticism. Concerns have focused on the curtailment of civil liberties, illegal executions and the treatment of Kurds. Recent reforms have sought to bring Turkey in line with EU standards. Civil liberties have been improved since 1995. 2002 saw the banning of executions except in times of war and the lifting of the last states of emergency in the south-east.

WORLD AFFAIRS

 OIC, OSCE, CE, NATO, OECD

 1945

Turkey has close ties with former Communist neighbours, particularly Bulgaria and Georgia, and with Turkic-speaking central Asian states. It has joined the BSEC, and has tried to mediate between Armenia and Azerbaijan. In 2000 Turkey agreed to send arms to Uzbekistan – its first military involvement in central Asia since the collapse of the Soviet Union. Before 1991 Turkey's chief trading partner was Iraq, and relations were improving until September 2001, when Turkey became the first Muslim country to join the "war on terrorism". It took over leadership of the peacekeeping force in Afghanistan in 2002.

Negotiations on joining the EU, although aided by recently improving relations with Greece, are impeded over the Turkish-backed partition of Cyprus and, particularly, EU concerns over human rights.

PEOPLE & SOCIETY

 231 people per sq mile

 66% urban 34% rural

 Sunni Muslim 99% Other 1%

 Death penalty not used

The Turks are racially diverse. Many are the descendants of refugees, often from the Balkans, but a strong sense of national identity is rooted in a shared language and religion. Most are Sunni Muslim, although a Shi'a community is growing fast, including the heterodox Alawite sect. The largest minority are the Kurds, while there are some 500,000 Arabic speakers. While women have equal rights in law, men dominate political and even family life. In 2002 women gained the right to an equal portion in the case of divorce. With a birth rate of 2%, Turkey is projected to have a larger population than any EU country by 2020.

ECONOMIC FOCUS

EXPORTS

Italy 6%
France 6%
UK 7%
USA 9%
Other 51%
Germany 21%

IMPORTS

Russia 6%
France 8%
Italy 8%
USA 8%
Other 56%
Germany 14%

STRENGTHS

Liberalized economy resulted in strong growth in the 1990s. Self-sufficient in agriculture. Textiles, manufacturing and construction sectors competitive on world markets. Tourism industry. Dynamic private sector economy. Skilled labour force. Customs union with EU since 1995.

WEAKNESSES

Persistently high inflation. Unsound public finances. Large government bureaucracy. Uneven privatization programme. Ailing banking sector. Influence of organized crime. High cost of military action against Kurds.

PROFILE

Turkey has one of the oldest and most advanced emerging market economies. In the 1990s it grew strongly, but continued to suffer from persistently high inflation. Despite structural reforms the economy reached crisis in February 2001, with a collapse of the banking system and the loss of over 500,000 jobs. This was compounded by the economic impact of the September 11 attack on the US. IMF rescue packages were agreed in return for banking reform and privatizing debt-laden state companies, and growth returned in 2002

The Church of the Holy Cross, *on Akdamar Island in Lake Van, was built in the 10th-century when Christianity was dominant.*

SYRIA

1941 1967 April 17 SYR +2 +963 .sy

OFFICIAL NAME **Syrian Arab Republic** CAPITAL **Damacus**
POPULATION **17m** CURRENCY **Syrian pound** OFF. LANG. **Arabic**

SYRIA SHARES BORDERS WITH Lebanon, Israel, Jordan, Iraq and Turkey. Many Syrians regard their country as an artificial creation of French mandated rule, which lasted from 1920 to independence. They identify instead with a Greater Syria, successor to the medieval Ummayad caliphate, encompassing Lebanon, Jordan and Palestine. Since independence, Syria's foreign relations have been turbulent, but the authoritarian Ba'athist regime of Hafez al-Assad (1970–2000) brought a measure of internal stability.

POLITICS

 2003/2007   President Bashar al-Assad   One-party state

Syria is in effect a single-party state. Its military-backed leader from 1970 to 2000 was Hafez al-Assad, a lifelong Ba'ath Party militant. His personal dominance ensured the succession of his son Bashar after his death in June 2000.

AT THE LAST ELECTION

People's Assembly 250 seats

67% Ba'ath Party   **33% Other Ba'ath**

Ba'ath Party = Members of the National Progressive Front (allies of the Ba'ath Party)   **Other Ba'ath** = Parties allied to the Ba'ath Party

Martial law has not been rescinded since 1963, but the regime has improved its human rights record in recent years. Political prisoners are released under frequent amnesties, and in 1994 all members of the Jewish minority were granted exit visas to travel abroad.

Assad dominated Syrian politics for 30 years. His military-backed regime, drawn mainly from his own Alawi minority grouping, kept a tight hold on power, although in his last decade Sunnis gained high political posts. Despite promises made under international pressure Assad never permitted genuine multi-partyism. Shortly before Assad's death the modernizing Mohammed Miro replaced prime minister Mahmoud az-Zoubi, who was forced from office. Assad's death was immediately followed by his son's election to the party leadership, which was overwhelmingly approved by referendum. Initial tentative reforms – such as the spread of "discussion clubs" and a more varied cabinet – were later curtailed.

The Ba'athist military swept to power in 1963 with a vision of uniting all Arab nations under a single Syrian-dominated socialist system. The coup ended the power of city elites and promoted citizens from rural areas.

Assad consolidated the Ba'ath Party as the major political force. Unrest among Islamic militants was crushed, notably in the army-led massacre at Hamah in 1982. Assad focused on foreign affairs, bidding to make Syria a major power, but plans to unite with fellow Ba'athist Iraq ended in 1981 amid mutual recriminations.

WORLD AFFAIRS

 Damasc, NAM, G24 OIC, AL   1945

Syria backed Iran in the 1980s Iran–Iraq War. It regained a measure of respectability in the eyes of the West by securing the release of hostages from Shi'a militants in Lebanon. Syria joined the US-led allies in the 1991 Gulf War, legitimizing the action in the eyes of the Arab world. In 2000, however, Syria sent humanitarian aid to Iraq, in defiance of the UN blockade. The US has since accused it of supporting international terrorists and of giving support to the ousted regime of Saddam Hussein during the 2003 invasion.

ECONOMICS

 75th $1.06bn

 $940   0.3%

Rapid growth after Gulf War. Healthy oil production rates are increasing. Despite international cash injections, Syria lacks foreign investment. Agriculture is improved, but the water supply is vulnerable.

RESOURCES

 19.7bn kwh   Comb. 86% Hydro 14% Nuclear 0%

Sheep 12.4m Goats 979,325 Cattle 836,868   551,000 b/d (reserves of 2.5bn bbl)

Syria hopes to reverse a trend of declining oil production since 1996 through intensifying oil and natural gas exploration efforts, and effecting a switch from oil- to natural gas-fired power plants.

DEFENCE

 $1.88bn   Compulsory

None   259,000

Syria sees its extensive military capability as a significant deterrent to Israel's territorial expansion. It has fought four wars against Israel since 1948, and is the Arab world's strongest military power after Egypt.

MEDIA

 Censorship   Medium

 10 daily 20 per 1,000 people   TV: 1/0 Radio 1/0

Information became freer after Jordanian papers were again allowed into Syria in 1999, and with the advent of satellite TV, which is widely watched.

EDUCATION

 74%   227,926 students

 12 years   Primary 100% Secondary 42% Tertiary 6%

The development of a modern and universally accessible system of education remains an important objective. Higher education is provided by seven state universities, notably at Damascus, Aleppo and Tishrin.

HEALTH

 1 per 769 people   71 years

 90 per 1,000 people   24 per 1,000 live births

An adequate system of primary health care has been set up since the Ba'ath Party came to power. Hospitals often lack modern equipment and medical services are in need of further investment.

SPENDING

 9 per 1,000 people   10.9%

 3.1%   0.9%

The gulf between Syria's rich and poor is widening. The political elite is more numerous and richer than ever before. Palestinian refugees and the urban unemployed make up the poorest groups.

Syria sees itself as the major barrier to Israel's regional dominance. Syria has considerable control over Lebanon and hosts radical Palestinian factions, as well as forging alliances with north African states. The biggest issue with Israel remains the strategically vital Golan Heights, seized by Israel during the Six-Day War in 1967. Peace negotiations foundered when Ariel Sharon became prime minister of Israel in 2001.

There are enduring tensions with Turkey over attitudes to Israel and to Turkish Kurdish guerrillas, access to water, and Syria's desire for the return of its former coastal Alexandretta Province.

PEOPLE & SOCIETY

 239 people per sq mile

 52% urban 48% rural

 Sunni Muslim 74% Other Muslim 16% Christian 10%

 Death penalty used

Most Syrians live in the west, where the largest cities are sited. About 90% are Muslim. They include the politically dominant Alawis, a heterodox offshoot of Shi'a, comprising 12% of the population, based in Latakia and Tartous provinces. There is also a sizable Christian minority. In the west and north a mosaic of groups includes Kurds, Turkic-speakers and Armenians, the latter based in cities. Damascus, Al Qamishli and Aleppo have small Jewish communities, and there are three villages where Aramaic is spoken. In addition, some 300,000 Palestinian refugees have settled in Syria. Minorities were initially attracted to the ruling Ba'ath Party because of its emphasis on the state over sectarian interests. However, disputes between factions led to the Alawis taking control, creating resentment among the Sunni Muslim majority.

The emancipation of women, promoted initially in the late 1960s, was carried forward under President Hafez al-Assad. His first woman cabinet minister was appointed in 1976.

Total Land Area : 184 060 sq. km
(71 066 sq. miles)

LAND HEIGHT

2000m/6562ft
1000m/3281ft
500m/1640ft
200m/656ft
Sea Level

POPULATION

over 500 000
over 100 000
over 50 000
over 10 000
under 10 000

0   100 km
0   100 miles

ECONOMIC FOCUS

EXPORTS

Turkey 8%
Saudi Arabia 9%
France 10%
Italy 12%
Germany 21%
Other 40%

IMPORTS

South Korea 5%
Turkey 5%
Germany 7%
Italy 7%
France 10%
Other 66%

STRENGTHS

Exporter of crude oil – production increasing as a result of new oil strikes. Manufacturing base has grown. Thriving agricultural sector.

WEAKNESSES

Defence spending is a major drain on economy. Large black market. Domination of inefficient state-run companies. Lack of foreign investment; foreign currency accounts banned. High population growth. Vulnerable water supply.

PROFILE

Billions of dollars flowed into the economy from the US, Japan, the EU and Saudi Arabia and other Gulf states after the 1990–1991 Gulf War. This cash injection, along with increased oil revenue, led to rapid growth. Diversion of water from the Euphrates River toward fertile plains, rather than poorer land, led to a rise in agricultural output. However, long-term economic prospects remain uncertain. The public sector employs 20% of the work force, and state controls inhibit private enterprise and investment, and have created a booming black market. Businessmen often channel funds through the freer Lebanese economy. An economic reform package in 2000 created a stock exchange and permitted private banks.

The ancient city of Palmyra, *in Syria's central region, was once the capital of the kingdom of Queen Zenobia.*

JORDAN

| 1946 | 1967 | May 25 | HJK | +2 | +962 | .jo |

OFFICIAL NAME: Hashemite Kingdom of Jordan CAPITAL: **Amman**
POPULATION **5.2m** CURRENCY **Jordanian dinar** OFF. LANG. **Arabic**

SURROUNDED ON ALL SIDES by the deserts of the Middle East, Jordan has just 26 km (16 miles) of maritime coastline. The vast majority of the population lives in the north-west of the country, on the east bank of the river Jordan. Jordan ceded its claim to the West Bank of the river to the aspiring Palestinian state in 1998. Tourism associated with important historical sites such as Petra is a mainstay of the economy.

ECONOMICS

 92nd $59m

 $1,710   1.8%

Major exporter of phosphates. Skilled work force. Unemployment, exacerbated by influx of refugees from Kuwait after Gulf crisis. Little arable land. Tourism badly affected by regional insecurity.

RESOURCES

 6.7bn kwh   Comb 100% Hydro 0% Nuclear 0%

Sheep 1.85m Goats 640,000 Cattle 65,400   40 b/d (reserves of 4,000,000 bbl)

Oil deposits have been discovered. Phosphates, livestock and crops such as tomatoes, wheat, olives and vegetables are the main resources.

DEFENCE

 $740m   Not compulsory

None   100,240

The armed forces are loyal to the monarchy. They have a reputation for professionalism and thorough training. The forces are dependent on Western support for credit in purchasing arms and equipment.

MEDIA

 Some censorship   Medium

 8 daily 42 per 1,000 people   TV: 1/0 Radio 1/0

A restrictive press and publications law was enacted by the government in 1998. All radio stations and TV channels are controlled by the state.

EDUCATION

 90%   142,190 students

16 years   Primary 69% Secondary 66% Tertiary 18%

Female students fare better than in some states in the area; men and women receive the same education. Jordanian teachers work all over the Middle East.

HEALTH

 1 per 588 people   70 years

25 per 1,000 people   25 per 1,000 live births

Primary health care is subsidized by the government. There are numerous hospitals, all well distributed throughout the country.

SPENDING

 49 per 1,000 people   8.5%

6.8%   3.6%

Poverty is relatively rare, though refugee camps still exist and 25% unemployment damaged many family incomes in the late 1990s.

POLITICS

 L. House 1997/2003 U. House 2001/2005   HM King Abdullah II   Constitutional monarchy

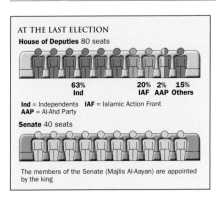

AT THE LAST ELECTION
House of Deputies 80 seats

63% Ind   20% IAF   2% AAP   15% Others

Ind = Independents   IAF = Islamic Action Front
AAP = Al-Ahd Party

Senate 40 seats

The members of the Senate (Majlis Al-Aayan) are appointed by the king

King Abdullah II acceded to the throne in February 1999 upon the death of his father, King Hussein. Although lacking in political experience, he is respected by the army and enjoys the support of Jordan's tribal leaders. Multi-party elections, initiated in 1993, have benefited pro-government parties, despite a strong Islamist opposition lobby. The appointment in 2000 of Prime Minister Ali Abu al-Ragheb marked a shift toward a modernizing and pro-business government.

WORLD AFFAIRS

 NAM, OIC, AMF, AL, WTO   1955

Jordan's position as a key player in Middle East politics is under question since the death of King Hussein. Policy toward the emerging Palestinian state is uncertain since its relations with Israel remain much less aggressive than those of other Arab countries. The US signed a free trade agreement in 2000.

PEOPLE & SOCIETY

 151 people per sq mile   79% urban 21% rural

 Sunni Muslim 92% Christian & others 8%   Death penalty used

POPULATION
over 100 000
over 50 000
over 10 000
under 10 000

LAND HEIGHT
1000m/3281ft
500m/1640ft
200m/656ft
Sea Level
-200m/-656ft

Total Land Area : 88 930 sq. km (34 336 sq. miles)

Jordan is a predominantly Muslim country drawn from Bedouin roots, with a Christian minority. About half the population are Palestinian in origin. The monarchy's power base lies among the rural tribes, which also provide the backbone of the military. National identity is strong.

LEBANON

1941 | 1941 | Nov 22 | RL | +2 | +961 | .lb

OFFICIAL NAME **Republic of Lebanon** CAPITAL **Beirut**
POPULATION **3.6m** CURRENCY **Lebanese pound** OFF. LANG. **Arabic**

LEBANON IS DWARFED by its two powerful neighbours, Syria and Israel. The country's coastal strip is fertile and the hinterland mountainous. Maronite Christians have traditionally ruled Lebanon. A civil war between Muslim and Christian factional groups which began in 1975 threatened to lead to the breakup of the state. However, Saudi Arabia brokered a peace agreement in 1989; politics became more stable and reconstruction began.

POLITICS

 2000/2004

 President Émile Lahoud

 Multi-party republic

AT THE LAST ELECTION

National Assembly 128 seats

6% MLU

| 18% RD | 16% Ind | 14% D | 8% BH | 6% NS | 32% Others |

RD = Resistance and Development List   Ind = Independents
D = Dignity   BH = Baalbek–Hermel List   NS = National
Struggle List   MLU = Mount Lebanon Unity

The Arab-brokered 1989 Taif peace agreement ending the civil war in Lebanon redressed the constitutional balance between Christian and Muslim groups and guaranteed a power-sharing structure. Syria remains the main power-broker in Lebanon, especially following the withdrawal of Israeli troops in 2000. Relative stability has been maintained under President Rafiq al-Hariri, who won the first post-war legislative elections in 1992, and was re-elected with a landslide for a third term in 2000. However, a worsening economic situation has led to clashes between Harari and General Émile Lahoud, who has been president since 1998.

WORLD AFFAIRS

 AL, G24, OIF, NAM, OIC

 1945

The agreement ending the civil war has left Syria with enormous influence in domestic politics. Until mid-2000, when Israeli troops withdrew, clashes in the south between Israeli occupying forces (and their proxy militias) and the Hezbollah militia were frequent and bloody.

PEOPLE & SOCIETY

 911 people per sq mile

 90% urban 10% rural

Muslim 70% Christian 30%

Death penalty used

The Lebanese population is fragmented into sub-sects of Christians and Muslims, but retains a strong sense of national identity. There has been a large Palestinian refugee population in the country since 1948. Islamic fundamentalism is influential among poorer Shi'a Muslims, who constitute the largest single group.

LAND HEIGHT

3000m/9843ft
2000m/6562ft
1000m/3281ft
500m/1640ft
200m/656ft
Sea Level

POPULATION

over 1 000 000
over 100 000
over 10 000
under 10 000

Quobaïyat
El Mina
Tripoli Zgharta
Amioun 3087m Hermel
Batroûn Bcharré
Jbaïl Qartaba Oranges
Joûnié Baalbek
BEIRUT
Baabda Aaley Zahlé
Bhamdoun Rayak
Damoûr Aanjar
Saïda
Jezzîne Lac de Qaraoun
Rachaïya
Nabatîyé Marjayoun
Soûr El Khiyam
Tibnine GOLAN HEIGHTS
En Nâqoûra Bent Jbail
ISRAEL

SYRIA
MEDITERRANEAN SEA

Total Land Area :
10 230 sq. km
(3950 sq. miles)

N

0   20 km
0   20 miles

ECONOMICS

 72nd

$-3.07bn

 $4,010

0.5%

Peace will allow Lebanon to regain its position as an Arab centre for banking and services. Potentially a major producer of wine and fruit. Dependent on imported oil and gas. High public debt.

RESOURCES

 7.1bn kwh

Comb. 87% Hydro 13% Nuclear 0%

Sheep 380,000 Goats 445,000 Cattle 74,000

Produces no oil Refines 37,500 b/d

Wine, cotton, fruit and vegetables are the main crops. Thermal power stations are fuelled by imported petroleum.

DEFENCE

$576m

Compulsory

None

71,830

The army has over 60,000 troops. There is a UN peacekeeping force on the Israeli border. Syrian forces, whose dominant security role had been formalized in 1991, withdrew from Beirut in 2001.

MEDIA

 Some censorship

 High

41 daily 74 per 1,000 people

TV: 1/4 Radio: 1/0

In the late 1990s the government banned news and political programmes on private satellite television channels.

EDUCATION

86%

81,588 students

11 years

Primary 100% Secondary 89% Tertiary 38%

Lebanon has one of the highest literacy rates in the Arab world. Education programmes were severely disrupted by war.

HEALTH

1 per 476 people

73 years

20 per 1,000 people

26 per 1,000 live births

An adequate system of primary health care exists in most areas of Lebanon. Hospital staffing is returning to pre-war levels.

SPENDING

 313 per 1,000 people

 3.5%

2.1%

2.2%

The high average income per capita statistics conceal the fact that a huge gulf exists between the poor and a small, massively rich elite.

SAUDI ARABIA

OFFICIAL NAME **Kingdom of Saudi Arabia** CAPITAL **Riyadh**
POPULATION **21.7m** CURRENCY **Saudi riyal** OFF. LANG. **Arabic**

O CCUPYING MOST OF THE Arabian peninsula, Saudi Arabia covers an area as large as western Europe. Over 95% of its land is desert, with the most arid part, known as the Empty Quarter or Rub al Khali, being in the south-east. Saudi Arabia has the world's largest oil and gas reserves. It includes Islam's holiest cities, Medina and Mecca, visited each year by two million Muslims performing the pilgrimage known as the *hajj*. The al-Sa'ud family have been Saudi Arabia's absolutist rulers since 1932. In theory, Islamic *sharia* law underpins the constitution.

POLITICS

 Not applicable   HM King Fahd ibn Abd al-Aziz   Monarchy

Since 1993 a Consultative Council (*Majlis ash-Shoura*) has been appointed by the king. The royal family rules by carefully manipulating appointments in all sectors of government. Frequent changes of personnel within the armed forces ensure that officers do not build personal followings. All influential cabinet portfolios, apart from those of oil and religious affairs, are held by members of the royal family.

LEGISLATIVE OR ADVISORY BODIES
Consultative Council 120 seats

Saudi Arabia is an absolute monarchy. The king rules with the assistance of an appointed Council of Ministers and the Consultative Council

Absolutist rule means that domestic politics are virtually nonexistent. The regime retains feudal elements: weekly *majlis*, or councils, are held where citizens can present petitions or grievances to leading members of the royal family. Large cash sums are often dispensed at these meetings.

The legitimacy of the regime is built on its adherence to Islamic values, and the backing of the *ulema* (scholars). It is the stress on Islam that colours Saudi life most. The 5,000-strong *mutawa* (religious police) enforce the five-times-a-day call to prayer, when businesses must close. During Ramadan the *mutawa* are especially active.

Following the 1991 Gulf War, a civil rights campaign emerged to challenge the authority of the ruling family, demanding closer adherence to Islamic values. The movement objected to the presence of US troops on Saudi territory and the consequent exposure to "corrupt" Western culture. The al-Sa'uds moved swiftly to quash the protest but exiled opponents have continued their activities using fax machines and e-mail. The most vociferous denunciations have come from Osama bin Laden, formerly part of the inner circle, operating from bases abroad.

The question of succession and the possibility of a future power struggle, rooted in rivalries endemic to the House of Sa'ud, emerged in 1996, when King Fahd suffered a stroke. The management of day-to-day affairs passed briefly to his half brother, Crown Prince Abdullah, who remains in effective if no longer formal control.

WORLD AFFAIRS

 AL, Damasc, GCC, OIC, OPEC   1945

Saudi Arabia's strategic importance is derived largely from its oil reserves and worldwide investments. Relations with the US, although close, have been frayed by recent US military campaigns in Afghanistan and Iraq. After Iraq's invasion of Kuwait in 1990, the

ECONOMICS

27th $14.5bn

$7,230   -0.5%

Rise of oil prices in 2000 signalled recovery from 1986 collapse, though the country continues to reduce its dependency on oil exports. Large income from pilgrims travelling to Mecca.

RESOURCES

113bn kwh   Comb. 100%
Hydro 0%
Nuclear 0%

Sheep 7.58m
Goats 4.31m
Camels 400,000   8.77m b/d
(reserves of 261.8bn bbl)

With the world's biggest oil and gas reserves, Saudi Arabia plays a key role in the global economy. Attempts at diversification have not altered heavy dependency on the oil markets.

DEFENCE

$24.3bn   Not compulsory

None   106,500

Saudi Arabia's substantial military contribution to the 1991 Gulf War, at a cost of $55 billion, enhanced its image as a major regional power. Military equipment is purchased mostly from the US, the UK and France.

MEDIA

Censorship   High

11 daily
59 per 1,000 people   TV: 2/0
Radio: 1/1

The government imposes total press censorship. The international *Sharq Al Awsat* is a leading Arabic daily. In 2001 the government announced strict rules regarding state and religion on the Internet.

EDUCATION

77%   273,992 students

Schooling is free but not compulsory   Primary 71%
Secondary 66%
Tertiary 19%

Growing numbers of Western-educated Saudis have intensified pressure for social and political change. Women have had equal opportunities in education since the 1950s.

HEALTH

 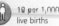

1 per 588 people   72 years

37 per 1,000 people   18 per 1,000 live births

Infant mortality has dropped and endemic disease has been nearly eradicated. Health care outside major centres still remains relatively undeveloped, given Saudi Arabia's huge economic resources.

SPENDING

93 per 1,000 people   14.1%

7.5%   6.4%

Saudi citizens are among the most prosperous in the world. The al-Sa'uds have used their wealth to create a cradle-to-grave welfare system. Ownership of TVs, telephones and VCRs is among the region's highest.

Saudis had taken a leading role in consolidating the Arab coalition against Iraq. Saudi Arabia sheltered the Kuwaiti royal family, provided military bases to the Western allies, and supplied more troops than any other Arab country. The continued presence of foreign forces then provoked hostility from Islamic militants. This gained world attention through statements by Osama bin Laden at the time of the September 2001 terrorist attacks on the US. The US pledged to withdraw its troops in 2003 following the successful invasion of Iraq.

A pact signed with Yemen in June 2000 ended a simmering border dispute. In early 2002 Crown Prince Abdullah's new peace plan for Israel/Palestine won praise from Arabs and the West – and hinted at a major change in Saudi foreign policy.

PEOPLE & SOCIETY

27 people per sq mile	87% urban 13% rural	Sunni Muslim 85% Shi'a Muslim 15%	Death penalty used

The Saudis, who take their name from the ruling al-Sa'ud family, were united by conquest between 1902 and 1932 by King Abd al-Aziz al-Sa'ud, who expelled the Turks. The vast majority of Saudis are Sunni Muslims who follow the *wahhabi* (puritan) interpretation of Islam and embrace *sharia* (Islamic law). The politically dominant Nejadi tribes from the central plateau around Riyadh are Bedouin in origin. The Hejazi tribes, from the south and west, have a more cosmopolitan, mercantile background, but are largely displaced from politics. In the eastern Al-Hasa province there is a Shi'a minority of some 300,000, many of whom are employed in the oilfields. Women have to wear the veil, cannot hold a driver's licence, and have no role in public life. They are effectively barred from the workplace except as teachers and nurses. However, in 2000 Saudi Arabia decided to sign the UN convention on women's rights – provided it did not contradict *sharia*, and issued women with identity cards in 2001.

Total Land Area : 2 114 690 sq. km (816 480 sq. miles)

LAND HEIGHT

3000m/9843ft
2000m/6562ft
1000m/3281ft
500m/1640ft
Sea Level

POPULATION

over 1 000 000
over 500 000
over 100 000
over 50 000
over 10 000
under 10 000

ECONOMIC FOCUS

EXPORTS

France 4%
Singapore 6%
South Korea 11%
Japan 16%
USA 17%
Other 46%

IMPORTS

Italy 4%
Germany 7%
UK 8%
Japan 9%
USA 19%
Other 53%

STRENGTHS

Vast oil and gas reserves. Soaring world oil prices in 2000. World-class associated industries. Accumulated surpluses and steady current income. Large income from two million pilgrims to Mecca annually.

WEAKNESSES

Lack of indigenous skilled workers. Food production requires heavy subsidy. Most consumer items and industrial raw materials imported. Up to 20% youth unemployment. Large national debt. Royal family technically owns most of national wealth.

PROFILE

Since the 1970s, great efforts have been made to reduce dependence on oil and to provide employment for young Saudis. By 2000, Saudi Arabia had steered OPEC towards controlling oil prices to avoid recession in industrialized countries or spurring a drive to develop alternative energy. Since 2000, foreigners have been allowed complete ownership of Saudi businesses and rights to property. Large sums have been spent on creating a US-standard infrastructure to provide the basis for a manufacturing economy. It remains, however, dependent on foreign workers.

Network of modern road junctions *spread out across the desert landscape near the* hajj *pilgrimage destination of Mecca.*

IRAQ

 1932   1990 July 17   IRQ +3 +964   .iq

OFFICIAL NAME **Republic of Iraq**   CAPITAL **Baghdad**
POPULATION **24.2m**   CURRENCY **Iraqi dinar**   OFF. LANG. **Arabic**

O IL-RICH IRAQ is divided down its middle by the Euphrates and Tigris Rivers. While the river valleys are fertile, most of the country is inhospitable desert or mountains. The modern state encompasses Kurds in the north, Sunni Muslims in the centre and a Shi'a Muslim majority to the south. The Arab nationalist regime of Saddam Hussein maintained power through fear from 1979 until its ouster in the 2003 US-led invasion.

ECONOMICS

 64th

 $950

No data available

60%

The US has promised substantial aid to Iraq following the invasion of 2003. The once thriving agricultural sector has been devastated by war.

RESOURCES

30.6bn kwh

Comb. 98% Hydro 2% Nuclear 0%

Sheep 6.78m Goats 1.6m Cattle 1.35m

2.41m b/d (reserves of 112.5bn bbl)

Iraq has huge reserves of oil and gas. Before the 1990 invasion of Kuwait and subsequent war and sanctions, Iraq supplied 80% of the world's trade in dates.

DEFENCE

 $1.37bn

 None

 Compulsory

 372,000

The failure of weapons inspectors to find any real weapons of mass destruction was brushed aside by the persistently obstructionist tendencies of the regime and prompted the invasion of 2003.

MEDIA

 Censorship

 9 daily 20 per 1,000 people

 Medium

 TV: 1/0 Radio: 1/0

The media were strictly controlled under Saddam Hussein, and his own son Uday controlled two major newspapers. The 2003 war was covered by the international media in unprecedented detail.

EDUCATION

 56%

 11 years

 209,818 students

Primary 88% Secondary 20% Tertiary 13%

The education system was interconnected with the Ba'athist regime. University scientists worked closely with the regime on weapons research programmes. Education will be a priority for aid agencies.

HEALTH

  1 per 2,000 people

34 per 1,000 people

 61 years

 93 per 1,000 live births

Deaths among children and the elderly had already spiralled sharply before 2003 as UN sanctions led to shortages of medical supplies and equipment. Hospitals in major cities were damaged by looters.

SPENDING

 36 per 1,000 people

 5.1%

 9.3%

 3.8%

The most vulnerable sections of society were disproportionately affected by the decade of UN sanctions. The elite of the Ba'athist regime displayed their wealth ostentatiously.

POLITICS

 2000/In transition   Vacant   In transition

Two decades of political upheaval followed the removal of the monarchy in 1958. Saddam Hussein overthrew his predecessor in 1979 and held power through a brutal dictatorship until his dramatic defeat in 2003. His period in office was dominated by

AT THE LAST ELECTION
National Assembly 250 seats

The National Assembly is composed of Ba'athists and their allies. Thirty seats representing the Kurdish region were not elected.

warfare and its consequences; he launched a war against neighbouring Iran within a year of coming to power. His invasion of Kuwait was defeated in 1991 by a US-led alliance, and his regime was besieged under a harsh policy of international sanctions. Viciously crushing dissent, he remained in power throughout the 1990s, and even succeeded in drawing support from previously hostile Arab neighbours and other countries against the sanctions. In March 2003, with UN weapons inspectors still failing to uncover the alleged arsenal of weapons of mass destruction (WMD), a US-led coalition invaded Iraq and ousted Saddam Hussein within three weeks.

The standard of living in Iraq dropped dramatically under the UN sanctions in the 1990s. Supplies of food and medicines were greatly curtailed. This, coupled with the brutality of the Ba'athist regime, paved the way for the government's rapid fall in 2003. Many welcomed the ouster of Saddam Hussein, but few were happy at the prospect of a US-controlled puppet state. Even before the invasion was begun US companies were pushed to the front of the queue for contracts to reconstruct Iraq's shattered infrastructure, prompting accusations of a new economic imperialism. Potential future leaders for Iraq are likely to be drawn from the previously exiled opposition.

Although the Ba'athist regime drew its members from across Iraqi society, and began by asserting its secularity, in reality much power was concentrated in the hands of the Sunni Muslim Tikriti tribe of Saddam Hussein. Domestic opposition became centered on the Kurds in the north and the Shi'a Marsh Arabs in the south. Suppression was ruthless. Chemical agents were used against the Kurds in the late 1980s and the ecosystem of the southern marshes was purposefully destroyed in the early 1990s. It was feared that the potential for ethnic tensions would be unleashed by the 2003 invasion.

WORLD AFFAIRS

  AL, OAPEC, OPEC, OIC, NAM   UN 1945

During the 1980–1988 Iran–Iraq war, Saddam Hussein was armed by the West as an ally against Islamic fundamentalism. However, his invasion of Kuwait in 1990 was decried the world over. A US-led military force, assisted by several Arab states, repelled Iraq in 1991.

While Russia and France led the way in undermining the resultant UN sanctions on humanitarian grounds, the US increased the rhetoric against Saddam Hussein after 2001. It counted Iraq among the "axis of evil" states sponsoring international terrorism. France, Germany and Russia were joined by most of Iraq's neighbours in opposing the war launched, without UN backing, by the US in 2003. The post-war regime is likely to have extremely close ties to the US. Iran, Syria and Muslim extremists are deeply suspicious of a potential US puppet state in their midst while Turkey fears a resurgence of pan-Kurdish nationalism.

PEOPLE & SOCIETY

143 people per sq mile	67% urban 33% rural	Shi'a Muslim 62% Sunni Muslim 33% Christian & other 5%	Death penalty used

Carved out of the remnants of the Ottoman Empire, Iraq is home to three distinct ethno-religious groups as well as smaller minorities, including Turkmen and Persians. There a variety of Christian sects, but most Iraqi Jews emigrated following the creation of Israel.

The Arab Muslims are divided between the Shi'a and Sunni sects. Iraq is home to some of the holiest sites of Shi'a Islam. Religious tensions have been largely suppressed, but resentment exists over previous minority Sunni control of government. The homeland and culture of the Shi'a Marsh Arabs was purposefully attacked and largely destroyed after an abortive uprising in 1991.

The Kurdish community, based in the north, was granted de facto self-rule under the protection of the no-fly zones after 1991, but was riven by internal conflict. The long-held desire for a separate Kurdish homeland has been politically suppressed to ensure the viability of post-war Iraq.

ECONOMIC FOCUS

EXPORTS

Netherlands 7%
Japan 7%
Italy 8%
France 8%
USA 44%
Other 26%

IMPORTS

Russia 4%
Italy 5%
China 11%
Australia 12%
France 21%
Other 47%

STRENGTHS

Second-largest crude oil and natural gas reserves in OPEC. Large labour force. Promises of substantial US aid.

WEAKNESSES

Infrastructure devastated by war. Legacy of sanctions. War-ravaged agricultural sector.

PROFILE

Before 1990, Iraq was the world's third-largest oil supplier. Under sanctions, oil was produced only for domestic consumption. Limited oil exports under strict UN supervision were resumed for the first time in 1996, and in 2000 the UN Security Council approved a resolution permitting Iraq to buy parts and equipment for the oil industry. The denial of Western assistance following the 1991 Gulf War stifled Iraq's economy. The once-thriving agricultural sector was devastated. The manufacturing industry remains at a standstill. The introduction of draconian penalties, including the death sentence, failed to curb the black market or halt the sharp depreciation in the value of the dinar. Efforts at recovery, such as the resumption of some informal economic links and the revision of UN sanctions in 2002, were undermined by the return of war in 2003.

Golden Mosque *at Sāmarrā' on the Tigris. Among the extensive remains of its ancient city are those of the Great Mosque built in 847CE.*

KUWAIT

1961 **1961** **Feb 25** **KWT** **+3** **+965** **.kw**

ECONOMICS

54th $8.57bn

$18,030   1.7%

Recovery of oil and gas production. Large overseas investments. Stable banking system. Adverse consequences of Iraqi invasion. Reliance on imported skilled labour, food and raw materials.

RESOURCES

31bn kwh   Comb. 100% Hydro 0% Nuclear 0%

Sheep 360,000 Goats 130,000 Cattle 21,000   2.14m b/d (reserves of 96.5bn bbl)

The oil industry is Kuwait's most profitable sector, accounting for over 80% of export earnings. Although badly hit by the Gulf War, when a number of wells were deliberately fired, it was quickly rehabilitated.

DEFENCE

$5.03bn   Compulsory

None   15,500

In August 1990 Kuwait's 11,000-strong, partly volunteer army was easily overrun by vastly superior Iraqi forces. Since its liberation, defence pacts have been signed with the US, the UK, France and Russia.

MEDIA

Some censorship   High

7 daily 377 per 1,000 people   TV: 1/0 Radio 1/0

All radio and terrestrial TV transmissions are controlled by the state, but satellite TV is freely available. Freedom of the press exists in theory.

EDUCATION

83%   29,509 students

14 years   Primary 77% Secondary 65% Tertiary 19%

Kuwaiti citizens receive free education from nursery to university. Since the liberation, more emphasis has been placed on technology in the curriculum.

HEALTH

1 per 526 people   76 years

1 per 1,000 people   9 per 1,000 live births

Despite theft of equipment during the Iraqi invasion, Kuwait has restored its Western-standard health care service. Nationals receive free treatment.

SPENDING

317 per 1,000 people   12.1%

6.5%   3.4%

As well as the oil-rich elite, most Kuwaitis enjoy high incomes, and the government has repeatedly rescued citizens who have suffered stock market or other financial losses.

OFFICIAL NAME State of Kuwait   **CAPITAL** Kuwait City
POPULATION 2m   **CURRENCY** Kuwaiti dinar   **OFF. LANG.** Arabic

A T THE NORTH-WEST EXTREME of the Gulf, Kuwait is dwarfed by its neighbours. The flat, almost featureless landscape conceals huge oil and gas reserves, which put Kuwait among the world's first oil-rich states. In 1990 Iraq invaded, claiming Kuwait as its 19th province. A US-led alliance, under the aegis of the UN, expelled Iraqi forces following a short war in 1991. Kuwait served as the launching point for the 2003 invasion of Iraq.

POLITICS

1999/2003   Amir Shaikh Jaber al-Ahmad al-Jaber al-Sabah   Constitutional monarchy

AT THE LAST ELECTION

National Assembly 50 seats

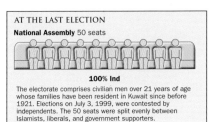

100% Ind

The electorate comprises civilian men over 21 years of age whose families have been resident in Kuwait since before 1921. Elections on July 3, 1999, were contested by independents. The 50 seats were split evenly between Islamists, liberals, and government supporters.

In 1992 Amir Shaikh Jaber restored the National Assembly. There was then a government of "national unity" until 1999, when elections strengthened the amir's Islamist and liberal opponents. The Council of Ministers resigned in 2001 in the face of Assembly criticism. In the new cabinet the ruling al-Sabah family still holds the top posts.

WORLD AFFAIRS

AL, Damasc, GCC, OIC, OPEC   1963

Kuwait's strategic importance is as a major exporter of crude oil and natural gas. As such, it has always maintained very close links with the West, which have deepened since the war with Iraq, and on which it depends for its future security. Kuwait still awaits the return of POWs from Iraq.

PEOPLE & SOCIETY

291 people per sq mile   96% urban 4% rural

Muslim 85% Christian, Hindu & others 15%   Death penalty used

Total Land Area: 17 820 sq. km (6880 sq. miles)

LAND HEIGHT
over 100 000
over 50 000
over 10 000
under 10 000
200m/656ft
Sea Level
0 25 km
0 25 miles

Kuwait is a conservative Sunni Muslim society (27% of the population are Shi'a). Women have considerable freedom, although the amir's decree providing for female enfranchisement is repeatedly rejected by the National Assembly.

Kuwait's oil wealth has drawn in thousands of workers from south Asia and other Arab countries. The PLO's support for the Iraqi invasion led to most Palestinians, hitherto more numerous in Kuwait than elsewhere in the Arabian peninsula, being driven out. Now native Kuwaitis are outnumbered by resident foreign nationals.

BAHRAIN

 110th $113m

 $7,640 -1.5%

OFFICIAL NAME **State of Bahrain** CAPITAL **Manama**
POPULATION **663,000** CURRENCY **Bahraini dinar** OFF. LANG. **Arabic**

B AHRAIN IS AN ARCHIPELAGO of 33 islands situated between the Qatar peninsula and the Saudi Arabian mainland. Only three of the islands are inhabited. Bahrain Island is connected to Saudi Arabia's eastern province by a causeway opened in 1986. Bahrain was the first Gulf emirate to export oil; its reserves are now almost depleted. Services such as offshore banking, insurance and tourism are major employment sectors for skilled Bahrainis.

ECONOMICS

Bahrain has been the Arab world's major offshore banking sector since the 1980s. Depleted oil reserves and insufficient diversification. High levels of government borrowing.

POLITICS

 2002/2006
 HM Shaikh Hamad bin Isa al-Khalifa
Multi-party republic

RESOURCES

 5.8bn kwh Comb. 100% Hydro 0% Nuclear 0%

 Sheep 17,500 Goats 16,300 Cattle 11,000 — 37,473 b/d (reserves of 219m bbl)

Bahrain remains dependent on its oil and gas production. As oil has declined, so gas has assumed greater importance. Most is used to supply local industries, particularly the aluminium plant.

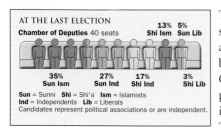

AT THE LAST ELECTION		
Chamber of Deputies 40 seats	13% Shi Ism	5% Sun Lib
35% Sun Ism	27% Sun Ind	17% Shi Ind	3% Shi Lib

Sun = Sunni Shi = Shi'a Ism = Islamists
Ind = Independents Lib = Liberals
Candidates represent political associations or are independent.

DEFENCE

 $364m Not compulsory

 None 10,700

There is a small but well-equipped air force. The navy is hard-pressed to patrol the 49-island archipelago. Bahrain is home to the US 5th Fleet and US air bases have been used in recent conflicts.

The al-Khalifa family has dominated politics since 1783 by means of an effectively autocratic system, although the amir has been advised since 1993 by an appointed Consultative Council. A national charter of political reforms was approved by the council in 2000 and backed in a 2001 referendum. The country was declared a constitutional monarchy in February 2002, and elections for a Chamber of Deputies in October were won by Islamist candidates. The repeal of the State Security Law in 2001 promised an end to the detention of political dissidents. Many were Shi'a opponents of the regime, traditionally backed by Iran.

MEDIA

 Some censorship High

 5 daily 117 per 1,000 people — TV: 1/0 Radio: 1/1

Bahrain has a less authoritarian media regime than most of the Gulf states, although government critics have been prosecuted. CNN and BBC satellite TV are freely available.

WORLD AFFAIRS

AL, Damasc, GCC, OIC, OAPEC
 1971

Total Land Area : 680 sq. km (263 sq. miles)

Bahrain has good relations with the UK and the US, but is uneasy with their stance on Iraq. There is residual tension with Iran. A dispute with Qatar over the Hawar islands was resolved in Bahrain's favour in 2001.

EDUCATION

 88% 7,676 students

 15 years Primary 100% Secondary 94% Tertiary 20%

Female literacy rates are well above the Gulf average. The University of Bahrain opened in 1986 after a series of funding problems.

PEOPLE & SOCIETY

 2,429 people per sq mile
 93% urban 7% rural

Shi'a Muslim 70% Sunni Muslim 30%
 Death penalty used

HEALTH

 1 per 1,000 people 73 years

 20 per 1,000 people 7 per 1,000 live births

The high-quality health service is free to Bahraini nationals. Some go abroad for advanced care. The Muharraq Health Centre was upgraded in 2001.

Bahrain is the smallest and most densely populated Arab state. The key division is between Sunni and Shi'a Muslims. Sunnis hold the best jobs in business and government. Shi'a Muslims tend to do menial work and have a lower standard of living. The most impoverished Shi'a Muslims tend to be of Iranian descent.

LAND HEIGHT
100m/328ft
Sea Level

POPULATION
over 100 000
over 50 000
over 10 000
under 10 000

Hawar Islands

SPENDING

 255 per 1,000 people 4.8%

 4.4% 2.6%

Beneficiaries of the amir's extensive patronage form the wealthiest group in society. The country's largest religious community, the Shi'a Muslims, is also the poorest.

OMAN

ECONOMICS

 80th

$3.35bn

$4,778

-1.1%

Oman has benefited from staying out of OPEC and selling oil at spot prices without quotas. Rich Indian Ocean coastal waters have potential for sizable fishing industry. Overdependence on oil.

RESOURCES

11bn kwh

Comb. 100%
Hydro 0%
Nuclear 0%

Sheep 335,000
Goats 980,000
Cattle 290,000

959,000 b/d
(reserves of
5.56bn bbl)

The government invested $3 billion in 2003 in a number of projects to encourage diversification and cut down dependence on oil revenues.

DEFENCE

$2.83bn

Not compulsory

None

33,300

The UK is the main supplier of equipment. In the Gulf War, Oman provided communications and services to US and UK forces. Oman's Defence Council has replenished tanks, ships and aircraft in recent years.

MEDIA

  Censorship

High

6 daily
28 per 1,000
people

TV: 1/0
Radio: 2/0

Nothing which is critical of the government may be published in Oman, despite a 1984 law allowing for "freedom of opinion".

EDUCATION

 72%

16,032 students

 Schooling not compulsory

Primary 75%
Secondary 67%
Tertiary 8%

Education has improved since 1970, but rural illiteracy is still high. Over 200 new schools were built between 1996 and 2000.

HEALTH

  1 per 769 people

71 years

  38 per 1,000 people

17 per 1,000 live births

Oman has a policy of replacing expatriate medical staff with Omani nationals. There are no hospitals in rural areas, which are served by clinics.

SPENDING

  97 per 1,000 people

14.4%

  3.9%

2.9%

Omanis in urban areas enjoy the same high living standards that are to be found in other Gulf states. Hunting trips are popular among the Omani elite, and a khanjar, a curved dagger, is seen as a status symbol.

OFFICIAL NAME **Sultanate of Oman** CAPITAL **Muscat**
POPULATION **2.7m** CURRENCY **Omani rial** OFF. LANG. **Arabic**

SHARING BORDERS WITH Yemen, the United Arab Emirates and Saudi Arabia, Oman occupies a strategic position at the entrance to the Gulf. It is the least developed of the Gulf states. The most densely populated areas are the northern coast and the southern Salalah plain. Oil exports have given Oman modest prosperity under a paternalistic sultan, who defeated a Marxist-led insurgency in the 1970s.

POLITICS

  2000/2003

 Sultan Qaboos bin Said

Monarchy

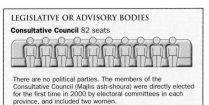

LEGISLATIVE OR ADVISORY BODIES

Consultative Council 82 seats

There are no political parties. The members of the Consultative Council (Majlis ash-shoura) were directly elected for the first time in 2000 by electoral committees in each province, and included two women.

Sultan Qaboos is an authoritarian but paternalistic monarch, whose dynasty traces its roots to the 18th century. As well as being head of state, the sultan is prime minister and minister for foreign affairs, defence and finance. The regime faces no serious challenge, although Qaboos keeps a careful eye on the religious right wing. In 1991, he created the Consultative Council (*Majlis ash-shoura*), which gives a semblance of democracy. From 2000 its members were directly elected by provincial committees, rather than being appointed. Major political issues include the planned privatization of medium-sized government projects, and improving Oman's self-defence capability.

WORLD AFFAIRS

 Damasc, GCC, AMF, OIC, AL

 1971

Relations with Israel were cut off after an outbreak of the renewed Palestinian *intifada* in 2000. Oman has ties with Iran and called for an easing of sanctions against Iraq, but is basically pro-Western and supportive of the US-led military action against Iraq.

PEOPLE & SOCIETY

 33 people per sq mile

 77% urban
23% rural

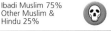 Ibadi Muslim 75%
Other Muslim &
Hindu 25%

 Death penalty used

Strait of Hormuz
Al Khasab • Musandam Peninsula
OMAN ENCLAVE
Shinas • Al Khaburah
Suhar As Sib Matrah
Al Buraymi • Barka' **MUSCAT**
Al Qabil Jabal ash Sham Quravyat
Ibri 2980m Ar Rustaq Al Hadd • Sur
Bahla • Izki Ibra • Al Kamil
Nazwa RAMLAT AHL Ashkharah
Adam WAHIBAH
Umm as Samin
Dawwah
Khaluf Jazirat Masirah
Khalij Masirah
Duqm
Al Jawarah
Sawqirah Suqrah Bay
ZUFAR
(DHOFAR)
JABAL AL QAMAR • Mirbat
Raysut • Salalah

POPULATION
○ over 50 000
• over 10 000
• under 10 000

LAND HEIGHT
2000m/6562ft
1000m/3281ft
500m/1640ft
200m/656ft
Sea Level

Total Land Area :
212 460 sq. km
(82 030 sq. miles)

0   100 km
0   100 miles

Native Omanis, who include Arab refugees who fled Zanzibar in the 1960s, make up three-quarters of the population. Expatriates pose no threat to the regime and Westerners enjoy considerable freedom. Urban drift has taken place, and most Omanis now live in cities. Most Omanis are Ibadi Muslims who follow an appointed leader, the Imam.

QATAR

 1971   1971   Sept 3   Q   +3   +974   .qa

OFFICIAL NAME **State of Qatar** CAPITAL **Doha**
POPULATION **584,000** CURRENCY **Qatar riyal** OFF. LANG. **Arabic**

PROJECTING NORTH FROM the Arabian peninsula into the Gulf, Qatar is mostly flat, semi-arid desert. Oil production in the late 1940s quickly transformed Qatar from an impoverished pearl producer into a prosperous shaikhdom and a founder member of OPEC. Plentiful oil and natural gas reserves have made it one of the wealthiest states in the region. Politics is being democratized gradually under the ruling al-Thani clan.

POLITICS

 Not applicable   Amir Shaikh Hamad bin Khalifa al-Thani   Monarchy

Qatar is a traditional emirate. The government and religious establishment is dominated by the amir, Shaikh Hamad, who took power from his father, Shaikh Khalifa, in 1995. The pro-democracy movement has called for reform of the 35-member Advisory

LEGISLATIVE OR ADVISORY BODIES
Advisory Council 35 seats

Qatar is an absolute monarchy and has no legislature. The amir rules with the assistance of the Council of Ministers and the Advisory Council.

Council. Shaikh Hamad responded by authorizing Qatar's first elections, to a new municipal council for Doha, in 1999, in which all adults, including women, were able to vote and stand as candidates. The creation of a partially elected Consultative Council was approved by referendum in 2003.

WORLD AFFAIRS

 AL, GCC, OIC, OPEC, OAPEC   1971

Although keen to retain strong links with the West and supportive of the 2003 invasion of Iraq, the amir has been critical of previous US and UK air strikes. Qatar supplied liquified natural gas (LNG) to Israel in the late 1990s, but relations have suffered greatly since the renewal of the Palestinian *intifada* in 2000.

PEOPLE & SOCIETY

 138 people per sq mile   93% urban / 7% rural

Sunni Muslim 95% Other 5%   Death penalty used

Since the advent of oil wealth, the Qataris, who were formerly nomadic Bedouins, have become a nation of city-dwellers. Almost 90% of the population now inhabit the capital Doha and its suburbs. As a result, northern Qatar is dotted with depopulated and abandoned villages.

Ar Ru'ays
Al Khuwayr
Madinat ash Shamāl
Al Ghāriyah
Al. Fuwayriṭ
Al Ghuwayrīyah
Madīnat al Ka'bān
Al Buşayyir
T H E
Al Jumaylīyah
Al Khawr
Hawar (to Bahrain)
Dawhat al Huşayn
Ar Rufayq
Abū Thaylah
Dukhān
Umm Şalāl 'Alī
Umm Şalāl Muḥammad
G U L F
Ash Shaḥānīyah
Al Gharrāfah
Madīnat Khalīfah
Ar Rayyān
DOHA
Umm Bāb
Al Wukayr
Al Wakrah
J A B A L D U K H A N
Musay'īd
Dawḥat as Salwā
Al Kir'ānah
Al Kharrārah
As Salwā
Mazra'at Turaynā
103m
S A U D I   A R A B I A
Khawr al 'Udayd

POPULATION
over 100 000
under 10 000 •

Total Land Area : 11 000 sq. km
(4247 sq. miles)

0   30 km
0   30 miles
N

LAND HEIGHT
200m/1640ft
Sea Level

ECONOMICS

 96th $-1.66bn

 $11,570   2%

A steady supply of crude oil and huge gas reserves. Dependence on foreign work force. Potential threat to security from Iraq and Iran makes some multinationals wary of investment.

RESOURCES

 8.2bn kwh   Comb. 100% Hydro 0% Nuclear 0%

 Sheep 214,531 Goats 179,000 Camels 50,000   783,000 b/d (reserves of 15.2bn bbl)

Qatar has the third-smallest reserves of crude oil within OPEC but abundant reserves of gas (the third-largest in the world), including the world's largest field of gas unassociated with oil.

DEFENCE

 $1.24bn   Not compulsory

None   12,400

The estimated 12,000-strong armed forces are too small to play a significant role in Qatari affairs, even in the event of political turmoil. A defence agreement with the US was extended in 2002.

MEDIA

 Some censorship   High

 6 daily 161 per 1,000 people   TV: 1/1 Radio: 1/0

Qatari TV is the most independent in the region. *Al Jazeera* provides the leading Arab perspective in the international media, especially since the events of September 11, 2001.

EDUCATION

 81%   8,475 students

 Schooling free but not compulsory   Primary 86% Secondary 80% Tertiary 27%

Education is free, all the way from primary to university level. The government finances students to study overseas.

HEALTH

 1 per 794 people   70 years

 16 per 1,000 people   14 per 1,000 live births

Primary health care is free to Qataris. Hospitals operate to Western standards of care and the government also funds treatment abroad.

SPENDING

 205 per 1,000 people   7.1%

3.4%   2.9%

Qataris have a high income per capita. There is no income tax, public services are free, and the government guarantees jobs for school-leavers. There are no exchange controls.

UAE (UNITED ARAB EMIRATES)

       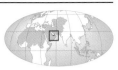

OFFICIAL NAME **United Arab Emirates** CAPITAL **Abu Dhabi**
POPULATION **2.7m** CURRENCY **UAE Dirham** OFF. LANG. **Arabic**

THE UNITED ARAB EMIRATES (UAE), created in 1971, is the Arab world's only working federation. Six of its seven emirates cluster around the north-eastern corner of the country, while Abu Dhabi has a larger hinterland of semi-arid desert relieved by occasional oases. Prosperity once relied on pearls, but the UAE is now a sizable gas and oil exporter, and has a growing services sector.

ECONOMICS

 49th

 $24.6bn

 $17,870

 4.5%

Oil and gas reserves are the third-biggest in OPEC. Development of service industries and manufacturing sector. Lack of skilled manpower. Most raw materials and foodstuffs have to be imported.

RESOURCES

 31bn kwh

 Comb. 100%
Hydro 0%
Nuclear 0%

Sheep 467,281
Goats 1.2m
Cattle 200,000

2.42m b/d
(reserves of 97.8bn bbl)

The UAE is a major exporter of crude oil and natural gas. Mina Jabal Ali in Dubai is the world's largest man-made port. Saadiyat Island off Abu Dhabi is being developed as a financial resort.

DEFENCE

$3.07bn

Not compulsory

 None

41,500

Training of UAE forces is limited, and personnel are mainly drawn from other Arab states and the Indian sub-continent. US air bases in the UAE have been used persistently in regional conflicts.

MEDIA

Censorship

High

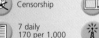 7 daily
170 per 1,000
people

TV: 4/0
Radio: 7/0

Satellite TV programming is unrestricted in the UAE. Dubai Media City, opened in 2001, promotes greater press freedoms.

EDUCATION

 76%

16,213 students

12 years

Primary 94%
Secondary 78%
Tertiary 13%

UAE citizens enjoy completely free education from primary to tertiary level. Zayed University was set up in three emirates in 1998.

HEALTH

 1 per 556 people

75 years

   people

 7 per 1,000 live births

A high-quality system of primary health care is in place for all UAE citizens, with hospitals able to carry out most operations.

SPENDING

 82 per 1000 people

 4.6%

 1.9%

 0.8%

UAE nationals have one of the highest per capita incomes in the Arab world. There is no income tax and oil revenues subsidize public services. Government policies encourage entrepreneurs.

POLITICS

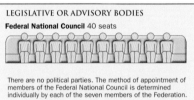

Not applicable

President Shaikh Zayed bin Sultan al-Nahyan

Monarchy

The UAE's seven emirates – Abu Dhabi, Dubai, Sharjah, Ras al Khaimah, Ajman, Umm al Qaiwain and Fujairah – are dominated by their ruling families. The main personalities are the ruler of Abu Dhabi, Shaikh Zayed, who holds the UAE presidency, and the four al-Maktoum brothers who control Dubai. The eldest, Shaikh Maktoum al-Maktoum, is ruler of Dubai as well as vice president and prime minister of the UAE.

President Zayed has relaunched the advisory Federal National Council in response to criticism of the lack of democracy. The growth of Islamic fundamentalism is also a concern. The freedoms granted to Westerners have aroused some anger but, for economic reasons, they are unlikely to be withdrawn.

LEGISLATIVE OR ADVISORY BODIES

Federal National Council 40 seats

There are no political parties. The method of appointment of members of the Federal National Council is determined individually by each of the seven members of the Federation.

WORLD AFFAIRS

 AL, OPEC, GCC, OAPEC, OIC

 1971

The UAE is an advocate of moderation within the Arab world. It maintains close links with most OECD states. In 1992, conflict flared when Iran seized control of three islands in the Strait of Hormuz. Attempts are being made to settle the dispute through diplomacy.

Total Land Area : 83 600 sq. km (32 278 sq. miles)

POPULATION
over 100 000
under 10 000

LAND HEIGHT
1000m/3281ft
500m/1640ft
Sea Level

PEOPLE & SOCIETY

 84 people per sq mile

 87% urban
13% rural

Sunni Muslim 96%
Christian, Hindu & others 4%

 Death penalty used

UAE nationals are largely city dwellers, with Abu Dhabi and Dubai the dominant centres. They are mostly conservative Sunni Muslims of Bedouin descent. They are greatly outnumbered by expatriates who arrived in the 1970s during the oil boom. Poverty is rare in the UAE. Women in theory enjoy equal rights with men.

YEMEN

| 1990 | 1990 | May 22 | ADN | +3 | +967 | .ye |

OFFICIAL NAME Republic of Yemen **CAPITAL** Sana
POPULATION 19.9m **CURRENCY** Yemeni rial **OFF. LANG.** Arabic

YEMEN IS LOCATED in southern Arabia. The north is mountainous, with a fertile strip along the Red Sea. The south is largely arid mountains and desert. Until 1990 Yemen was two countries, the Yemen Arab Republic in the north and the People's Democratic Republic of Yemen in the south. The north was run by successive military regimes; the poorer south was the Arab world's only Marxist state. Post-unification conflict between the two ruling hierarchies, nominally in coalition, led to a two-month civil war in 1994, the ousting of the former Marxists, and a new constitution.

POLITICS

 2003/2009   President Ali Abdullah Saleh   Multi-party republic

AT THE LAST ELECTION
House of Representatives 301 seats
1% 1% Ind NUPO
79% GPC   15% YAR 3% YSP 1% Ba'ath

GPC = General People's Congress **YAR** = Yemeni Alliance for Reform (al-Islah) **YSP** = Yemen Socialist Party **Ind** = Independents **NUPO** = Nasserite Unionist Popular Organization **Ba'ath** = Arab Socialist Ba'ath Party

The merger of North and South Yemen in 1990 united Yemenis under one ruler for the first time since 1735. At first, President Ali Saleh skillfully maintained unity. Then, in 1994, a bloody civil war erupted, fuelling a secessionist movement in the south. By mid-1994, the fighting had subsided and the southerners were crushed. In 1999 President Saleh won the region's first ever direct election of a head of state. However, Saleh's regime still faces threats from disgruntled southern tribesmen angry at levels of poverty in their oil-rich country. Since 1992, tribesmen have kidnapped more than 100 foreigners, including diplomats and tourists.

WORLD AFFAIRS

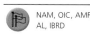 NAM, OIC, AMF, AL, IBRD   1947

Yemen has tried to break its international isolation since the 1991 Gulf War with active support for the US-led "war on terrorism". However, it did question the 2003 invasion of Iraq.

PEOPLE & SOCIETY

 92 people per sq mile   25% urban 75% rural

 Sunni Muslim 55% Shi'a Muslim 42% Others 3% Death penalty used

N
POPULATION
over 500 000
over 100 000
over 10 000
under 10 000

Total Land Area :
562 970 sq. km
(217 362 sq. miles)

0   200 km
0   200 miles

LAND HEIGHT
3000m/9843ft
2000m/6562ft
1000m/3281ft
500m/1640ft
200m/656ft
Sea Level

Yemenis are almost entirely of Arab and Bedouin descent, though there is a small, dwindling, Jewish minority and people of mixed African and Arab descent along the south coast. In rural areas and in the north, Islamic orthodoxy is strong and most women wear the veil. In the south, however, women still claim the freedoms they had under the Marxist regime.

 102nd $1.86bn

 $370   10%

Since the 1994 civil war, Yemen has increasingly had to import food supplies. Lack of central control, poor integration and the persistence of patronage politics are hampering economic revival.

 2.5bn kwh   Comb. 100% Hydro 0% Nuclear 0%

 Sheep 4.8m Goats 4.25m Cattle 1.34m   458,000 b/d (reserves of 4bn bbl)

Oil reserves are considerable, though initial estimates were exaggerated. Salt is the only other mineral commercially exploited. Yemen's high population growth is a severe strain on resources.

 $531m   Compulsory

 None   66,500

Following unification in 1990, mutual suspicion hampered the integration of the two separate defence forces. Sporadic, bitter clashes have taken place, most notably in 1994.

 Some censorship   High

 4 daily 15 per 1,000 people   TV: 1/0 Radio: 1/0

The government keeps a tight control on the media and vets the entry of foreign journalists. TV and radio are state-controlled and have a limited range. Satellite TV is not generally available.

 46%   65,675 students

 15 years   Primary 78% Secondary 45% Tertiary 10%

Some 80% of the population have no formal classroom education. Schooling barely extends into the rural areas. Illiteracy is especially high among women: 74% cannot read or write.

 1 per 5,000 people   61 years

 43 per 1,000 people   76 per 1,000 live births

The major cities have an adequate primary health care system. A new 300-bed hospital in Sana is due to be completed in 2004. Rural areas are less well served. Health services are under threat from tribal gangs.

 15 per 1,000 people   8.1%

 6.7%   2.4%

Most Yemenis suffered a fall in living standards after Saudi Arabia expelled its Yemeni workers. A lack of jobs in other Gulf states has fuelled unemployment, estimated at around 30%.

IRAN

| 1502 | 1990 | Feb 11 | IR | +3.5 | +98 | .ir |

OFFICIAL NAME **Islamic Republic of Iran** CAPITAL **Tehran**
POPULATION **72.4m** CURRENCY **Iranian rial** OFF. LANG. **Farsi (Persian)**

IRAN IS SURROUNDED by turbulent neighbours, with republics of the former Soviet Union to the north, Afghanistan and Pakistan to the east and Iraq and Turkey to the west. The south faces the Persian Gulf and the Gulf of Oman. Since 1979, when a revolution led by Ayatollah Khomeini deposed the shah, Iran has become the world's largest theocracy and the leading centre for militant Shi'a Islam. Iran's active support for Islamic fundamentalist movements has led to strained relations with central Asian, Middle Eastern and north African states, as well as the US and western Europe.

POLITICS

 2000/2004   President Mohammad Khatami   Islamic theocracy

A power struggle between the clergy and the secular state has arisen from the ill-defined division of power between the two. The conservative faction in parliament lost its overall majority in 1996 and has been steadily displaced by reformists, who in 2000 made sweeping gains in parliamentary elections. In 2001 reformist president Mohammad Khatami was re-elected, this time with an overwhelming 77% of the vote.

Khatami is committed to modernizing the economy, but is strongly opposed by the mullahs, for whom adherence to religious values is more important than material welfare. Student pro-reform protests were heavily suppressed by hardliners, who remain a force, despite the 2000 elections, through the powerful Council of Guardians.

AT THE LAST ELECTION

Consultative Council (Majlis) 290 seats

65% IIPF 17% C 11% Ind 5% Vacant 2% Rel

IIPF = Islamic Iran Participation Front (reformists)
C = Coalition of Followers of the Line of Imam (conservatives)
Ind = Independents **Rel** = Religious Minorities

Iran's religious revolution of 1979 was fuelled by popular outrage at the corruption, repression, and inequalities of the shah's regime. Since the time of Ayatollah Khomeini, successive Iranian governments have maintained that the clergy have a religious duty to establish a just social system. Accordingly, the legislature, the executive and the judiciary may, in theory, be overruled by the religious leadership; former president Hashemi Rafsanjani's moderate policies were questioned by radical clergymen advocating "permanent revolution". However, the mullahs' failure to address Iran's economic problems has eroded their political standing. Reformists were encouraged by the election of President Khatami in 1997, but the clergy remains powerful. Huge student demonstrations in 1999 and 2000 in favour of reform were offset by crackdowns on reformist politicians and newspapers. The mullahs, so far unbowed by reformist election victories, have continued to confront the modernizers.

WORLD AFFAIRS

 OPEC, OIC, G24, ECO, NAM   1945

Iran has assumed international significance as the voice of militant Shi'a Islam. It is accused of backing terrorist activity by Muslim extremists and fostering unrest throughout the Middle East and central Asia. Iran's main security problem is with Iraq, which allows *mujahideen* guerrillas to mount attacks on Iran from its territory.

ECONOMICS

 34th $12.6bn

 $1,680   11.3%

OPEC's second-biggest oil-producer. Traditional exports include carpets, pistachio nuts and caviar. Theocratic authorities restrict contact with the West and access to technology.

RESOURCES

 103bn kwh   Comb. 93% Hydro 7% Nuclear 0%

Sheep 53m Goats 25.2m Cattle 7m   3.69m b/d (reserves of 89.7bn bbl)

Iran has substantial oil reserves. It also has metal, coal and salt deposits, but these are relatively undeveloped. Principal crops are wheat, barley, rice, sugar beet, tobacco and pistachio nuts.

DEFENCE

 $4.7bn   Compulsory

 None   395,000

Iran has almost 500,000 men under arms, including the 125,000-strong Revolutionary Guard Corps (*Pasdaran Inquilab*), and is regarded by neighbouring states as a serious military threat.

MEDIA

 Censorship   Medium

33 daily 26 per 1,000 people   TV: 1/0 Radio: 1/0

Radio and TV are state-controlled. Satellite dishes are banned. Closures of reformist newspapers by the conservative Council of Guardians, and prosecutions of their editors, continue.

EDUCATION

 77%   679,000 students

 14 years   Primary 98% Secondary 77% Tertiary 18%

In Tehran's classrooms, since 2002, female students and staff have been permitted to lower their veils. There are 36 universities; their students are strong supporters of liberalization and reform.

HEALTH

 1 per 1,111 people   69 years

18 per 1,000 people   33 per 1,000 live births

Although an adequate system of primary health care exists in the cities, conditions in rural areas are basic. AIDS is spreading; some 20,000 adults were estimated to be living with HIV/AIDS in 2001.

SPENDING

 30 per 1,000 people   5.8%

$ 4.6%   1.7%

After the 1979 revolution, living standards in Iran declined markedly. A shortage of foreign exchange has stifled imports of consumer goods. Rationing, brought in during the war with Iraq, is still partly in force.

Under President Khatami, Iran has tried to convey a less confrontational image. Improved relations with Saudi Arabia, troubled since Iran's seizure of the islands of Abu Musa and the Tumbs in 1970, resulted in the signing of a pact in 2001. Ties with the West have also improved, although relations with the US remain tense and suffered a setback in 2002 after President George W. Bush cast Iran as part of an international "axis of evil".

PEOPLE & SOCIETY

 115 people per sq mile   65% urban / 35% rural   Shi'a Muslim 95% / Sunni Muslim 4% / Other 1%   Death penalty used

The people of the north and centre – about half of all Iranians – speak Farsi (Persian), while about a quarter speak related languages, including Kurdish in the west and Baluchi in the south-east. Another quarter of the population speaks Turkic languages, primarily the Azeris and the Turkmen in the north-west. Smaller groups, such as the Circassians and Georgians, are found in the northern provinces.

Until the 16th century, much of Iran followed the Sunni interpretation of Islam, but since then the Shi'a sect has been dominant. Religious minorities, accounting for just 1% of the population, include followers of the Bahai faith, who suffer discrimination, Zoroastrians, Christians and Jews. The regime has a remarkably liberal attitude to refugees of the Muslim faith. Nearly three million Afghan refugees were received during the height of the Afghan civil war, although many have since been repatriated. In Khorosan province in the east, refugees account for nearly a quarter of the population; near the Turkish border they constitute half the total population. Many are young, resulting in intense competition with Iranians for jobs and consequent ethnic tensions.

ECONOMIC FOCUS

EXPORTS

Singapore 4% — France 5% — Italy 9% — South Korea 9% — Japan 19% — Other 54%

IMPORTS

China 6% — France 6% — South Korea 7% — Italy 7% — Germany 11% — Other 63%

STRENGTHS

OPEC's second-biggest oil producer; soaring world oil prices in 2000. There is potential for related industries and the increased production of traditional exports: carpets, pistachio nuts and caviar.

WEAKNESSES

Theocratic authorities restrict contact with Western countries and access to technology. High unemployment and inflation. Excessive foreign debts.

PROFILE

With few industries other than oil, US sanctions and fluctuations in oil prices made foreign earnings volatile; higher prices in 2000 held out the prospect of being able to invest in diversification.

Total Land Area :
1 636 000 sq. km
(631 660 sq. miles)

LAND HEIGHT

3000m/9843ft
2000m/6562ft
1000m/3281ft
500m/1640ft
200m/656ft
Sea Level

POPULATION

☐ over 1 000 000
◉ over 500 000
◎ over 100 000
○ over 50 000

The Reshteh-ye Kuhhā-ye Alborz
(Elburz Mountains) in northern Iran. Their Caspian Sea slopes are rainy and forested; the south-facing slopes are dry.

TURKMENISTAN

1991 | 1991 | Oct 27 | TM | +5 | +993 | .tm

OFFICIAL NAME **Turkmenistan** CAPITAL **Ashgabat**
POPULATION: **4.9m** CURRENCY **Manat** OFF. LANG. **Turkmen**

ORIGINALLY THE POOREST state among the former Soviet republics, Turkmenistan has adjusted better than most to independence, exploiting the market value of its abundant natural gas supplies. A largely Sunni Muslim area, Turkmenistan is part of the former Turkestan, the last expanse of central Asia incorporated into tzarist Russia. Much of life is still based on tribal relationships.

POLITICS

 L. House 1999/2004
U. House 2003/2008

 President Saparmurad Niyazov

 One-party state

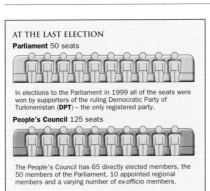

AT THE LAST ELECTION
Parliament 50 seats

In elections to the Parliament in 1999 all of the seats were won by supporters of the ruling Democratic Party of Turkmenistan (**DPT**) – the only registered party.

People's Council 125 seats

The People's Council has 65 directly elected members, the 50 members of the Parliament, 10 appointed regional members and a varying number of ex-officio members.

Officially, Turkmenistan became a multi-party democracy at independence, although President Niyazov has banned the formation of new parties. As in other ex-Soviet states, former communists, regrouped as the Democratic Party of Turkmenistan, still dominate the political process. The DPT harbours the traditional communist suspicion of Islamic fundamentalism. Turkmenistan's main concern is to prevent the social and nationalistic conflicts that have blighted other CIS republics. Russian remains the bureaucratic language.

WORLD AFFAIRS

 EAPC, OIC, ECO, OSCE, CIS

 1992

Turkmenistan is concentrating on establishing good relations with Iran and Turkey, but is wary of Islamic fundamentalism. President Niyazov opposes economic union with the CIS, and has also expressed caution about closer political union with other Turkic-speaking Asian states.

Total Land Area :
488 100 sq. km
(188 455 sq. miles)

POPULATION
over 100 000
over 50 000
over 10 000
under 10 000

LAND HEIGHT
1000m/1640ft
500m/1640ft
200m/656ft
Sea Level
-200m/-656ft

PEOPLE & SOCIETY

 26 people per sq mile

 45% urban
55% rural

 Sunni Muslim 87%
Eastern Orthodox 11%
Other 2%

Death penalty not used

Before tzarist Russia annexed Turkmenistan in 1884, the Turkmen were a largely nomadic tribal people, and the tribal unit remains strong. Tribal conflicts among the Turkmen, rather than tensions with the two main minorities – Russians and Uzbeks – are a source of strife. Since 1989, Turkmenistan has been rehabilitating its traditional language and culture, as well as reassessing its history. Islam is again central to the Turkmen.

ECONOMICS

 119th

 $412m

$750

10%

Decision to abolish collective farms is gradually encouraging private initiative and enterprise. Cotton monoculture has forced rising food imports. Thriving black market all but wiped out value of manat.

RESOURCES

 9.4bn kwh

 Comb. 100%
Hydro 0%
Nuclear 0%

 Sheep 6m
Goats 375,000
Cattle 860,000

 162,000 b/d
(reserves of 500m bbl)

Under a ten-year programme, Turkmenistan aims to raise its oil production to nearly one million barrels per day by the year 2010.

DEFENCE

 $222m

 Compulsory

None

 17,500

Turkmenistan is totally dependent on Russia for defence. The military is under the joint control of both countries. Turkmen pilots are trained in Pakistan.

MEDIA

 Censorship

Medium

2 daily
No data for circulation

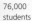 TV: 1/0
Radio: 1/0

Iranian and Afghan radio stations, beaming in Islamic programmes, are popular. TV channels are only available in urban areas.

EDUCATION

 98%

 76,000 students

17 years

Primary 94%
Secondary ?
Tertiary 22%

University students must know the life and works of President Niyazov. They now have to work for two years after their first two years of study.

HEALTH

 1 per 333 people

 66 years

 28 per 1,000 people

 27 per 1,000 live births

Spending is now high for the central Asian region, but Turkmenistan's health indicators remain among the worst.

SPENDING

 No data

 3.2%

4.5%

4.1%

The wealthiest groups are those connected to the government. The transition to a liberal economy has attracted high spending.

UZBEKISTAN

1991 | 1991 | Sept 1 | UZ | 5 to +6 | +998 | .uz

OFFICIAL NAME Republic of Uzbekistan **CAPITAL** Tashkent
POPULATION 25.6m **CURRENCY** Som **OFF. LANG.** Uzbek

SHARING THE ARAL SEA COASTLINE with its northern neighbour, Kazakhstan, Uzbekistan has common borders with five countries, including Afghanistan to the south. It is the most populous central Asian republic and has considerable natural resources. Uzbekistan contains the ancient cities of Samarqand, Bukhara (Bukhoro), Khiva and Tashkent. The dictatorship of President Karimov has prevented the spread of Islamic fundamentalism.

POLITICS

 1999/2004   President Islam Karimov   Presidential democracy

AT THE LAST ELECTION
National Parliament 250 seats   4% NT   1% Vac

44% Ind   19% PDP   14% F   8% FP   6% LN   4% A

Ind = Independents   **PDP** = People's Democratic Party
F = Fidorkorlar   **FP** = Fatherland Progress Party
LN = Local nominees   **A** = Adolat
NT = National Renaissance   **Vac** = Vacant

President Karimov's PDP has not been willing to devolve or share power. A constitution adopted in December 1992 appeared to endorse multi-party politics along Western lines. However, Karimov took advantage of greater powers granted to his office by banning a number of opposition parties, including the nationalist Birlik (Unity) movement and the Islamic Renaissance Party. Erk (Will), the only legal opposition party, was proscribed in 1993, and in 1995 a group of activists, found guilty of political subversion, received stiff prison sentences. Opposition is now entirely underground.

WORLD AFFAIRS

 SCO, CIS, NAM, OSCE, OIC   1992

Uzbekistan's ties with the US were strengthened when it played host to US forces during the war in Afghanistan in 2001. Relations with Turkey are also developing. It has border disputes with its neighbours over the laying of land mines to deter terrorism.

Total Land Area : 447 400 sq. km
(172 741 sq. miles)

POPULATION
over 1 000 000
over 100 000
over 50 000
over 10 000

LAND HEIGHT
3000m/9843ft
2000m/6562ft
1000m/3281ft
500m/1640ft
200m/656ft
Sea Level

PEOPLE & SOCIETY

 148 people per sq mile   37% urban 63% rural

Sunni Muslim 88% Eastern Orthodox 9% Other 3%   Death penalty used

Among the former Soviet republics, Uzbekistan has a relatively complex makeup. In addition to the Uzbeks, Russians, Tajiks and Kazakhs, there are small minorities of Tatars and Karakalpaks. The proportion of Russians has been declining since the 1970s. Tensions among ethnic groups have the potential to create regional and racial conflict.

 89th $184m

 $360   23%

Well-developed cotton market. Current production of natural gas makes significant contribution to electricity generation. Dependent on grain imports, as domestic production meets only 25% of needs.

 45.8bn kwh   Comb. 88% Hydro 12% Nuclear 0%

 Sheep 8.1m Goats 830,000 Cattle 5.34m   172,00 b/d (reserves of 600m bbl)

Uzbekistan has the world's largest gold mine, and also large deposits of natural gas, petroleum, coal and uranium. An important oilfield was discovered in 1992 and production will rise with further investment.

 $1.76bn   Compulsory

 None   55,000

A policy of mining the land borders with Kyrgyzstan and Tajikistan to thwart incursions by Islamic militants has drawn international criticism.

 Censorship   High

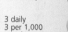 3 daily 3 per 1,000 people   TV: 2/0 Radio: 1/0

Restrictions on independent publications, designed to encourage the personality cult and policies of Karimov, manifest themselves both in overt censorship and self-censorship by media outlets.

 89%   638,200 students

 18 years   Primary 78% Secondary 94% Tertiary 32%

The state system still follows the Soviet model, though some instruction is in Uzbek. In the late 1980s, there were a few ethnic Tajik schools and a university in Samarqand. These were closed down in 1992.

 1 per 323 people   69 years

 23 per 1,000 people   22 per 1,000 live births

The health service has been in decline since the dissolution of the USSR. Some rural areas are not served at all. Serious respiratory diseases among cotton growers are increasing.

 No data   2.6%

 7.7%   3.4%

Former Communists are still the wealthiest group, since they retain control of the economy. Many rural poor live below the poverty line.

KAZAKHSTAN

1991 · 1991 · Oct 25 · KZ · +5 to+6 · +7 · .kz

OFFICIAL NAME **Republic of Kazakhstan** CAPITAL **Astana**
POPULATION **16m** CURRENCY **Tenge** OFF. LANG. **Kazakh**

THE SECOND-LARGEST of the former Soviet republics, Kazakhstan extends almost 3,000 km (1,900 miles) from the Caspian Sea in the west to the Altai Mountains in the east, and 1,600 km (1,000 miles) north to south. It borders Russia to the north and China to the east. Kazakhstan was the last Soviet republic to declare its independence, in 1991. In 1999, elections confirmed the former communist Nursultan Nazarbayev and his supporters in power. Kazakhstan has considerable economic potential, and many Western companies seek to exploit its mineral resources.

ECONOMICS

 68th $-1.75bn

 $1,260   8.4%

First of the former Soviet states to establish a free market economy. Energy and consumer goods must be imported. A mass privatization programme was launched in 1994.

RESOURCES

 49.1bn kwh   Comb. 88%
Hydro 12%
Nuclear 0%

 Sheep 8.94m
Pigs 1.08m
Cattle 4.11m   828,000 b/d
(reserves
8bn bbl)

Mining is the single most important industry in Kazakhstan. Joint ventures to exploit substantial oil and gas reserves in the Caspian Sea were agreed with Russia in 1995, and the US and Japan in 1998.

DEFENCE

 $1.27bn   Phasing out conscription

 None   60,000

A restructuring of Kazakhstan's armed forces was launched in 2001. This included moves to end conscription, the duration of which had been halved, from two years to one in 1998.

MEDIA

Censorship Medium

 7 daily
30 per 1,000
people   TV: 1/several
Radio: 1/several

The state-owned media compete with independent publications and privately owned radio and television stations. Amendments in 2001 to the Media Law strengthened state control of smaller media outlets.

EDUCATION

 99% 419,460
students

 15 years   Primary 97%
Secondary 87%
Tertiary 23%

Education remains based on the Soviet model. Since the adoption of Kazakh as the state language in 1995, Russian is gradually being replaced by Kazakh as the main medium of instruction in schools.

HEALTH

 1 per 286
people   65 years

18 per 1,000
people 21 per 1,000
live births

The health system is limited in terms of facilities and coverage. Rural people have minimal access to clinics. The country's size means that extending coverage and improving the quality of care will be costly.

SPENDING

 65 per 1,000
people   1.3%

 4.4% 2.7%

Life for the majority of Kazakhs is hard, and has grown even more difficult since 1989. Living standards have deteriorated and employment has risen as a result of market-oriented reforms.

POLITICS

 L. House 1999/2004
U. House 2002/2005   President Nursultan
Nazarbayev   Presidential
democracy

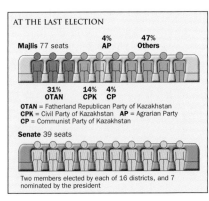

AT THE LAST ELECTION

Majlis 77 seats

4% AP   47% Others

31% OTAN   14% CPK   4% CP

OTAN = Fatherland Republican Party of Kazakhstan
CPK = Civil Party of Kazakhstan   AP = Agrarian Party
CP = Communist Party of Kazakhstan

Senate 39 seats

Two members elected by each of 16 districts, and 7 nominated by the president

The increased powers of President Nazarbayev are the focus of political controversy, prompting his critics to accuse him of developing a personality cult. The 1995 constitution strengthened presidential powers, conferring a veto over the decisions of the Constitutional Council. Nazarbayev, who was due to face re-election in 1996, also won a referendum which extended his term of office until 2000. However, in 1998 the legislature approved constitutional amendments forcing him to hold a presidential election in 1999.

Despite a democratic government, the president enjoys political dominance, and the patronage of the Kazakh clans is still important. Since coming to power in 1989, Nazarbayev has concentrated on market reforms. There have been allegations of electoral fraud, and domestic and international criticism of Nazarbayev's attempts to expand the scope of presidential powers. In 2000 the Assembly granted him special powers to advise future presidents after his term expires in 2006, and opposition parties were effectively neutered in 2002 by party registration reforms.

WORLD AFFAIRS

 CIS, EAPC, SCO,
OIC, OSCE 1992

Kazakhstan's earlier enthusiasm for more integration of the former Soviet states has cooled. Lying between the massive states of Russia and China, it has signed major treaties with both countries in the hope of improving relations.

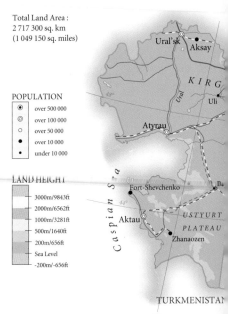

Total Land Area :
2 717 300 sq. km
(1 049 150 sq. miles)

POPULATION
- over 500 000
- over 100 000
- over 50 000
- over 10 000
- under 10 000

LAND HEIGHT
- 3000m/9843ft
- 2000m/6562ft
- 1000m/3281ft
- 500m/1640ft
- 200m/656ft
- Sea Level
- -200m/-656ft

Relations with Russia, although strained at times by Moscow's concern over Kazakhstan's ethnic Russians, have been cemented by a 25-year cooperation treaty, which includes currency convertability between the rouble and the tenge.

Relations with China have improved, with agreements in 1998 and 1999 on border issues, and Kazakhstan joins China, Russia and three other central Asian republics in the Shanghai Cooperation Organization. However, it competes with Uzbekistan to be the acknowledged central Asian regional power.

The country's location bridging Europe and Asia has led to close relations with a variety of other partners, and its rich mineral resources have attracted investors from Europe, the US and Asia, particularly South Korea.

PEOPLE & SOCIETY

 15 people per sq mile

 56% urban 44% rural

 Muslim 50% Russian Orthodox 13% Others 37%

 Death penalty used

Kazakhstan's ethnic diversity arose from the forced settlement during the Soviet era of Germans, Tatars and Russians. By 1959, Kazakhs were outnumbered by ethnic Russians. This balance has been redressed by the immigration of ethnic Kazakhs from neighbouring states and the departure in the 1990s of some 1.5 million ethnic Russians. In addition, a majority of ethnic Germans have opted to live in Germany, although in 2000 the government announced a campaign to try to lure some of them back.

In 1995, ethnic Russians criticized the country's new constitution for preventing dual citizenship with Russia and refusing to recognize Russian as an official language. Central control over ethnic Russians has been reinforced by shifting the capital to Astana (formerly Akmola) in the north, where the majority of ethnic Russians reside.

ECONOMIC FOCUS

EXPORTS

Turkey 5%
Italy 9%
Germany 10%
Other 41%
China 11%
Russia 24%

IMPORTS

USA 5%
Germany 7%
Russia 32%
Italy 11%
China 13%
Other 32%

STRENGTHS

Mineral resources, notably oil, gas, and bismuth and cadmium, used in electronics industry. Joint oil and gas ventures with Western companies. Mass privatization programme launched in 1994.

WEAKNESSES

Collapse of former Soviet economic and trading system. Reliance on imported consumer goods. Rapid introduction of the tenge in 1993 increased instability and fuelled sharp price rises.

PROFILE

Kazakhstan has moved faster than other former Soviet republics to establish a market economy. Prices have been freed, foreign trade deregulated and the tax system reformed. Petroleum revenues have been the main engine of growth, and inflation, at one time rising sharply, has been brought under control. Foreign direct investment is mainly in the energy sector. Outdated equipment and inadequate distribution networks mean that energy has to be imported, although Kazakhstan exports fossil fuel. An oil price boom set the tone for the country's first "five-year plan" in 2000, part of Nazarbayev's "Kazakhstan 2030" programme. It promised long-term land leases, although not full private ownership, from 2001.

The Altai Mountains, *eastern Kazakhstan. Subject to harsh continental winters, the Altai range is a cold, inhospitable place. Rivers carry meltwater down onto the vast steppe.*

KYRGYZSTAN

 1991 1991 Aug 31 KS +6 +996 .kg

OFFICIAL NAME Kyrgyz Republic **CAPITAL** Bishkek
POPULATION 5m **CURRENCY** Som **OFF. LANG.** Kyrgyz & Russian

KYRGYZSTAN IS A SMALL and very mountainous state in central Asia. It is the least urbanized of the former Soviet republics and was among the last to develop its own cultural nationalism. Its increasingly autocratic government is treading uncertainly between Kyrgyz nationalist pressures and ensuring that the minority Russians are not alienated, since they tend to possess the skills necessary to run a market-based economy.

POLITICS

 L. House 2000/2005
U. House 2000/2005
 President
Askar Akayev
 Presidential
democracy

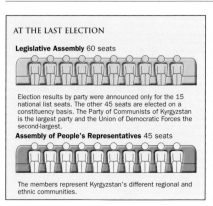

AT THE LAST ELECTION

Legislative Assembly 60 seats

Election results by party were announced only for the 15 national list seats. The other 45 seats are elected on a constituency basis. The Party of Communists of Kyrgyzstan is the largest party and the Union of Democratic Forces the second-largest.

Assembly of People's Representatives 45 seats

The members represent Kyrgyzstan's different regional and ethnic communities.

President Akayev's administration has become increasingly autocratic, ending Kyrgyzstan's reputation as one of the region's most liberal societies. During the 2000 legislative and presidential elections, the main opposition leader, Felix Kulov, was imprisoned only weeks before the presidential poll. The temporary imprisonment in March 2002 of his successor, Azimbek Baknazaro, prompted mass protests, when five demonstrators were shot dead by police.

WORLD AFFAIRS

 SCO, CIS, OSCE,
OIC, EAPC
 UN 1992

Kyrgyzstan is working to reduce its dependence on Russia. Turkey is developing close links aimed at restraining the fundamentalist influence in the region. Relations with Uzbekistan, which allegedly supports some of the anti-government forces in Kyrgyzstan, are tense.

Total Land Area:
198 500 sq. km
(76 640 sq. miles)

ECONOMICS

 148th $-158m

 $270   6.9%

Agricultural self-sufficiency. Gold and mercury exports. Hydro-power potential. Dominant state and collective farming mentality. Sharp decline since breakup of USSR, on which it depended for trade and supplies.

RESOURCES

 11.6bn kwh   Comb. 14%
Hydro 86%
Nuclear 0%

 Sheep 4.16m
Goats 346,000
Cattle 985,000
 1,544 b/d
(reserves of
37m bbl)

Kyrgyzstan has small quantities of coal, oil and gas, and hydro-electric power potential. Energy policy is primarily aimed at developing these further to eventually achieve self-sufficiency.

DEFENCE

 $255m   Phasing out
conscription

 None   10,900

A national army was set up in 1992. Conscription is to be phased out by 2005. Kyrgyzstan is home to the new military alliance of six ex-Soviet states.

MEDIA

 Some
censorship
 Low

 4 daily
9 per 1,000
people
 TV: 1/1
Radio: 1/3

Television programming relies mainly on Russian transmissions. The Kyrgyz press is increasingly under pressure from the government's efforts to silence opposition.

EDUCATION

 97%   49,744
students

 15 years   Primary 100%
Secondary 86%
Tertiary 30%

Replacing Russian as the main teaching language is proving an enormous task. Russian is likely to survive at tertiary level, as the Kyrgyz language lacks key technical and scientific terms.

HEALTH

 1 per 333
people
 68 years

26 per 1,000
people
25 per 1,000
live births

Kyrgyzstan has one of the least developed public health systems in central Asia, and the country's infant mortality rate is high.

SPENDING

 39 per 1,000
population
 2%

5.4%   2.2%

In 2000, almost 90% of the population were estimated as living in poverty. The old Communist Party *nomenklatura* are the main beneficiaries of privatization.

PEOPLE & SOCIETY

65 people per
sq mile
 34% urban
66% rural

 Sunni Muslim 70%
Russian Orthodox 30%
 Death penalty
not used

POPULATION   LAND HEIGHT

over 500 000		4000m/13 124ft
over 100 000		3000m/9843ft
over 50 000		2000m/6562ft
over 10 000		1000m/3281ft
under 10 000		500m/1640ft

Like other former Soviet republics, Kyrgyzstan has witnessed the rise of militant nationalism. Relations are most strained with the large Uzbek minority. The preference given to Kyrgyz in the political system has aggravated ethnic tensions. The trend in politics is towards greater Islamization, which is linking religion and race issues more closely.

TAJIKISTAN

OFFICIAL NAME **Republic of Tajikistan** CAPITAL **Dushanbe**
POPULATION **6.2m** CURRENCY **Somoni** OFF. LANG. **Tajik**

TAJIKISTAN LIES ON the western slopes of the Pamirs in central Asia. Language and traditions are similar to those of Iran rather than those of Turkic Uzbekistan. Tajikistan decided on independence only when neighbouring Soviet republics declared theirs in late 1991. Fighting between Communist government forces and Islamist rebels, which erupted shortly afterwards, has been contained since 1997 by a tenuous peace agreement.

POLITICS

L. House 2000/2005
U. House 2000/2005

President
Imomali Rakhmanov

Presidential
regime

AT THE LAST ELECTION

Assembly of Representatives 63 seats

71% PDPT
21% CPT
2% Vac
3% IRP
3% Others

PDPT = People's Democratic Party of Tajikistan and allies
CPT = Communist Party of Tajikistan   IRP = Islamic Revival Party   Vac = Vacant

National Assembly 33 seats

Five deputies are elected by each regional assembly, and a further eight deputies are appointed by the president.

The lull in fighting between government forces and Islamist rebels, aided by a 1997 peace accord, has consolidated the regime of former Communists led by President Rakhmanov. In 1998, the Islamist United Tajik Opposition (UTO) joined the government in accordance with the accord, which provided for a National Reconciliation Commission along with parliamentary elections. In the 2000 elections the pro-Rakhmanov PDPT, which headed the poll, claimed some support from former UTO members.

WORLD AFFAIRS

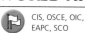
CIS, OSCE, OIC, EAPC, SCO

1992

Tajikistan remains heavily dependent on Russia for economic and military assistance. A joint operation with Uzbekistan and Kyrgyzstan began in 2000 to combat the Islamic Movement of Uzbekistan, based in northern Tajikistan.

Total Land Area : 143 100 sq. km (55 251 sq. miles)

POPULATION
over 500 000
over 100 000
over 50 000
over 10 000
under 10 000

LAND HEIGHT
4000m/13 124ft
3000m/9843ft
2000m/6562ft
1000m/3281ft
500m/1640ft
200m/656ft

PEOPLE & SOCIETY

112 people per sq mile

28% urban
72% rural

Sunni Muslim 80%
Shi'a Muslim 5%
Other 15%

Death penalty used

The main ethnic conflict in Tajikistan is between the Tajiks and Uzbeks, of Persian and Turkic origin respectively. As in neighbouring Uzbekistan, however, Russians are discriminated against, and their population has thinned from 400,000 in 1989 to fewer than 200,000. It is estimated that about 50,000 refugees remain in Afghanistan.

ECONOMICS

151st

$-61m

$180

33%

Tajikistan has 14% of known world uranium reserves. Hydro-electric power has considerable potential. Little diversification in agriculture; only 6% of land is arable. Exodus of skilled Russians.

RESOURCES

14bn kwh

Comb. 2%
Hydro 98%
Nuclear 0%

Sheep 1.36m
Goats 575,000
Cattle 1.05m

381 b/d
(reserves of 15m bbl)

Tajikistan has one key resource – uranium – which accounted for 30% of the USSR's total production before 1990. The end of the nuclear arms race has reduced its value, however.

DEFENCE

$127m

Compulsory

None

6,800

Security along the Afghan border is bolstered by the presence of some 20,000 international (mostly Russian) peacekeepers. The civil war left almost 20,000 land mines across the country.

MEDIA

Some censorship

High

3 daily
21 per 1,000 people

TV: 1/4
Radio: 3/0

The underdeveloped media are prone to self-censorship and pro-government reporting. Foreign broadcasts may not be retransmitted.

EDUCATION

99%

108,203 students

17 years

Primary 95%
Secondary 78%
Tertiary 20%

School attendance figures are high in Tajikistan. The university at Dushanbe has been weakened by the departure of its Russian academics.

HEALTH

1 per 500 people

68 years

33 per 1,000 people

21 per 1,000 live births

Theoretically health provision is free of charge; however, massive underfunding means that patients invariably have to pay to get treatment.

SPENDING

1 per 1,000 population

1.7%

2.2%

5.2%

More than half of Tajik people live below the UN-defined poverty line; the war against the Islamist rebels worsened conditions. The former Communist bureaucrats continue to be the wealthiest group.

AFGHANISTAN

1919 | 1919 | Aug 19 | AFG | +4.5 | +93 | .af

OFFICIAL NAME **Islamic State of Afghanistan**   CAPITAL **Kābul**
POPULATION **23.3m**   CURRENCY **New afghani**   OFF. LANG. **Pashtu & Dari**

AFGHANISTAN LIES LANDLOCKED IN CENTRAL ASIA, sharing land borders with Pakistan, Iran, China, Tajikistan, Turkmenistan and Uzbekistan. Three-quarters of its territory is inaccessible terrain. Its political system, economy and infrastructure have been devastated by decades of armed conflict. In the 1980s Islamic *mujahideen* factions defeated the Soviet-backed Communist regime, but rivalries undermined their fragile power-sharing agreement and the hard-line *taliban* militia swept to power in 1996. Islamic dress codes and behaviour were vigorously enforced and women were left with few rights or opportunities. Notorious for harbouring extremists, the *taliban* regime crumbled in the face of the US-led "war on terrorism" launched in late 2001.

POLITICS

 1988/2004   President Hamid Karzai   In transition

The political system had virtually collapsed in Afghanistan prior to the 1996 *taliban* takeover. Rival *mujahideen* factions had been in control since April 1992, when the Communist President Najibullah was forced to step down. According to the 1993 Islamabad peace accord, elections were to be held by the end of the year. These were indefinitely postponed owing to factional fighting, which led in early 1995 to the emergence of a potent new force, the extremist Islamic *taliban*. Initially the product of Islamic schools in the refugee camps on the Pakistan border, the *taliban* were mostly ethnic Pashtuns, and their support strongest around Kandahar. Kabul fell to them in 1996, and an opposition Northern Alliance headed by the former president, Burhanuddin Rabbani, failed to reverse the position. On assuming power the *taliban* declared Afghanistan to be a "complete" Islamic state, and imposed a strict Islamic code.

AT THE LAST ELECTION

House of Representatives (dissolved)

Following the downfall of Najibullah's regime in April 1992, both houses were dissolved and an interim *mujahideen* legislature formed.

Senate (dissolved)

The US-led intervention in late 2001 helped replace the *taliban* regime with groups allied to the Northern Alliance, which succeeded in gaining control of most major cities, including Kabul. Later that year UN-sponsored talks led to the formation of an interim government headed by Pashtun leader Hamid Karzai, who is committed to implementing the decisions of a Loya Jirga (grand council), pending elections in 2004. Ex-king Zahir Shah returned in April 2002, where he endorsed Karzai's election as head of state.

WORLD AFFAIRS

 ECO, NAM, OIC, IBRD, CP   1946

Afghanistan was a pariah state under the *taliban* government. The regime defied international opinion, and UN sanctions, by harbouring Saudi extremist Osama bin Laden, the head of anti-US terrorist network al-Qaeda. It was also condemned over human rights, particularly the treatment of women, and the destruction of ancient Buddhist statues in Bamian. When a worldwide "war on terrorism" became the top US

 ECONOMICS

 104th $-143m

 $270   56.7%

Continued warfare since 1979 destroyed the economy, which was largely agricultural. Under the *taliban* production of opium poppies was the most lucrative cash crop.

 RESOURCES

 485m kwh   Comb 35% Hydro 65% Nuclear 0%

 Sheep 14.3m Goats 2.2m Cattle 1.5m   No oil No refineries

Natural gas and coal are Afghanistan's most important strategic resources. Restoring the power generation system, which has suffered widespread deterioration and destruction, is a priority.

DEFENCE

 $245m   Compulsory

 None   None   58,000

The new regime is establishing a national army. Private armies have been banned. An international peacekeeping force maintains security in Kabul, while effective control elsewhere is maintained by warlords.

MEDIA

Some censorship   Low

10 daily 6 per 1,000 people   TV: 1/0 Radio: several

Various factions run newspapers and radio stations. Television and the Internet were banned under the *taliban*, and although television broadcasts restarted in 2001, cable TV was banned as un-Islamic in 2003.

EDUCATION

37%   12,800 students

13 years   Primary 49% Secondary 22% Tertiary 2%

Under the *taliban*, education for women was strictly limited and segregation rigidly enforced. The Northern Alliance announced the lifting of restrictions on female education in November 2001.

HEALTH

 1 per 10,000 people   43 years

 41 per 1,000 people   163 per 1,000 live births

The health service has collapsed completely and almost all medical professionals have left the country. Infant and maternal mortality rates are among the highest in the world, and life expectancy is very low.

 SPENDING

 0.2 per 1,000 people   12.2%

 2%   1.6%

The vast majority of Afghans live in conditions of extreme poverty. The country does not have the resources to feed its people at present – a situation exacerbated by the severe drought of 2000.

priority after the New York and Washington attacks of September 2001, Afghanistan became the first target, leading to its destruction. The new interim government is consequently heavily dependent on the countries which effectively installed it, making good relations with them essential for future aid. Pakistan was the last country to break off its links with the *taliban* and remains Afghanistan's most delicately placed partner, with a history of religious as well as ethnic sympathies with the ousted, Pashtun-dominated, Islamic regime.

PEOPLE & SOCIETY

 93 people per sq mile

 22% urban 78% rural

 Sunni Muslim 84% Shi'a Muslim 15% Others 1%

 Death penalty used

Ethnicity largely determined intra-*mujahideen* feuding after 1992. Pashtuns have traditionally been the rulers of Afghanistan, and dominated the *taliban*. The fall of that regime in 2001 provide the opportunity for the Tajik–Uzbek alliance to enforce a power-sharing agreement. Pashtuns have since faced reprisal attacks, particularly in the north, where they are a minority. Religious differences between Sunnis and Shi'as became acute under the Sunni taliban regime.

Some two million people were killed in the ten-year conflict which followed the invasion by Soviet Union forces in 1979 and in the post-1992 civil war. As many people again were maimed. A further six million people were forced to flee to neighbouring Pakistan and Iran; many returned, but the fighting in 2001 created a fresh wave of refugees and left hundreds of thousands more people internally displaced.

Women enjoyed few rights under the rigid Islamic regime of the *taliban*. The interim government has lifted the ban on women in employment and allowed girls to resume schooling, but social restrictions still exist.

ECONOMIC FOCUS

EXPORTS

Russia 5% | Belgium 7%
USA 7%
India 8%
Other 41%
Pakistan 32%

IMPORTS

Turkmenistan 6% | South Korea 7%
Kenya 9%
Japan 16%
Other 43%
Pakistan 19%

STRENGTHS

Afghanistan has very few strengths, apart from illicit opium trade. Revalued currency was released in 2002, and all overseas assets were unfrozen in the same year.

WEAKNESSES

Decades of fighting have destroyed the economy; Afghanistan's agriculture and industry are in ruins. Communication links were damaged by the 1998 earthquakes and devastated by bombing in 2001.

PROFILE

The protracted fighting has left Afghanistan one of the poorest and least developed countries in the world. Estimates suggest that $4 billion is needed to rebuild the country and that 80% of its infrastructure has been destroyed. Agricultural activity has fallen back from pre-1979 levels; the Soviets' "scorched earth" policy laid waste large areas, and much of the rural population fled to the cities. Many farmers turned back to growing poppies for opium production, but saw little profit from the trade, despite Afghanistan being one of the world's largest sources of opium. Although prohibited, poppy cultivation has increased under the new, less intimidating regime.

Total Land Area : 652 090 sq. km
(251 770 sq. miles)

LAND HEIGHT | POPULATION
3000m/9843ft | over 1 000 000
2000m/6562ft | over 100 000
1000m/3281ft | over 50 000
500m/1640ft | over 10 000
200m/656ft | under 10 000

Mujahideen guerrillas, *members of just one of the many factions who vied for power in Afghanistan under the* taliban, *prepare to launch a rocket attack.*

PAKISTAN

 1947   1971   March 23   PK   +5   +92   .pk

OFFICIAL NAME **Islamic Republic of Pakistan**   CAPITAL **Islamabad**
POPULATION **149m**   CURRENCY **Pakistani rupee**   OFF. LANG. **Urdu**

ONCE A PART OF BRITISH INDIA, Pakistan was created in 1947 in response to the demand for an independent and predominantly Muslim Indian state. Initially the new nation included East Pakistan, present-day Bangladesh, which seceded from Pakistan in 1971. In eastern and southern Pakistan, the flood plain of the Indus River is highly fertile and produces cotton, the basis of the large textile industry.

ECONOMICS

 45th $-96m

$440   3.1%

One of the world's leading producers of cotton and a major exporter of rice. Corruption at all levels of government undermined economic confidence throughout the 1990s.

RESOURCES

 62.4bn kwh   Comb. 64%
Hydro 35%
Nuclear 1%

Sheep 24.2m
Goats 49.1m
Buffaloes 23.3m   55,258 b/d
(reserves of
222m bbl)

Apart from cotton and rice, Pakistan's major resources are oil, coal, gas and water. Steps are being taken to attract more foreign investment in oil and gas exploration, extraction and distribution.

DEFENCE

 $2.4bn   Not compulsory

Undisclosed :
Weapons tested
in May 1998   620,000

Pakistan has emerged as a significant regional arms trader. It established itself as a nuclear power after conducting a number of successful nuclear tests in May 1998. Defence spending has a high priority.

MEDIA

 Censorship   Medium

264 daily
21 per 1,000
people   TV: 1/1
Radio: 2/1

Private broadcasts were licensed in 2001. Journalists who challenge official views are systematically harassed.

EDUCATION

 46%   1.14 students

Schooling is not compulsory   Primary 86%
Secondary 37%
Tertiary 3%

Although universal free primary education is a constitutional right, education is not compulsory. Literacy rates in Pakistan are among the lowest in the world. The education system is heavily Islamized.

HEALTH

 1 per 1,667 people   60 years

30 per 1,000
people   85 per 1,000
live births

Availability of doctors and hospital beds is among the lowest in the world, and there is a shortage of equipment and medicines. Pakistan has a high incidence of heroin addicts.

SPENDING

 8 per 1,000 people   4.4%

 2.7%   0.7%

Members of the bureaucratic and political elite tend to be extremely rich, as are some of the top military. Despite Pakistan's considerable economic potential, much of its population lives below the poverty line.

POLITICS

 L. House 2002/2007
U. House 2003/2006   President
Pervez Musharraf   Multi-party
democracy

Multi-party democracy was suspended from 1999–2002. The current regime has committed to restore democracy by 2003. The military-dominated National Security Council advises the president. The popularity of the 1999 coup, which removed PML Prime Minister Nawaz Sharif, indicated the loss of respect for the country's much-abused democratic institutions. In 2001 coup leader General Pervez Musharraf appointed himself president, and in 2002 he was endorsed for a further five years in a controversial referendum. He has since restored the constitutional powers of the presidency.

The 2002 elections were won by the pro-Musharraf PML(Q), which outmanoeuvred the PPP and the Islamist MMA to secure the appointment of Zafarullah Jamali as prime minister.

Under pressure to curb the ambitions of radical Islamists in Kashmir, the regime treads a tightrope in domestic politics, where militant Islam has a powerful grip on the poor. Although Islamist parties had previously failed to convert this grass-roots backing into electoral success, the MMA became the third-largest group in parliament in 2002.

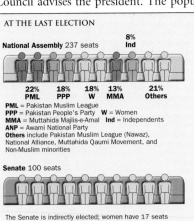

AT THE LAST ELECTION

National Assembly 237 seats

8% Ind

22% PML   18% PPP   18% W   13% MMA   21% Others

PML = Pakistan Muslim League
PPP = Pakistan People's Party   W = Women
MMA = Muttahida Majlis-e-Amal   Ind = Independents
ANP = Awami National Party
Others include Pakistan Muslim League (Nawaz), National Alliance, Muttahida Qaumi Movement, and Non-Muslim minorities

Senate 100 seats

The Senate is indirectly elected; women have 17 seats

WORLD AFFAIRS

 IAEA, SAARC, ECO,
NAM, OIC   1947

In 1998, Pakistan carried out a series of nuclear tests in response to similar tests by India, provoking international condemnation and three years of US sanctions. The last of three wars between India and Pakistan was three decades ago, but their dispute over Kashmir and Jammu has repeatedly stoked tensions, and has almost led to full-scale war between the two countries. In late 2001–early 2002, a series of attacks by Muslim Kashmiri separatists, allegedly supported by Pakistan, pushed the two countries yet again to the brink of war. Pakistan's membership of the Commonwealth was suspended after the 1999 coup.

One of only three countries to recognize the Afghan *taliban* regime, Pakistan in September 2001 urged the *taliban* to hand over terrorism suspect Osama bin Laden, and then backed US-led action against the regime despite internal dissent.

PEOPLE & SOCIETY

 500 people per sq mile   33% urban 67% rural   Sunni Muslim 77% Shi'a Muslim 20% Hindu & Christian 3%   Death penalty used

Punjabis account for 50% of the population, while Sindhis, Pathans and Baluch are also prominent. *Mohajirs* – Urdu-speaking immigrants from pre-partition India – predominate in Karachi and Hyderabad. Punjabi political and military dominance of the centralized state has spawned many separatist and autonomy movements. Pathans have frequently threatened to establish a homeland with ethnic kin in Afghanistan. Tensions between the Baluch and Pathan refugees from Afghanistan sporadically erupt into violence, as do those between native Sindhis and immigrant *mohajirs*.

The gap between rich and poor, as exemplified by the feudal land-owning class, which dominates the ruling elite, and their serfs, is considerable. There is an expanding middle class of small-scale merchants and manufacturers.

Recent years have witnessed a marked increase in Islamist militancy, accompanied by growing discrimination against religious minorities. After the 1999 coup, the Musharraf regime trod a fine line in trying to avoid conflict with Islamic militants, both over issues such as the strict application of Islamic *sharia* law and over foreign policy.

The extended family is an enduring institution, and ties between its members are strong, reflected in the dynastic and nepotistic nature of the political system. Although some women hold prominent positions, and Benazir Bhutto has twice been prime minister, relatively few are allowed to work by their religiously conservative menfolk. Pakistan has one of the world's lowest ratios of females to males, implying widespread neglect and some female infanticide. Amnesty International criticized Pakistan in 2000 for its failure to give women's rights sufficient protection.

Total Land Area : 770 880 sq. km
(297 637 sq. miles)

LAND HEIGHT

6000m/19 686ft
4000m/13 124ft
3000m/9843ft
2000m/6562ft
1000m/3281ft
500m/1640ft
200m/656ft
Sea Level

POPULATION

over 5 000 000
over 1 000 000
over 500 000
over 100 000
over 50 000
over 10 000

0   200 km
0   200 miles

ECONOMIC FOCUS

EXPORTS

UAE 6%
Germany 6%
Hong Kong 6%
UK 7%
Other 52%
USA 23%

IMPORTS

USA 6%
UAE 7%
Kuwait 8%
Japan 8%
Saudi Arabia 8%
Other 63%

STRENGTHS

Gas, water, coal, oil. Substantial untapped natural resources. Low labour costs. Potentially huge market. One of the world's leading producers of cotton and a major exporter of rice.

WEAKNESSES

Production of cotton and rice vulnerable to weather conditions. History of inefficient and haphazard government economic policies. Weak and overstretched infrastructure.

PROFILE

Pakistan has yet to show progress in tackling its considerable economic problems. Although successive governments have reversed the nationalization policies instituted in the 1970s, private enterprise has been stifled by the rules of a massive bureaucracy. There is some foreign investment in previously state-only sectors such as banking, and water and other utilities. However, corruption at all levels of government undermined economic confidence throughout the 1990s, and it was particularly acute under the administration of Benazir Bhutto. Efforts by the military government to tackle corruption and poverty were praised by the World Bank in 2001. Defence spending remains high.

Paddy fields, *with monsoon rains threatening from the Himalayas. Rice is the second most valuable agricultural export after cotton.*

COMOROS

ECONOMICS

 184th $-1m

 $380   3.5%

Vanilla, ylang-ylang and cloves are the main cash crops. Subsistence level farming. Over 50% of food requirements are imported. Lack of basic infrastructure, especially electricity and transport.

RESOURCES

 17m kwh   Comb. 88% / Hydro 12% / Nuclear 0%

 Sheep 21,000 / Goats 172,000 / Cattle 52,000   Not an oil producer

There are few strategic resources. Most fuel for energy is imported. There is potential for HEP and geothermal generation. Fishing remains a neglected source of future growth.

DEFENCE

 $3m (estimate)   Not compulsory

 None   Small number of presidential guard

France and South Africa finance the small presidential guard, the principal security force. Mauritian aid was also sought after clashes on Anjouan.

MEDIA

 Some censorship   Low

 No daily papers   TV: 1/0 / Radio: 1/some

China helped to fund the islands' first national TV station. Radio is strictly controlled, and there is no single national newspaper.

EDUCATION

 60% 649 students

16 years Primary 76% / Secondary 25% / Tertiary 1%

There is a very limited education system beyond secondary level. Schools are equipped to teach only basic literacy, hygiene and agricultural techniques. Pupil–teacher ratios are high.

HEALTH

 1 per 14,000 people   60 years

 people   60 per 1,000 live births

Health care is rudimentary. Although there are a good number of regional health centres, their poor facilities have deterred their use.

SPENDING

 13 per 1,000 people   No data

4.2% 4.9%

A political and business elite controls most of the wealth. Bridegrooms win social status according to the size of their weddings. Government workers often suffer from wage arrears.

 1975   1975   July 6   COM   +3   +269 .km

OFFICIAL NAME **Union of the Comoros** CAPITAL **Moroni** POPULATION **749,000**
CURRENCY **Comoros franc** OFF. LANG. **Arabic, French & Comoran**

THE ARCHIPELAGO REPUBLIC of the Comoros lies off the east African coast, between Mozambique and Madagascar. It consists of three main islands and a number of islets. Most of the population are subsistence farmers. In 1975, the Comoros Islands, except for Mayotte, became independent of France. Since then instability has plagued this poor region, with several coups and counter-coups, and repeated attempts at secession by smaller islands.

POLITICS

 1996/2000 (postponed)   President Assoumani Azzali Military-based regime

AT THE LAST ELECTION

Federal Assembly 43 seats

2% Ind

91% RND 5% FNJ 2% VA

RND = National Rally for Development
FNJ = National Front for Justice
Ind = Independent VA = Votes annulled

The Senate was abolished under the 1996 constitution.

Attempts to introduce democracy have been consistently undermined by repeated coups. Anjouan declared independence in 1997, since when rival militias have favoured either co-habitation with Grande Comore or reattachment to France. Renewed violence in April 1999 provided Colonel Assoumani Azzali with the pretext to install himself as president. In a new "Union of the Comoros" a loose confederation gives each island its own president and legislature, with a federal president having overall authority. Azzali was returned to power unopposed in 2002, although his victory was undermined by low voter turnout.

WORLD AFFAIRS

 OIC, FZ, AL, AU, COI   1975

France remains the Comoros' main benefactor, although economic ties with South Africa have strengthened in recent years. An OAU assessment team visited strife-torn Anjouan in February 1999, but had to be evacuated after fighting on the island intensified.

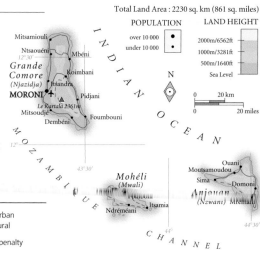

Total Land Area : 2230 sq. km (861 sq. miles)

POPULATION
over 10 000
under 10 000

LAND HEIGHT
2000m/6562ft
1000m/3281ft
500m/1640ft
Sea Level

Mitsamiouli
Ntsaouéni
Mbéni
Grande Comore (Njazidja)
Koimbani
MORONI
Itsandra
Pidjani
Le Kartala 2361m
Mitsoudjé
Dembéni
Foumbouni

INDIAN OCEAN
MOZAMBIQUE CHANNEL

Mohéli (Mwali)
Fomboni
Itsamia
Ndréméani

Ouani
Moutsamoudou
Sima
Domoni
Anjouan (Nzwani)
Mrémani

PEOPLE & SOCIETY

 870 people per sq mile   34% urban / 66% rural

Sunni Muslim 98% / Roman Catholic 1% / Other 1%   Death penalty used

The Comoros has absorbed Polynesians, Africans, Indonesians, Persians and Arabs over time, as well as immigrants from Portugal, Holland, France and India. Some communities retain their individual character. Ethnic tension is rare, partly owing to the unifying force of Islam, the predominant religion. A more potent divisive factor is regionalism.

MALDIVES

1965 | 1965 | July 26 | MV | +5 | +960 | .mv

OFFICIAL NAME **Republic of Maldives** CAPITAL **Male'**
POPULATION **309,000** CURRENCY **Rufiyaa** OFF. LANG. **Dhivehi**

AN ISLAMIC SULTANATE UNTIL 1968, the Maldives is an archipelago of 1,190 small coral islands or atolls (a word derived from the local Dhivehi language), set in the Indian Ocean south-west of India. The islands, none of which rise above 1.8 m (6 ft), are protected by encircling reefs or *faros*. Only 200 are inhabited. Tourism has grown in recent years, though vacation islands are separate from settled islands.

POLITICS

 1999/2004   President Maumoon Abdul Gayoom   Non-party democracy

AT THE LAST ELECTION
Citizens' Assembly 50 seats

There are no political parties. 42 members of the Majlis (Assembly) are elected, and 8 appointed by the president

Politics in the Maldives is the reserve of a small group of influential families. Most were already dominant under the sultanate. Formal parties with ideological objectives are virtually non-existent, politics being organized around family and clan loyalties.

Former president Ibrahim Nasir abolished the premiership in 1975 and substantially strengthened the presidency. The main figure now is Maumoon Abdul Gayoom, a wealthy businessman who has been president since 1978.

A young Westernized elite has increased the pressure for political reform. Rival candidates may now seek to be parliament's presidential nominee; only one name then goes forward for popular endorsement in a referendum.

WORLD AFFAIRS

 OIC, SAARC, NAM, WTO, Comm   1965

The Maldives is a long-standing member of the NAM. The government rejects the view that the organization does not have a role to play in the post Cold War world. The Maldives' international standing was enhanced in 1990, when it hosted the fifth SAARC summit meeting.

PEOPLE & SOCIETY

 2,664 people per sq mile   28% urban 72% rural

 Sunni Muslim 100%   Death penalty not used

The people live on only 200 of the 1,190 islands. About 25% of the total population live on the island capital of Male'. It is estimated that 12,000 guest workers from Sri Lanka and India work in the Maldives. The country's new-found prosperity has seen the emergence of a commercial elite.

Eight Degree Channel

Ihavandippolhu Atoll
Thiladhunmathi Atoll
Makunudhoo Atoll
North Miladummadulu Atoll
North Maalhosmadulu Atoll
South Miladummadulu Atoll
Faadhippolhu Atoll
South Maalhosmadulu Atoll
Horsburgh Atoll
Rasdu Atoll
Male' Atoll
Ari Atoll
MALE'
Felidhu Atoll
North Nilandhe Atoll
South Nilandhe Atoll
Mulaku Atoll
Kolhumadulu Atoll
Hadhdhunmathi Atoll

N

One and Half Degree Channel
North Huvadhu Atoll
South Huvadhu Atoll

Total Land Area : 300 sq. km (116 sq. miles)

Equatorial Channel — *Equator*
Fuammulah

POPULATION
• over 10 000
• under 10 000

Addu Atoll
Gan

LAND HEIGHT
100m/328ft
Sea Level
0 — 100 km
0 — 100 miles

INDIAN OCEAN

 170th $-63m
 $1,960   0.6%

Economic reforms since 1989 have eased import restrictions and encouraged foreign investment. Cottage industries employ 25% of work force; there is little scope for expansion.

 82m kwh   Comb. 100% Hydro 0% Nuclear 0%
 Sheep 11,000 Goats 20,000 Cattle 31,000   Not an oil producer

Natural resources include abundant stocks of fish, particularly tuna. Fishing employs over 10% of the working population. Coconut production is important. Oil products and nearly all staple foods are imported.

 $36m   Not compulsory
 None   0

The British military presence ended in 1975, when troops were withdrawn from the staging post on Gan, in the Addu atoll. In 1998 the Maldives called on India for military assistance to help suppress a coup attempt.

 Some censorship   Low
 3 daily 19 per 1,000 people   TV: 1/0 Radio: 3/0

There is a marked degree of press self-censorship. In the past, journalists have been imprisoned. An Internet café opened in Male' in 1998.

 96%   No data
 Schooling is not compulsory   Primary 100% Secondary 69% Tertiary No data

Primary education has been improved. Secondary education is less developed in the outer islands; the first school outside Male' was opened in 1992.

 1 per 1,328 people   67 years
 21 per 1,000 people   28 per 1,000 live births

There is a lack of general equipment and facilities throughout the Maldives. Health care is less developed on the outlying islands.

11 per 1,000 people   6.7%
6.4%   3.7%

Great disparities of wealth exist between the people who live in the capital, Male', and those who live on the more distant outer islands.

BANGLADESH

1971 | 1971 | March 26 | BD | +6 | +880 | .bd

OFFICIAL NAME **People's Republic of Bangladesh** CAPITAL **Dhaka**
POPULATION **143m** CURRENCY **Taka** OFF. LANG. **Bengali**

BANGLADESH LIES AT the north of the Bay of Bengal and shares borders with India and Burma. Most of the country is composed of fertile alluvial plains; the north and north-east are mountainous, as is the Chittagong region in the south-east. After its secession from Pakistan in 1971, Bangladesh had a troubled history of political instability, with periods of emergency rule. Effective democracy was restored in 1991.

POLITICS

 2001/2006   Iajuddin Ahmed   Parliamentary democracy

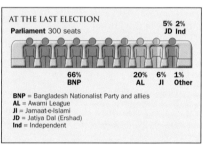

AT THE LAST ELECTION
Parliament 300 seats
5% 2% JD Ind
66% BNP   20% AL   6% JI   1% Other
BNP = Bangladesh Nationalist Party and allies
AL = Awami League
JI = Jamaat-e-Islami
JD = Jatiya Dal (Ershad)
Ind = Independent

Between 1975 and 1990 the military was in power in Bangladesh. The overthrow of President Ershad in 1990 saw a return to multi-party politics. Bangladesh's first woman prime minister, Begum Khaleda Zia, head of the BNP, was elected in 1991. The AL, which had steered Bangladesh to independence in 1971, mounted a sustained campaign against her regime, forcing a rerun of elections in 1996. It won the largest number of seats and its leader, Sheikh Hasina Wajed, became the first prime minister to complete a full term. The revived BNP returned to power in the October 2001 poll, amid much electoral violence.

WORLD AFFAIRS

 OIC, SAARC, NAM, WTO, Comm   1974

Good relations with the West, the main source of essential aid, are a priority. Relations with Pakistan have slowly improved since Pakistan's agreement in 1991 to accept the 250,000 pro-Pakistan Bihari Muslims in Bangladeshi refugee camps since 1971. Relations with India are improving.

PEOPLE & SOCIETY

 2,774 people per sq mile   26% urban 74% rural

 Sunni Muslim 87% Hindu 12% Other 1%   Death penalty used

Bangladesh is one of the most densely populated countries in the world, despite the fact that three-quarters of the population is rural. As in India, there is considerable Muslim–Hindu tension; in 2001 thousands of Hindus claimed persecution from the new nationalist government.

Total Land Area : 133 910 sq. km (51 703 sq. miles)

POPULATION
◙ over 1 000 000
◉ over 500 000
◎ over 100 000
○ over 50 000
• over 10 000

LAND HEIGHT
500m/1640ft
200m/656ft
Sea Level

0   100 km
0   100 miles

BRUNEI

 1984   1984   Feb 23   BRU   +8   +673   .bn

OFFICIAL NAME **Sultanate of Brunei** CAPITAL **Bandar Seri Begawan**
POPULATION **341,000** CURRENCY **Brunei dollar** OFF. LANG. **Malay**

LYING ON THE north-western coast of the island of Borneo, Brunei is divided in two by a strip of the surrounding Malaysian state of Sarawak. The interior is mostly rainforest. Independent from the UK since 1984, Brunei is ruled by decree of the sultan. It is undergoing increasing Islamicization. Oil and gas reserves have brought one of the world's highest standards of living.

POLITICS

 Not applicable   HM Sultan Haji Sir Hassanal Bolkiah Mu'izzadin Waddaulah   Monarchy

Since a failed rebellion in 1962, a state of emergency has been in force and the sultan has ruled by decree. Hopes for democracy were dashed when political parties were banned in 1988. In 1990, "Malay Muslim Monarchy" was introduced, promoting

LEGISLATIVE OR ADVISORY BODIES

Brunei is an absolute monarchy; the sultan consults four advisory councils: Religious Council, Privy Council, Council of Cabinet Ministers, and Council of Succession, which he appoints. Political parties have been banned since 1988.

Islamic values as the state ideology. This further alienated the large Chinese and expatriate communities. Power is closely tied to the royal family. One of the sultan's brothers holds the foreign affairs portfolio and the sultan himself looks after defence and finance.

WORLD AFFAIRS

 OIC, APEC, WTO, ASEAN, Comm   1984

Brunei's claims to part of the Spratly Islands are disputed with China, Taiwan, Vietnam, Malaysia and the Philippines. Political exiles opposed to the government and based in Malaysia are a main concern. Relations with the UK, the ex-colonial power, are good. Japan is an important economic ally, taking over 50% of Brunei's total exports.

PEOPLE & SOCIETY

 168 people per sq mile   73% urban / 27% rural

 Muslim 66% / Buddhist 14% / Christian & other 20%   Death penalty not used

Malays are the beneficiaries of positive discrimination; many in the Chinese community are either stateless or hold British protected person passports. Among indigenous groups, the Murut and Dusuns are favoured politically over the Ibans. Women, less restricted than in some Muslim states, are obliged to wear headscarves but not the veil. Many women hold influential posts in the civil service.

Total Land Area : 5270 sq. km (2035 sq. miles)

LAND HEIGHT   POPULATION
1500m/4921ft   ○ over 50 000
1000m/3281ft   ● over 10 000
500m/1640ft   ● under 10 000
200m/656ft
Sea Level

Pekan Muara
Perkemahan Berakas
Kampong Parit BANDAR SERI BEGAWAN
SOUTH CHINA SEA
Kampong Labu
Bangar
Tutong
Kampong Kuala Abang
Kampong Lumut
Kampong Benutan
Kuala Belait Pekan Seria
Badas Kampong Bukit Sawat
Kampong Batang Duri
Kampong Tanajor
Kampong Kuala Balai Kampong Labi
Kampong Sukang
Kampong Teraja
Bukit Pagon 1618m
MALAYSIA
SARAWAK
N
0   20 km
0   20 miles

 95th $2.09bn

 $24,762   1.0%

ECONOMICS

Earnings from massive overseas investments, mainly in the US and Europe, now exceed oil and gas revenues. Single-product economy. Failure of diversification programmes could lead to problems in the future.

 1.7bn kwh   Comb. 100% / Hydro 0% / Nuclear 0%

 Ducks 40,000 / Pigs 6,000 / Cattle 8,000   195,000 b/d (reserves of 1.4bn bbl)

RESOURCES

Oil and gas are the major resources. Energy policy is now focused on regulating output in order to conserve stocks, since reserves are of limited duration. Almost all food is imported.

 $279m   Not compulsory

 None   7,000

DEFENCE

As well as being head of the 5,900-strong armed forces, the sultan has a personal bodyguard of 2,000 UK-trained Gurkhas. The UK and Singapore are close defence allies.

 Some censorship   Medium

 3 daily / 69 per 1,000 people   TV: 1/0 / Radio: 1/0

MEDIA

State controls were relaxed somewhat in 2000, but self-censorship on political and religious content continues.

 92%   2,080 students

 12 years   Primary 100% / Secondary 77% / Tertiary 7%

EDUCATION

Free schooling is available to the entire population, with the exception of the stateless Chinese, who do not qualify. The University of Brunei Darussalam was opened in 1985.

 1 per 939 people   76 years

 23 per 1,000 people   7 per 1,000 live births

HEALTH

The national health service is free, although if major surgery is required many Bruneians tend to travel to Singapore.

 538 per 1,000 people   5.5%

3.1%   5.7%

SPENDING

The wealthiest people in Brunei are those close to the sultan. A high standard of living keeps discontent to a minimum. Bruneians are major consumers of high-tech equipment and designer labels.

MALAYSIA

1963 | 1965 | Aug 31 | MAL | +8 | +60 | .my

OFFICIAL NAME **Federation of Malaysia** CAPITAL **Kuala Lumpur**
POPULATION **23m** CURRENCY **Ringgit** OFF. LANG. **Bahasa Malaysia**

COMPRISING THE THREE territories of Peninsular Malaysia, Sarawak and Sabah, Malaysia stretches over 2,000 km (1,240 miles) from the Malay Peninsula to the north-eastern end of the island of Borneo. A central mountain chain divides Peninsular Malaysia, separating fertile western plains from an eastern coastal belt. Sarawak and Sabah have swampy coastal plains rising to mountains on the border with Indonesia. Putrajaya, just south of Kuala Lumpur, is a high-tech new development intended as the future capital. The United Malays National Organization has dominated politics since independence.

ECONOMICS

42nd	$8.41bn
$3,380	1.4%

Fastest-growing south-east Asian economy until the 1997 financial crisis. Major disk-drive producer. Shortage of skilled labour. Multimedia centre is expected to attract major foreign investment.

RESOURCES

60.8bn kwh	Comb. 92% Hydro 8% Nuclear 0%
Ducks 13m Pigs 1.83m Cattle 723,346	788,000 b/d (reserves of 3bn bbl)

Palm oil, of which Malaysia is the world's largest producer, and petroleum are the key resources. Malaysian timber, mostly from Sarawak, accounts for nearly half of world exports.

DEFENCE

$3.25bn	Not compulsory
None	100,000

The main defence concerns are Singapore, with its large and highly mechanized army, and, more recently, Indonesia. Also important to Malaysia is the growing Chinese influence in the South China Sea.

MEDIA

Some censorship	Medium
38 daily 112 per 1,000 people	TV: 3/4 Radio: 3/3

Almost all the newspapers are controlled by the state and UMNO, which claims a need to protect the country from un-Islamic influences. The Internet provides a medium for free reporting.

EDUCATION

88%	230,000 students
15 years	Primary 99% Secondary 98% Tertiary 12%

Racial integration in multi-ethnic schools is encouraged, but teaching is to remain in separate languages. Plans for a private Chinese university were finally realized in 2002.

HEALTH

1 per 1,429 people	73 years
24 per 1,000 people	9 per 1,000 live births

There is growing disparity between the modern facilities available in cities and the traditional medicine practised in rural areas. Acupuncture and herbs continue to be used by the Chinese community.

SPENDING

181 per 1,000 people	3.8%
4.9%	1.4%

The Chinese remain the wealthiest community in Malaysia. However, the UMNO government embarked on a deliberate programme of achieving 30% Malay ownership of the corporate sector.

POLITICS

L. House 1999/2003
U. House varying

Raja Tuanku Syed Sirajuddin ibni al-Marhum Syed Putra Jamalullail

Parliamentary democracy

AT THE LAST ELECTION

House of Representatives 193 seats

5% DAP | 2% PBS

76% BN | 14% PAS | 3% PKN

BN = National Front (dominated by the United Malays National Organization – **UMNO**) **PAS** = Pan-Malaysian Islamic Party **DAP** = Democratic Action Party **PKN** = National Justice Party (Keadilan) **PBS** = United Sabah Party

The DAP, the PAS and the PKN form the Alternative Front.

Senate 69 seats

The Senate comprises 26 members indirectly elected by the State Legislative Assemblies, and 43 appointed by the head of state

Supreme power rests in theory with the monarch, who acts on the advice of parliament. Opposition parties, while legal, are under tight control.

Mahathir's administration has declared that it no longer wishes to discriminate positively in favour of Malays, but the Chinese community accuses the government of corruption and uncompetitive practices, declaring that Malays are still favoured for the placing of government contracts. The Chinese are further alienated by the more restrictive nature of Islamic society.

Malaysia has long been dominated by the United Malays National Organization (UMNO), part of the ruling BN coalition, since Malay independence in 1957. It controls a huge network of patronage. In 2002, Prime Minister Mahathir Mohamed shocked the country by tearfully announcing that he would retire in 2003, after 22 years at the helm. He had appeared unassailable, although his authority had been shaken by the economic

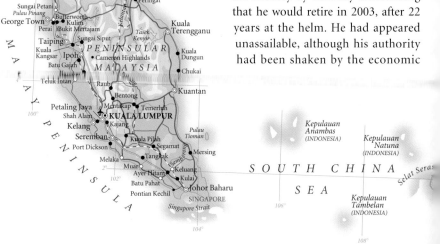

THAILAND

Kangar
Pulau Langkawi
Alor Setar
Tumpat · Kota Bharu
Pasir Mas · Peringat
Sungai Petani
Pulau Pinang · Butterworth
George Town · Kulim
Perai · Bukit Mertajam
Taiping · Sungai Siput
Tasek Kenyir
Kuala Terengganu
Kuala Kangsar · Ipoh · Cameron Highlands
Batu Gajah
Teluk Intan · Raub
Bentong
Petaling Jaya · Mentakab · Temerluh
Shah Alam · Kajang
KUALA LUMPUR
Kelang · Kajang
Seremban · Kuala Pilah · Segamat
Port Dickson · Tangkak · Mersing
Melaka · Muar
Ayer Hitam · Keluang
Batu Pahat · Kulai
Pontian Kechil · Johor Baharu
SINGAPORE
Singapore Strait

PENINSULAR MALAYSIA
Kuala Dungun
Chukai
Kuantan

MALAY PENINSULA

Pulau Tioman
Pulau Tioman

Kepulauan Anambas (INDONESIA)
Kepulauan Natuna (INDONESIA)

SOUTH CHINA SEA

Selat Seras
Kepulauan Tambelan (INDONESIA)

crisis of 1997–1988 and dissent within the ruling coalition. In 1998, Anwar Ibrahim, deputy prime minister and once Mahathir's chosen successor, was dismissed after challenging the government's economic policy and calling for political reform. He was convicted in 1999 on corruption charges; his prison sentence was lengthened to 15 years in 2000 after his conviction for sodomy. The initial verdict sparked riots and gained support for the new opposition PKN headed by Anwar's wife, Wan Azizah. PKN activists have been hounded by the government. In the 1999 elections, the BN coalition retained its large majority but Mamathir's own UMNO lost ground.

WORLD AFFAIRS

 G15, ASEAN, APEC OIC, Comm   1957

Mahathir sees himself as one of the developing world's leading voices. He maintains a strongly anti-US line in his public speeches and has chastised the West for singling out Islamic countries in its campaign against international terrorism. Mahathir's pro-Malay policies have caused tensions with Singapore, exacerbated by the latter's dependence on Malaysia for water.

PEOPLE & SOCIETY

 181 people per sq mile   58% urban 42% rural   Muslim 53% Buddhist 19% Others 28%   Death penalty used

The key distinction in Malaysian society is between the indigenous Malays, termed the "Bumiputras" (literally, sons of the soil), and the Chinese. The Malays form the largest group, accounting for just under half of the population. However, the Chinese have traditionally controlled most business activity. The New Economic Policy (NEP), introduced in the 1970s, was designed to address this imbalance by offering positive opportunities to the Malays through the education system and by making jobs available to them in both the state and private sectors. There are estimated to be more than one million Indonesian and Filipino immigrants in Malaysia, attracted by its labour shortages and a dearth of employment in their own countries. In addition, nearly 255,000 Vietnamese refugees were offered temporary refuge in Malaysia between 1975 and 1997; most have now been resettled in third countries, but around 6,000 remain. Gender discrimination was only outlawed in 2001. Muslim women are encouraged to take the veil.

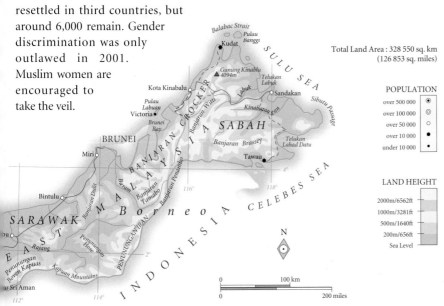

Total Land Area : 328 550 sq. km (126 853 sq. miles)

POPULATION

over 500 000 ◉
over 100 000 ◎
over 50 000 ○
over 10 000 ●
under 10 000 ·

LAND HEIGHT

2000m/6562ft
1000m/3281ft
500m/1640ft
200m/656ft
Sea Level

0   100 km
0   200 miles

N

ECONOMIC FOCUS

EXPORTS

Netherlands 5%
Taiwan 5%
Japan 12%
Other 38%
Singapore 17%
USA 23%

IMPORTS

Taiwan 5%
South Korea 5%
Other 38%
Singapore 14%
USA 17%
Japan 21%

STRENGTHS

Electronics, computer hardware, and electrical appliances. Tourism. Heavy industries such as steel. Palm oil. Latex, rubber, chemical products. Return to growth from 2000.

WEAKNESSES

High level of debt. Shortage of skilled labour. High interest rates deter private investors. High government budget spending. Competition from NICs.

PROFILE

From 1987, for almost a decade, Malaysia expanded faster than any other south-east Asian nation, at an average yearly rate of 8%, with much of the growth state-directed. However, plans for full industrialization, named "Vision 2020", were revised after the 1997 financial crisis. The construction of Putrajaya provided a renewed stimulus for growth at the end of the 1990s. A project for a Multimedia Super Corridor (MSC), located south of Kuala Lumpur and aimed at attracting world-class companies, is expected to be completed by 2003.

Tea plantations *and colonial-style houses and gardens make Cameron Highlands, in Peninsular Malaysia, one of Asia's most popular mountain resorts.*

INDONESIA

1949 | 1999 | Aug 17 | RI | +7 to +9 | +62 | .id

ECONOMICS

 32nd $7.99bn

$570   11.5%

Oil and natural gas play a major role, though output of oil is currently falling. Corruption and bureaucracy remain rife. There have been recent signs of a return to high growth.

RESOURCES

 89.6bn kwh

Comb. 81%
Hydro 16%
Other 3%

Ducks 28.1m
Goats 12.5m
Cattle 11.2 m

1.41m b/d
(reserves of
5bn bbl)

Indonesia is rich in energy sources. The main export earners are oil and liquefied natural gas. Indonesia's other main resources are coal, bauxite and nickel, and agricultural products such as rubber and palm oil.

DEFENCE

 $860m   Compulsory

None   297,000

Defence spending is low by regional standards, despite the military's high profile. The constitution enshrines the military's political role.

MEDIA

Some censorship   Medium

69 daily
23 per 1,000
people

TV: 1/5
Radio: 1/1

The 1999 press law prohibits censorship, but journalists can still be fined for violating "religious and moral norms". Independent press and broadcasting have flourished since 1998.

EDUCATION

87%   3.13m students

12 years

Primary 100%
Secondary 56%
Tertiary 11%

Primary education is compulsory, and is often provided by Islamic schools, but children in many rural areas are still deprived of secondary education.

HEALTH

1 per 5,000 people   66 years

22 per 1,000 people   41 per 1,000 live births

An extensive network of clinics, down to village level, means that access to health care is reasonable. However, malnutrition, particularly among children, continues to remain a real problem.

SPENDING

14 per 1,000 people   0.6%

1.4%   0.8%

  Since 1998 attempts have been made in the courts to tackle the issues of corruption and concentration of wealth in the hands of close associates and relatives of former President Suharto.

OFFICIAL NAME Republic of Indonesia   **CAPITAL Jakarta**
POPULATION 218m   **CURRENCY Rupiah**   **OFF. LANG. Bahasa Indonesia**

INDONESIA IS THE WORLD'S LARGEST ARCHIPELAGO. Its 18,108 islands stretch 5,000 km (3,100 miles) eastwards from the Indian Ocean to New Guinea. Java, Kalimantan, Papua, Sulawesi and Sumatra are mountainous, volcanic and densely forested. Politics after independence was dominated by the military for over three decades, until the fall of the Suharto regime in 1998. In outlying regions, the forcibly suppressed demands for greater autonomy have flared up, bringing renewed violence. East Timor voted for independence in 1999 and became a fully sovereign state in 2002.

POLITICS

 1999/2004   President Megawati Sukarnoputri   Multi-party republic

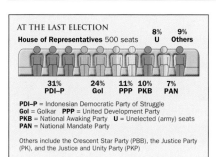

AT THE LAST ELECTION
House of Representatives 500 seats   8% U   9% Others

31% PDI–P   24% Gol   11% PPP   10% PKB   7% PAN

PDI–P = Indonesian Democratic Party of Struggle
Gol = Golkar   **PPP** = United Development Party
PKB = National Awaking Party   **U** = Unelected (army) seats
PAN = National Mandate Party

Others include the Crescent Star Party (PBB), the Justice Party (PK), and the Justice and Unity Party (PKP)

Under General Suharto, the autocratic ruler from 1968, Golkar – an amalgam of interest groups– and the army were dominant. Suharto was forced to resign in 1998 amid widespread protest over corruption, economic mismanagement and denial of democratic rights. After his fall, the mainly Muslim PDI–P, led by Megawati Sukarnoputri, won elections, but Abdurrahman Wahid of the PKB was elected president; Megawati became vice president. Disenchantment with Wahid pressured him

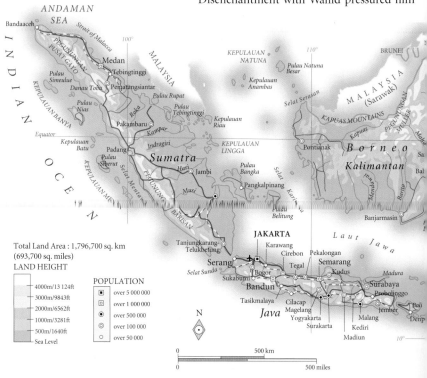

Total Land Area : 1,796,700 sq. km
(693,700 sq. miles)

LAND HEIGHT

4000m/13 124ft
3000m/9843ft
2000m/6562ft
1000m/3281ft
500m/1640ft
Sea Level

POPULATION

over 5 000 000
over 1 000 000
over 500 000
over 100 000
over 50 000

into devolving many of his duties to her in 2000. Increasingly vehement opposition culminated in his removal in July 2001 whereupon Megawati became president herself.

The army's involvement in politics remains a serious problem. In early 2000, the influential General Wiranto left the government, but the army refused to relinquish its 38-seat entitlement in the legislature any earlier than 2009.

WORLD AFFAIRS

 APEC, ASEAN, G15, OPEC, OIC 1950

Indonesia pursues a largely pro-Western foreign policy, although the government is under pressure to improve its human rights record and opposed the 2003 invasion of Iraq. The scale and nature of the East Timor massacres in 1999 severely damaged its standing. Internal security in the far-flung provinces tests regional relations.

China remains a concern, despite the restoration of diplomatic ties in 1990. Indonesia and Australia have co-operated on security since 1995, but the movement of illegal immigrants through Indonesia and recent Islamist terrorism create tensions.

PEOPLE & SOCIETY

 314 people per sq mile

 42% urban 58% rural

 Sunni Muslim 87% Christian 9% Others 4%

 Death penalty used

The basic Melanesian–Malay ethnic division disguises a diverse society. The national language, Bahasa Indonesia, co-exists with at least 250 other languages. Attempts by the Javanese political elite to suppress local cultures have been vigorously opposed by the East Timorese, the Aceh of northern Sumatra and the Papuans of Irian Jaya.

Religious and inter-ethnic hostility is increasing. In 1998 there were violent clashes between Muslims and Christians on Sulawesi, and in the Moluccas. Similar clashes occurred in Kalimantan in 1999 and 2001 between indigenous Dayaks and ethnic Madurese immigrants. Aceh introduced Islamic *sharia* law in 2000.

Discrimination against ethnic Chinese has encouraged vicious attacks on their businesses, as in Jakarta in 1998. Gender equality is enshrined in law, and women are active in public life.

ECONOMIC FOCUS

EXPORTS

China 5%
South Korea 6%
Singapore 11%
USA 16%
Japan 20%
Other 42%

IMPORTS

USA 7%
China 7%
Singapore 9%
South Korea 10%
Japan 19%
Other 48%

STRENGTHS

Varied resources, especially oil. Signs of return to high growth. Debt successfully rescheduled. International credit rating improved.

WEAKNESSES

High level of bureaucracy. Endemic corruption. Huge wealth disparities. Regional insecurity deters investment. High underemployment.

PROFILE

Under Suharto the economy grew rapidly, fuelled largely by oil, until its collapse in 1997–1998. State-owned corporations played a significant role, protected from foreign competition. Non-oil exports were diversified, but the debt burden used up a third of export earnings. Reform was delayed by conflict between "technologists" who favoured industrialization over profit for state concerns and advocates of deregulation. Further reforms have been stymied by the government's poor representation in parliament. Corruption remains rife, embroiling then president Wahid in 2001. Persistent weaknesses are likely to continue to hold back real growth. However, relations with the IMF and other donors were sufficiently improved by 2002 for Indonesia's international credit rating to be upgraded.

Rice terraces on Bali, *one of Indonesia's 18,108 islands and its most popular tourist destination. Rice is the staple food crop.*

600–800 CE

707 The Great Mosque in Damascus *was built. It is decorated with sumptuous mosaics in the Byzantine style.*

EUROPE AND AFRICA

624 Visigoths expel last Byzantine garrisons from southern Iberia
626 Constantinople besieged by Sasanids, Avars and Slavs

635–42 Conquest of Egypt by Arabs

642 Foundation of Fustat (Egypt) and Great Mosque by Amr ibn al-'As
647 Arab invasion of Tripolitania

663 Byzantine Emperor Constans II invades Italy and sacks Rome
669 Arab conquest of North Africa extended beyond Tripoli to the west
670 Annexation of Tunisia; foundation of Kairouan
680 Arab armies reach Atlantic at Morocco

711 Invasion of Iberian Peninsula by Tariq; conquest of Visigothic kingdom (by 714)
712 Muslim capture of Toledo
714 S and C Spain effectively under Muslim control
718 Christian victory at battle of Covadonga temporarily halts Muslim advance in Iberian Peninsula
732 Arab armies halted at Poitiers, France

755 Revived Umayyad dynasty established at Córdoba by Abd al-Rahman (to 1031)

785 Foundation of Great Mosque at Córdoba; extended in 4 phases (832-848; 929-961; 961-976; 987)
789 Idrisids establish power in NW Africa (Morocco, to 926)
790 Beginnings of Viking raids on western Europe

SOUTHWEST ASIA

570 Birth of Muhammad in Mecca
595 First marriage of Muhammad
610 Muhammad receives first revelation
611 Arabs invade Mesopotamia
611–626 Sasanid armies capture Jerusalem and overrun Asia Minor
622 Muhammad's emigration with followers to Yathrib (Medina), the Hegira: start of the Islamic era
622 *Qibla* oriented toward Jerusalem
624 Muhammad's rejection of links with Judaism
629 Muhammad's pilgrimage to Mecca
630 Orientation of *qibla* is altered toward Ka'ba in Mecca
632 Death of Muhammad in Medina; succession of Abu Bakr (to 634), beginning of Arab expansion in Arabian peninsula
633–37 Muslims conquer Syria
634 Caliphate of 'Umar (to 644); conquest of Palestine and Syria
635 Arab armies cross Euphrates
636 Byzantine army routed by Muslims on Yarmuk River
637 Arab conquest of Mesopotamia
637 Arabs capture Ctesiphon
637 Arabs defeat Persians at al-Qadisiya; Jerusalem seized
638 Foundation of first mosque in Kufa
641 Arabs capture Nineveh and invade Armenia
642 Muslims invade Persia; Sasanid empire falls
644 Death of 'Umar; 'Uthman appointed caliph
656 Assassination of 'Uthman; 'Ali, son-in-law of Muhammad, attempts to gain control of caliphate (to 661)
660 Mu'awiya proclaimed caliph in Damascus
661 'Ali assassinated; beginning of Umayyad Caliphate (to 750)
670 Reconstruction of mosque in Kufa
683 Anti-caliphate based in Mecca (to 693)
687 Foundation of Dome of the Rock in Jerusalem; completed 692
693 Burning of the Ka'ba; anti-caliph executed
707 Great Mosques of Damascus and Medina built; al-Aqsa Mosque in Jerusalem

711 'Abbasid Caliphate established
750 Umayyad Caliphate is overthrown in Damascus; succeeded by the 'Abbasid dynasty (to 1258)
754 al-Mansur becomes caliph in Baghdad (to 775)
756 Under 'Abbasid Caliphate, new interest in seafaring, focused on Persian Gulf routes
762 'Abbasid capital moved to Mesopotamia; founding of Baghdad
786 Harun al-Rashid becomes caliph; Baghdad becomes centre of arts and learning

CENTRAL AND EAST ASIA

SOUTH AND SOUTHEAST ASIA

618 Tang begin to unite China

664 Arab conquest of Kabul
671 Arab armies cross Oxus (Amu Darya)
681 Arabs cross into Transoxania and spend winter
683 Civil war in Khurasan
689 Eastern Turks invade Transoxania
691 Umayyad rule restored in Khurasan

687-692 The Dome of the Rock *was built in Jerusalem on orders of Umayyad caliph 'Abd al-Malik.*

705 Qutayba ibn Muslim marches into Khurasan
711 Eastern Turks conquer western Central Asia
712 Arabs conquer Khwarizm. Eastern Turks take Samarkand
713 Qutayba ibn Muslim reaches Ferghana. First mosque built in Bukhara

711–12 Arab conquest of Sind introduces Islam to South Asia

725 Restoration of Balkh
729 Muslim rule restored in Bukhara
733 Famine in Khurasan
737 Death of the Khan in Tukharistan
739 Fall of the Western Turkish empire
741 Sogdians restored to their native land
742 Congregational mosque built in Balkh
743 Partisans of 'Ali revolt in Khurasan
745 Foundation of Uighur Empire in C Asia (Chinese Turkestan, to 840)
747 Abu Muslim arrives in Khurasan
748 Chinese destroy Suyab
751 Defeat of Tang Chinese by Arab forces at battle of Talas River; end of Arab advances in C Asia
752 Prince of Ushrusana sends embassy to China
753 Walls and defensive towers constructed at Samarkand

c.750 Muslim merchants establish Islam in Kerala, SW India

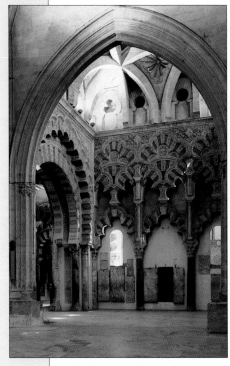

763 Tang China is invaded by Tibetans
766 Qarluqs occupy Suyab

783 Defensive walls constructed near Bukhara
792 Qarluqs expelled from Ferghana
794 Subjugation of Ushrusana. New congregational mosque built in Bukhara

785 The Great Mosque at Córdoba *in southern Spain was founded by Abd al-Rahman.*

800–1000 CE

EUROPE AND AFRICA

800 Start of Aghlabid dynasty in Tunis
c.800 Emergence of trading towns such as Manda and Kilwa on E African coast.
800 Charlemagne crowned Holy Roman Emperor by Pope Leo III in Rome
827 Crete and Sicily attacked by Aghlabids
830 Foundation of Great Mosque at Kairouan
839 Swedes travel through Russia to Constantinople; opening of riverine trade from Baltic to Black Sea
844 Vikings attack Seville
847 Muslim raiders burn outskirts of Rome
862 Novgorod founded by Rurik the Viking
863 Saints Cyril and Methodius sent as Orthodox Christian missionaries to Moravia
868 Ahmad Ibn Tulun founds the Tulunid dynasty in Egypt (to 905); control spreads to Syria
876 Mosque of Ibn Tulun, Cairo, based on Great Mosque at Samarra
884 Kiev becomes capital of new Russian state
896 Magyars start to settle in Danube basin
899–905 'Abbasid campaign against Egypt
c.900 Arab dhows (sailing ships) begin to ply the coastal routes of East Africa, as far south as Sofala
c.900 First sighting of Greenland by Viking seamen
905 'Abbasids take over Egypt
910 Shi'ite Fatimids expel Aghlabids from Tunis; extend power to Egypt and Syria and claim caliphate (to 1171)
928 Ruler of Córdoba, Abd al-Rahman III, takes title of caliph
936 Córdoba palace complex of Madinat al-Zahra begun

969 Fatimids conquer Egypt, found Cairo
970 Al-Azhar University established in Cairo
972 Zirid dynasty, of Berber origin, rule Tunisia and E Algeria, based at Kairouan (to 1148)
976–1009 Decline of Arab power in Iberia

992 Ghana captures Berber town of Awdaghost, gaining control of southern portion of trans-Saharan trade route

SOUTHWEST ASIA

809 Death of Harun al-Rashid; start of civil war between al-Amin and al-Ma'mun (ends 813).
813 Reign of al-Ma'mun, development of Arab science
820 Death of al-Shafi

836 Baghdad terrorized by Turkish slave troops; 'Abbasid Caliph al-Mu'tasim builds new capital at Samarra

848 Foundation of Great Mosque at Samarra, with monumental spiral minaret
860 Zaidi Imams rise to power in Yemen; rule intermittently to 1281
862 Qubba al-Sulaybiya mausoleum, Samarra; first monumental Islamic tomb
863 Byzantines annihilate Arab forces to stem Muslim advance in Anatolia
869 Revolt of black slaves in southern Iraq
892 Capital of 'Abbasid Caliphate shifts back from Samarra to Baghdad
894 Shi'ite Qarmatians establish power base in C Arabia

932 Shi'ite Buwayhids (Buyids) establish power base in Persia, Iraq; rule in name of 'Abbasid Caliphate (to 1082)
935 Final text of Qur'an codified
936 Turkic troops in pay of Buwayhids take effective control of 'Abbasid Caliphate
945 Persian Buwayhids conquer Baghdad but allow caliph to reign as figurehead
945 Hamdanids establish power base in Syria and Lebanon (to 1004)
950 Death of philosopher al-Farabi
956 al-Mas'udi's major historical/geographical work *The Meadows of Gold*
970 Fatimids establish control of Damascus
970 Seljuk Turks enter lands of caliphate
976 Byzantine forces threaten to take Jerusalem

c.950 Manuscripts of the Qur'an *of this period were all written in the heavy Kufic script.*

CENTRAL AND EAST ASIA

806 Rafi bin Layth revolts in Samarkand

816 Famine in Khurasan
819 Founding of Samanid dynasty in Khurasan and Transoxania (to 1005)
820 The Tughuzghuz take Ushrusana
830 Tahirids proclaim independence at Khurasan

867 Founding of Saffarid dynasty in E Persia (to 1495)
868 *The Diamond Sutra*, world's oldest surviving printed work

907 End of the Tang dynasty in China; Arab disruption of trans-Asian trade
916 Foundation of Khitan Empire

947 Khitans invade northern China, establishing Liao dynasty at Beijing

962 Foundation of Afghan Ghaznavid dynasty
970 Paper money introduced in China

979 Song dynasty unites China

992 Establishment of Qarakhanid dynasty in Transoxania (to 1211)

SOUTH AND SOUTHEAST ASIA

c.800 Arab ships sailing as far as China

977 Founding of Ghaznavid dynasty in India (to 1186)

997 Mahmud of Ghazni extends rule into northwest India

830 The Great Mosque at Kairouan *was begun. The Tunisian city, founded in 670, was a major Islamic centre in N Africa.*

876 The Mosque of Ibn Tulun *in Cairo set the style of north African Islamic architecture.*

1000–1200 CE

c.1199 The spectacular Qutb Minar *minaret in Delhi was built by the Ghurid conquerors of northern India.*

EUROPE AND AFRICA

c.1000 Arab merchants begin to set up trading states in Ethiopian Highlands
1015 Hammadids, offshoot of Zirids, rule E Algeria (to 1152)
1025 Death of great Byzantine emperor, Basil II (the Bulgar Slayer)
1031 Beginning of Christian reconquest *(Reconquista)* of Spain
1041 Zirids of Ifriqiyah gain independence
1048 Fatimids lose control of Ifriqiya (Tunisia)
1050 King of Takrur converts to Islam
1054 Final schism between Roman and Orthodox churches
1066 Battle of Hastings; Norman conquest of England
1071 Completion of St. Mark's basilica, focus of public religious life in Venice
1076 Ghana falls to Almoravids
1076 King of Ghana converts to Islam
1085 Christian forces under Alfonso VI of León take Toledo
1086 Almoravids enter Spain
1091 Completion of Norman conquest of Sicily
1094 Christian warlord El Cid takes Valencia
1095 Byzantine empire appeals for aid to pope, who preaches in France to raise support
c.1110 Onset of serious desiccation of Sahel region
1126 Birth of Muslim philosopher Averröes (Ibn Rushd) in Córdoba
1128 Almohad religious revival order starts takeover of Almoravid dominions in N Africa and Iberia (1130–1269)
1132 Palatine Chapel at Palermo; unique blend of Romanesque, Byzantine and Islamic architectural elements
1136 Independence of Russian state of Novgorod
1137 Union of Aragon and Catalonia
1147 Almohads established in Morocco and southern Spain
1147 Second Crusade; Lisbon taken from Moors, Holy Roman Emperor Conrad defeated by Turks at Dorylaeum
1154 Building of Chartres Cathedral
1169 Shi'ite Fatimid dynasty in Egypt suppressed by Saladin
1171 Founding of Ayyubid sultanate in Egypt (to 1260)
1172 Great Mosque at Seville, intended to be the largest in the world, and the Giralda, a great square minaret
1174 Saladin becomes Ayyubid sultan of Egypt and Syria (to 1193)
1184 Completion of citadel at Cairo
1189 Start of Third Crusade
1189 Succession of Richard I the Lionheart

1194 Emperor Henry VI crowned King of Sicily
1196 Marinids take control of Morocco (to 1485)

SOUTHWEST ASIA

1005 al-Sufi's *Geography*; (now in St. Petersburg) probably oldest extant illustrated Arabic manuscript
1009 Destruction of the Church of the Holy Sepulchre in Jerusalem
1055 Seljuks capture Baghdad, ruling in the name of the 'Abbasid caliph
1069 Seljuks take Konya (Iconium)
1071 Seljuks under Alp Arslan defeat Byzantines at Manzikert
1077 Seljuk province established in Anatolia with capital first at Nicaea and then Konya; dynasty comes to be known as the Seljuks of Rum (to 1307)
1078 Seljuks take Damascus
1079 Seljuks take Jerusalem
1084 Fall of Antioch to Seljuks

1092 'Abbasid vizier Nizam al-Mulk murdered by Ismaili Assassin
1094 Seljuk dynasty of Syria founded with capital at Aleppo
1096 First Crusade
1098 Crusaders take Antioch
1099 Jerusalem captured by crusaders; Godfrey of Bouillon elected King of Jerusalem
c.1118 Crusading order of Knights Templar founded in Jerusalem
1124 Crusaders capture Tyre
1127 Zangid dynasty of Seljuk governors control Syria and Mesopotamia to 1222; initiate Muslim counter-offensive against crusaders
c.1130 Hospital of St. John of Jerusalem (the Hospitallers) becomes military order
1144 Edessa conquered by Zangi, governor of Mosul
1145 The Friday Mosque at Isfahan
1148 Crusaders abandon siege of Damascus
1151 Last Christian stronghold in County of Edessa falls to Nur al-Din
1163 Iplici Mosque at Konya, probably the first to have a campanile (tower) minaret
1174 Saladin takes Damascus
1183 Saladin takes Aleppo
1187 Saladin defeats crusader armies at Hattin; takes Jerusalem and Acre
1188 Saladin completes conquest of Latin kingdoms in Levant; Christians reduced to coastal enclaves
1188 The Mosque at Rabat, like Seville, intended to be the largest in the world
1190 Frederick I (Barbarossa) drowned in Anatolia on way to Holy Land
1191–2 Third Crusade; Richard I of England recovers some of territory taken by Saladin, including Jaffa and Acre; fails to take Jerusalem
1192 Richard I of England makes treaty with Saladin
1193 Death of Saladin
1197 Order of Teutonic Knights established in the Holy Land

CENTRAL AND EAST ASIA

SOUTH AND SOUTHEAST ASIA

1020 Firdowsi's *Shahnama* – Book of Kings, Persia's national epic
1038 Beginning of Seljuk dynasty, the first major Turkish Muslim empire (to 1194)
c.1040 Seljuk Turks conquer Afghanistan and E Persia
c.1045 Movable type printing invented in China
1077 Seljuk governors in Oxus region establish separate state of Khwarizm Shah (to 1231)

c.1025 Conquest of Punjab by Ghaznavids
1030 Tower of Victory built by Mahmud of Ghazni, Muslim conqueror of N India

1090 Shi'a Ismailis (of Alamut, Assassins) emerge as major force in N Persia (to 1256)

1126 Averröes, *the influential Muslim philosopher is born in Córdoba.*

1123 *Rubaiyat* (quatrains) of Omar Khayyam; also his *Algebra*, for which he is more celebrated in his homeland, Persia

1188 Nizami's *Layla and Majnun*, a Persian recasting of perennially popular pre-Islamic love story in verse

1186 Raids by Muhammad al Ghur herald decline of Ghaznavid dynasty, and of Buddhism, in N India

1191–93 Afghan Ghurids defeat Rajputs and seize Delhi and much of N India

1172 The Giralda, *the bell-tower of Seville's cathedral, was originally the minaret of the Great Mosque.*

1200–1450 CE

1250–54 Louis IX of France
embarked on his first crusade,
but was captured and ransomed.
In 1270 he died on crusade
outside the walls of Tunis.

EUROPE AND AFRICA

1200 Emergence of Hausa city-states, which come to dominate sub-Saharan trade.
1200 Rise of Mali in West Africa
1204 Fourth Crusade never reaches Holy Land; crusaders sack Constantinople; Venetian gains in Adriatic and Peloponnese
1208 Crusade against Cathars, or Albigensians, in southern France
1212 Battle of Las Navas de Tolosa; decisive defeat of Almohads by Christians in Iberia
1226 Creation of the Golden Horde, Mongol state in S Russia (to 1502)
1228 Start of collapse of Almohad Empire in North Africa
1228 Hafsid dynasty established at Tunis (to 1574)
1230 Establishment of Nasrid kingdom of Granada, Muslim stronghold in S Spain (to 1492)
1230 Establishment of the Mali Empire
1236 Christian reconquest of Córdoba
1241 Mongols invade Poland and Hungary
1248 Christian reconquest of Seville
1250–54 First of Louis IX's crusades; invasion of Egypt ends in defeat at Mansura; Louis captured and ransomed
c.1250 Building of stone mosques in Swahili city-states
1250 Mali Empire at its greatest extent
1261 Michael Palaeologus recaptures Constantinople and restores Byzantine Empire
1269 Marinids inflict final defeat on Almohads in Morocco
1270 Death of Louis IX outside walls of Tunis
1273 Foundation of Alhambra Palace at Granada
1282 French driven from Sicily, which passes to Aragon
1306–10 Hospitallers conquer Rhodes, which becomes their base
1312 Knights Templar Order accused of heresy and suppressed by Pope
1324 Pilgrimage to Mecca by Mansa Musa of Mali
1325 Ibn Battuta's first pilgrimage to Mecca
1331 Ibn Battuta's voyage to the Swahili cities of East Africa
1347 Marinids take Tunis
1348–51 Black Death reaches Europe and N Africa
1352 Ibn Battuta's travels to the Mali Empire
1354 First Ottoman conquests in SE Europe at Gallipoli; Ottomans advance into Europe
1366 Capture of Edirne (Adrianople) by Ottomans
1378 Beginning of Great Schism in Catholic church (to 1417)
1381 Peasants' Revolt in England
1389 Battle of Kosovo; Ottomans gain control of Balkans
1393 Ottoman conquest of Bulgaria
1396 Bayezid defeats crusader army at Nicopolis
1415 Portuguese capture Ceuta in Morocco
1430 Sultans of Kilwa begin grand building programme
1442 al-Maqrizi writes detailed topographical survey of Egypt

SOUTHWEST ASIA

1204 Maimonides' *The Guide to the Perplexed*
1206 Citadel of Damascus completed
1225 Holy Roman Emperor Frederick II inherits Kingdom of Jerusalem
1229 Frederick negotiates agreement which wins back control over Jerusalem
1229 Rasulids control Yemen (to 1454)
1237 Huand Khatun Mosque, mausoleum, madrasa, and baths at Kayseri, C Turkey, major complex endowed by Seljuk noblewoman
1250 Mamluks, military caste from Caucasus, take over Syria, Egypt and Hejaz (to 1517)
1256–57 Assassins' stronghold at Alamut falls to Hülegü
1258 Sack of Baghdad and fall of 'Abbasid Caliphate; Hülegü founds Il-Khanate
1260 Hülegü invades Syria; Mongols suffer first major defeat at 'Ayn Jalut
1268 Mamluks capture Antioch from crusaders

1281 Succession of Osman I, beginning of Ottoman dynasty (to 1924) and first phase of expansion
c.1302 Last Christian territory in Levant falls to Mamluks
1314 Rashid al-Din's *Jami 'al-tawarikh*, Persian history of Mongol conquest
1326 Ottomans capture Byzantine city of Bursa and make it their capital
1336 Birth of Timur
1345 Ottomans annex Emirate of Karasi; empire reaches Dardanelles
1347 Black Death reaches Baghdad and Constantinople
1370 Beginning of Timur's conquests; Timurid successors rule his empire to 1506
1372 *Kitab hayyat al-hayyawan* by al-Damiri, encyclopaedic collection of tales, traditions and scientific observations concerning animals
1378 Foundation of Ak Koyunlu, state based on Turkoman tribesmen in E Anatolia, Azerbaijan, Zagros mountains (to 1508)
c.1380 Foundation of Janissary corps by Ottomans
1380 Timur launches series of attacks on Persia
1384 Herat rebels; Timur suppresses ruling dynasty
1387 Isfahan rebels; in reprisal, Timur kills 70,000 people, building towers with their skulls
1388–91 Timur wages war against Mongol Khanate of the Golden Horde
1389 Accession of Bayezid I

1393 Sack of Baghdad by Timur
1400 Sack of Aleppo and Damascus by Timur
1401 Sack of Baghdad by Timur
1402 Ottomans defeated by Timur at Ankara
1405 Death of Timur
1406 Ibn Khaldun's *Muqaddima*, the first attempt in any language to elucidate the laws governing the rise and fall of civilizations

CENTRAL AND EAST ASIA

1206 Mongols united by Temujin, proclaimed Genghis Khan. The Great Yasa, law code of the Mongols promulgated by Genghis Khan. Mongols begin conquest of Central Asia
1211 Mongols begin conquest of northern (Jin) China
1219 Mongol invasion of Khwarizm Empire
1227 Death of Genghis Khan
1229 Ögödei elected Great Khan
1231 Mongols reconquer resurgent Empire of the Khwarizm Shah
1233 Mongols take Jin capital, Kaifeng
1235 Walled city built at Karakorum as fixed Mongol capital
1237 Start of Mongol conquest of Russia
1253–55 William of Rubruck crosses Asia to Karakorum
1256 Il-Khanate established in Persia; successor state to Mongols (to 1353). Hülegü crosses Oxus
1258 Sa'di's *Gulistan*, major popular classic of Persian literature
1259 Great Khan Möngke dies
1264 Kublai defeats rival for title of Great Khan, ending civil war.
1265 Death of Hülegü
1271–95 Marco Polo travels throughout Asia, returning by ship through Persian Gulf
1274 First Mongol attempt to invade Japan defeated
1275 Marco Polo reaches Kublai Khan's summer palace at Shangdu (Xanadu)
1279 Foundation of Yuan dynasty; Yuan take over Southern Song
1281 Second failed Mongol invasion of Japan
1292 Marco Polo given task of escorting Mongol princess to Hormuz
1294 Death of Kublai Khan
1295 Conversion of the Il-Khan Ghazan to Islam
1320 Outbreak of plague in Yunnan province
1320–30 Mongol armies help spread plague throughout China
1330 Plague reaches northeastern China
1335 Rebellions against Mongol rule in China
1335 Demotte's *Shahnama*, fine example of Persian illuminated manuscript
1346 Plague reaches coast of Black Sea
1368 Establishment of the Ming dynasty
1379 Timur marches on Urgench
1395 Sack of New Sarai, capital of Golden Horde
1405 Beginning of Ming admiral Zheng He's seven voyages to Indian Ocean (to 1433)
1405 The Rigistan, Samarkand, built by Timur and one of the glories of his capital
1424 End of Ming campaign against Mongols
c.1433 Construction of ocean-going junks banned by Ming
1439 Poggio Bracciolini records Asian journeys of Niccolo Conti
1449 Mongols defeat Chinese and capture the emperor
1443 Great Library at Herat, Persia founded

SOUTH AND SOUTHEAST ASIA

c.1200 Muslim Sufi saint, Mu'in al-Din Chishti, founds first Sufi order in Indian subcontinent
1206 Breakaway Mamluk (Slave) dynasty, under Aibak, establishes Delhi Sultanate

1258 First Mongol expedition to Annam

c.1280 Mongol invasions of SE Asia destroy Pagan and eclipse Dai Viet
1283 Expeditions against Annam and Champa
1287 Mongol expedition to Pagan
1288 Kublai Khan abandons attempt to subdue Annam and Champa

1293 Failed Mongol invasion of Java
1295 Conversion of Sultan of Achin (Sumatra) to Islam, which spreads over much of the East Indies

1320 Muhammad ibn Tughluq succeeds to Sultanate of Delhi

1334–41 Ibn Battuta serves as *qadi* (judge) in Delhi
1336 Rebellion against Tughluqs marks beginning of Vijayanagara Empire

1345–46 Ibn Battuta visits Southeast Asia and China

1345 Hasan Gangu, governor of Tughluq Deccani domains, revolts and founds Bahmani kingdom
1398 Timur's invasion of India; sack of Delhi leads to fall of Tughluq dynasty

1445 Conversion of Malacca (Malaya) to Islam

1206-1227 Genghis Khan *led the Mongols in a spectacular series of conquests. Here he is depicted in battle, preceded by Jebe, one of his generals.*

1281 Osman I *founded the Ottoman dynasty, which would rule Turkey and a vast empire until the end of the First World War.*

1450–1700 CE

EUROPE AND AFRICA	SOUTHWEST ASIA
1453 Constantinople falls to Ottoman sultan Mehmed II	
1459 Annexation of Serbia by Ottomans	**1461** Ottomans take Christian city of Trebizond
1464 Beginning of Songhay expansion under Sunni Ali	
1469 Marriage of Ferdinand of Aragon and Isabella of Castile; union of Castile and Aragon (1479)	
1480 Muscovy throws off Mongol yoke	
1484 Ottoman Turks capture Akkerman at mouth of Dniester	
1492 Columbus, in search of Asia, reaches Caribbean	
1492 Muslim Granada falls to Spain	
1494 Treaty of Tordesillas divides western hemisphere between Spain and Portugal	
1502 First slaves taken to the New World	**1502** Italian Lodovico di Varthema visits Arabia disguised as an Arab
1505 First Portuguese trading posts in East Africa	**1512** Accession of Ottoman ruler Selim I
1511 Sa'dian dynasty comes to power in Morocco (to 1659)	**1514** Selim defeats Safavids at Çaldiran
1517 Ottomans conquer Mamluks in Egypt	**1516–17** Ottomans conquer Syria, Egypt, the Hejaz, and Yemen
1519 Charles V elected Holy Roman Emperor	**1517** Selim I orders construction of Ottoman fleet at Suez; Portuguese attack on Jedda repulsed
1519–22 Magellan begins and del Cano completes first global circumnavigation	**1520** Sulayman the Magnificent becomes Ottoman sultan (to 1566)
1521 Sulayman takes Belgrade	
1521 Siege of Rhodes under Knights of St. John by Ottomans	**1525** Ottomans defeat Portuguese fleet in Red Sea
1526 Battle of Mohács; Ottoman invasion of Hungary	**1528** Safavids take Baghdad from Kurdish usurper
1529 Ahmad Grañ leads *jihad* against Ethiopia	**1534** Sulayman retakes Baghdad from Safavids
1529 Unsuccessful Turkish siege of Vienna	**1538** Ottomans subjugate Yemen and Aden and occupy port of Basra on Persian Gulf
1538 Holy League against the Turks formed	
1540 Portuguese come to the aid of Ethiopia against Ahmad Grañ	
1543 Death of Ahmad Grañ, shot by a Portuguese musketeer	
1546 Songhay destroys Mali Empire	**1546** Ottomans retake Basra after revolt
1547 Negotiated peace acknowledges Ottoman control of most of Hungary	**1551–52** Ottomans fail to oust Portuguese from Hormuz
1562 After inconclusive skirmishes, Ottomans gain Transylvania	
1565 Ottoman siege of Malta fails	**1566** Sulayman succeeded by Selim II
1571 Ottomans take Cyprus from Venetians; at battle of Lepanto Ottoman navy defeated by united Christian fleet off Greek coast	
1578 Moroccans crush invading Portuguese	**1588** Abbas I (the Great) becomes Safavid shah
1580 Union of Spanish and Portuguese crowns	**1592** Zaidi Imams regain control of Yemen, and rule until 1962
1588 English defeat Spanish Armada	**1598** Isfahan becomes imperial Safavid capital
1591 Moroccan invaders destroy Songhay Empire	**1603–19** Safavid war with Ottomans; in first year Abbas recaptures Tabriz
1618 Thirty Years' War in Europe (to 1648)	**1604** Abbas conquers Erivan, Shirvan, and Kars
c.1660 Collapse of Mali Empire	**1672** Greatest extent of Ottoman Empire
1664 Turkish advance on Vienna turned back at battle of St. Gotthard	
1682 Peter the Great becomes tsar of Russia	
1683 Siege of Vienna ends in Ottoman defeat	
1698 Arabs from Oman capture Mombasa	
1699 Peace of Karlowitz confirms Austrian conquests from Ottomans	

1526 Sulayman the Magnificent *leads his troops against the Hungarians at the battle of Mohács.*

CENTRAL AND EAST ASIA

SOUTH AND SOUTHEAST ASIA

c.1450 Islam spreads over much of East Indies

1487–89 Portuguese Pero de Covilhã sails through Red Sea to India

1653 The Taj Mahal, *the mausoleum of Shah Jahan's wife was completed Agra. It is one of the greatest examples of Islamic architecture in the world.*

1499 Rise to power of Safavids in Persia
1500 Shaybanid dynasty, of Mongol descent, assumes control of Transoxania (to 1598)
1501 Accession of Shah Ismail I; beginning of Safavid dynasty in Persia (to 1732)

1498 Vasco da Gama rounds Cape of Good Hope and reaches India

1502 First published map to show correct general shape of India, by Alberto Cantino
1507 Portuguese victory over Ottoman and Arab fleet at Diu
1509–16 Portuguese voyages to Moluccas, Malacca, and Macao
1510 Portuguese conquest of Goa; Goa made capital of all Portuguese possessions in Asia
1511–12 Portuguese establish base in Malacca and reach Moluccas
1517 First Portuguese trading mission to China
1526 Babur conquers Delhi and founds Mughal Empire

1534–35 Safavid war with Ottomans, who capture Tabriz and Baghdad

1538 Failure of Ottoman blockade of Portuguese at Diu

1553–55 Safavid war with Ottomans

1556 Akbar becomes Mughal emperor (to 1605); Reign marked by territorial expansion and cordial Hindu-Muslim relations

1557 Foundation of Portuguese colony at Macao

1578–90 Safavid war with Ottomans

1581–82 Yermak begins Russian conquest of Siberia

1598 Anthony and Robert Sherley travel to Persia, where they meet Shah Abbas
1603 Foundation of Tokugawa Shogunate in Japan
1627 Herbert's travels in Persia
1636 Manchus establish Qing imperial rule at Mukden
1644 Qing forces enter Beijing

1600 Founding of British East India Company

1627 Shah Jahan becomes Mughal emperor
c.1647 Completion of *Atlas of India* by Sadiq Isfahani
1653 Completion of Taj Mahal
1658 Aurangzeb becomes Mughal emperor: empire reaches maximum extent during his reign (to 1701)
c.1660 Gujaratis make earliest known Indian nautical charts

1689 Treaty of Nerchinsk agrees Russian and Chinese spheres of influence in east Asia

1683 This Turkish banner *was captured by the Christian forces after the unsuccessful Ottoman siege of Vienna.*

1700–1900 CE

EUROPE AND AFRICA	SOUTHWEST ASIA
1701 Start of Asante's rise to prominence	
1705 Foundation of Husaynid dynasty in Tunis, which rules until 1957	
1716–18 Further Austrian victories, including capture of Belgrade from Ottomans	
1729 Portuguese leave East Africa following attacks from Oman	
1730 Revival of empire of Bornu in central Africa	
c.1730 Emergence of Fulbe confederation of Futa Jallon	**c.1750** Emergence of Wahhabi reform movement in Arabia
1757 Muhammad III becomes Sultan of Morocco	
1768 War between Russia and the Ottomans	**1774** Ottoman decline follows Treaty of Küçük Kaynarca
1776 Abd al-Kadir leads Muslims in *jihad* along the Senegal River	
1798 Occupation of Egypt by Napoleon Bonaparte; defeat of Egyptians at battle of the Pyramids. Battle of the Nile; British fleet defeats French	
1804 Fulani leader, Uthman dan Fodio declares *jihad* and conquers Hausa city-states	
1804 Muhammad Ali becomes Viceroy of Egypt	**1806** Wahhabis take Mecca
1804 Napoleon proclaimed Emperor of France	**1812** Burckhardt discovers Petra, ancient capital of Nabataea
1807 Hausa kings replaced by Fulani emirs	**1812** Egyptian forces retake Mecca and Medina
1816 Inspired by Uthman dan Fodio, Amadu Lobbo launches *jihad* in Masina	**1814** Burckhardt visits Mecca
1820 Egyptians invade Sudan	**1818** Sadleir is first European to make east-west crossing of Arabian peninsula
1820 Uthman dan Fodio establishes Sokoto Fulani Kingdom	**1818** Wahhabi movement suppressed by Egyptian forces
1821–33 Greek War of Independence from Ottomans	**1839–61** Sultan Abdul Majid I makes series of liberal Tanzimat decrees
1830 French invasion of Algeria; Algiers occupied	**1843** Fortunes of Sa'ud family restored by Faisal
1840 Ottoman Empire under threat from Egypt; saved by British and Austrian intervention	
1852 'Umar Tal conquers the Senegal valley	**1853** Richard Burton visits Mecca and Medina in Arab disguise
1853 Russians defeat Turkish navy at Sinop	
1854–56 Crimean War; French and British support Ottoman Turks against Russia	
1861 'Umar Tal's forces conquer Segu	
1861 Abolition of serfdom in Russia	
1863 Al-Hajj 'Umar Tal clashes with French in Senegal Valley and creates a Muslim empire; invades Timbuktu	
1864 'Umar Tal is killed attemping to suppress Fulani rebellion	
1869 Opening of Suez Canal	**1876–78** Doughty's Arabian journeys
1877–78 Russia, Serbia and Montenegro at war with Turkey	
1878 Treaty of San Stefano negotiated by Russia and Turkey	
1878 Berlin Congress: independence of Serbia, Montenegro, and Romania from Ottomans	
1881 Tunisia occupied by French	**c.1880** Birth of 'Abdal-'Aziz ibn Sa'ud in Kuwait
1882 Revolt in Egypt; occupation by British	
1882 Beginning of major Jewish emigration from Russian Empire	
1884 Berlin Conference on Africa; Samory Touré proclaims his Islamic theocracy in West Africa.	**1887** Riyadh taken by Rashidis, who dominate Nejd
1885 Bulgaria granted Eastern Rumelia	**1888** Publication of Doughty's classic *Travels in Arabia Deserta*
1887 Bulgaria independent of Ottoman empire	
1893 French conquer Dahomey	

1798 At the battle of the Pyramids *the Egyptian army was defeated by the French under Napoleon.*

CENTRAL AND EAST ASIA

1722–36 Subjugation of Afghans by Persia
1730–34 Suppression of Khazaks by Russia

1736 Nadir Shah becomes Shah of Persia
1747 Foundation of Afghanistan by Ahmad Khan Abdali
1751 Tibet, Dzungaria, Turkestan, and the Tarim Basin overrun by Qing Chinese
1758–59 Qing campaigns against Kalmyks
1786 Start of Qajar dynasty in Persia

1839–42 Afghans under Dost Muhammad defeat British in First Afghan War
1840–42 Opium War; British attacks force trading concessions from China
1850s Widespread Muslim rebellions against Qing rule in China
1855–73 *Jihad* of Yunnan Muslims; ends 1873

1863–73 Northwest uprising in Uighur domains of Qing empire; largest Muslim *jihad* in E Asia
1864 Establishment of Russian control in Kalmykia (Semipalatinsk)

1868–70 Suppression of Muslim states of Bukhara and Samarkand by Russia

1878–79 Second Afghan War; British attempt to invade Afghanistan, which is coming under Russian influence

SOUTH AND SOUTHEAST ASIA

c.1700 Probable commencement of Mughal military mapping
1707 Death of Aurangzeb heralds decline of Mughal power in India
c.1720 Marathas start to expand over most of India
1724 Independent rule over Deccan by Nizam of Hyderabad hastens disintegration of empire
1728 Marathas defeat Nizam of Hyderabad and gain supremacy over Deccan with subsequent territorial expansion
1739 Sack of Delhi by Persians and Afghans under Nadir Shah
1744–63 Anglo-French (Carnatic) wars; eclipse of French power in S Asia
1749 Mysore starts to become major power in southern India
1757 Expansion of Gurkha (Nepali) domains over much of Himalayas
1757 Battle of Plassey; British victory over combined French and Mughal force establishes British power in Bengal
1761 Defeat by Afghans temporarily ends Maratha hegemony over northern India
1761 British destroy French power in India following seizure of Pondicherry
1767 Appointment of James Rennell as first Surveyor-General of Bengal; beginning of Survey of India
1775 First Anglo-Maratha war (to 1782)
1782 Treaty ending first Anglo-Maratha war results in territorial losses for Marathas
1788 Occupation of Delhi; Maratha territorial apogee, Mughal rulers become puppets of Marathas
1799 Conquest of Mysore ends challenge to British power in southern India
1803 Second Anglo-Maratha war leads to British acquisition of Delhi
1815 Victory in Anglo-Gurkha war extends British possessions into the Himalayas
1818 Third Anglo-Maratha war ends in Maratha defeat
1819 Stamford Raffles, of the British East India company, founds Singapore
1849 British annex Punjab after two Sikh wars
1857 Last Mughal emperor, the Maratha puppet Bahadur Shah II, dethroned and exiled by British
1857–59 Revolt ("Mutiny") attempts to oust British from India. May 30, 1857: Lucknow mutiny. Jun 27, 1857: massacre of British evacuees at Cawnpore
1858 (Mar 22) British retake Lucknow after 20-day siege
1859 Timor divided between Netherlands and Portugal
1873 Dutch attack on Achin sultanate in Sumatra
1876 Queen Victoria declared Empress of India, and a viceroy appointed as her representative
1885 Foundation of Indian National Congress

1722 The Golden Mosque *with three gilt domes was built in Delhi in 1722. On March 22 1739, Nadir Shah stood on its roof to watch the massacre of the city's citizens.*

1804-1849 Muhammad Ali *ruled Egypt as an independent country, although it was still part of the Ottoman empire. This is the mosque he had built in Cairo.*

1900–1950 CE

EUROPE AND AFRICA

1904 French create federation of French West Africa

1908 Bulgaria declares full independence
1908 Bosnia-Herzegovina annexed by Austro-Hungarian Empire
1911 Libya occupied by Italy
1912 Serbia, Bulgaria, Greece and Montenegro form Balkan League; First Balkan War
1912–13 Balkan Wars; Ottomans lose most of their remaining European lands
1914 Assassination of Archduke Franz Ferdinand in Sarajevo precipitates start of First World War (to 1918)
1914 (Oct) Turkey closes Dardanelles
1915 Gallipoli landings. Establishment of Salonican front

1917 US declares war on Central Powers; Bolshevik revolution in Russia

1918 End of First World War

1919 Treaty of Versailles creates a new European order

1920 (Aug) Treaty of Sèvres
1920 Inauguration of League of Nations

1922 USSR (Union of Soviet Socialist Republics) is formed

1929 Wall Street Crash

1939 (Sep) Invasion of Poland by Germany and Soviet Union; outbreak of Second World War
1941 Germans and Italians advance into Egypt
1942 British defeat Germans at El Alamein
1942 Plans for Final Solution agreed at Wansee
1945 (May) Germany surrenders
1945 Yalta Conference; origins of Cold War

1949 Formation of NATO

SOUTHWEST ASIA

c.1900 Baku oil fields in Azerbaijan producing half the world's oil
1902 Ibn Sa'ud reclaims his patrimony by capturing Riyadh
1905 Jewish National Fund established to buy land in Palestine

1908 Ottoman sultan deposed in Young Turk Revolution

1914 Ottomans declare *jihad*; ally with Germany and Austria (Central Powers) against Allies
1915 About one million Armenians massacred or deported by Turks
1915 (Feb) First Turkish attempt to capture Suez
1916 (Feb) Russians take Erzurum
1916 (Apr) British surrender to Turks at Kut al Amara in Mesopotamia
1916–18 Arab Revolt; Saudi tribes supported by British rise against Turks
1917 Balfour Declaration commits Britain to creation of Jewish state in Palestine. British take Baghdad. British take Jerusalem
1918 Battle of Megiddo. Collapse of Ottoman empire; Turkish surrender
1919 Greek forces land at Smyrna. Kemal Pasha breaks away from authority of Istanbul government.
1920 Armenia cedes half its territory to Turkey
1921 Turkish Nationalist government established in Ankara
1922 Turks recapture Smyrna
1923 Foundation of modern Turkey by Kemal Atatürk
1923 (Jul) Treaty of Lausanne recognizes Turkish sovereignty over Smyrna and eastern Thrace

1926 Ibn Sa'ud crowns himself King of the Hejaz and Sultan of Nejd
1927 Oil discovered in Iraq

1932 Kingdom of Saudi Arabia proclaimed
1933 US company, Standard Oil of California, granted concession in Saudi Arabia
1936 Arab revolt in Palestine against Jewish immigration
1938 Commercial quantities of oil discovered in Saudi Arabia

1944 Standard reformed as ARAMCO (Arabian American Oil Company)
1945 Foundation of Arab League

1947 UN partition of Palestine
1948 Foundation of state of Israel leads to war; invading Arab armies repulsed in Israel; some 725,000 Arabs flee Palestine

1908 Abdul Hamid II, *having failed to modernize the Ottoman empire, was deposed by the Young Turks.*

CENTRAL AND EAST ASIA

1909 Anglo-Persian Oil Company (later BP) founded in Iran
1911 Qing dynasty overthrown by Sun Yat Sen's nationalists and Republic of China declared

1925 Reza Shah deposes last Qajar shah and is proclaimed ruler of Iran. He introduces Western-style reforms

1941 Abdication of Reza Shah; his son, Muhammad Reza Shah Pahlavi, succeeds him

1945 Atomic bombs at Hiroshima and Nagasaki force Japanese surrender
1945 (Aug) USSR declares war on Japan
1945 (Aug) Atom bomb dropped on Hiroshima
1945 (Sep) Japanese surrender
1945 Stalin begins transfer of ethnic-minority peoples to labour camps in Siberia

1946–49 Chinese Civil war between Nationalists and Communists

SOUTH AND SOUTHEAST ASIA

1904 Partition of Bengal: nationalist agitation in India
1906 Foundation of All-India Muslim League

1918 Indian contribution to First World War earns it membership in League of Nations
1919 Amritsar massacre leads to surge in Indian nationalism
1920 Mahatma Gandhi gains control of indian National Congress
1920 Start of civil disobedience campaigns by Gandhi in support of independence struggle

1926–27 Rebellion against Dutch rule in Java and Sumatra

1942 Indonesia, Indochina, Malaya, the Philippines, New Guinea and Singapore seized by Japan
1942 (Feb) Surrender of British forces to Japan in Singapore
1942 (Mar) Dutch surrender East Indies to Japan

1945 India becomes UN charter member
1945 Sukarno and Ho Chi Minh declare independence for Indonesia and Vietnam respectively

1947 India and Pakistan gain independence
1947 New independent dominions of India (Hindu) and Pakistan (Muslim) are born
1947 Start of Indo–Pakistani War fought over Jammu and Kashmir; UN ceasefire line agreed in 1949

1949 Indonesia gains independence from the Dutch

1916–18 Emir Faisal, *seen here with his bodyguard, united the Arabs and together with Colonel T.E. Lawrence led a successful revolt against the Turks. After the war, Faisal became king of Iraq under the British mandate.*

1948 The UK blockaded *the seas around Israel to prevent ships carrying Jewish refugees from landing. The 700 Jews aboard the ship swam safely to shore at Haifa, using a lifeline.*

1951–2003 CE

EUROPE AND AFRICA	SOUTHWEST ASIA
1954 Algerian uprising against French rule	**1956** Suez crisis; Israel, France and Britain invade Egypt; fail to block Egypt's nationalization of Suez Canal
	1958 Oil strikes in United Arab Emirates
	1961 Foundation of Organization of the Petroleum Exporting Countries (OPEC)
1960 Fifteen African countries gain independence	
1963 Foundation of Organization of African Unity (OAU)	**1967** Egypt closes Gulf of Aqaba to Israel; Israel defeats Egypt and other Arab nations in Six Day War; Israel takes Sinai, Gaza, Golan Heights, West Bank, and Jerusalem
	1973 Arab states fail to defeat Israel in Yom Kippur War
	1973 OPEC restricts flow of oil to world markets; raises price of crude oil by 200%; Oil crisis causes inflation and economic slowdown
1974 Revised Yugoslav constitution grants Kosovo autonomy	**1977** Start of Middle East peace process
	1978 Camp David summit between Egypt, Israel, and US
	1979 Egypt and Israel sign peace treaty based on Camp David accords
	1980 Start of Iran–Iraq War
	1981 52 American embassy staff held hostage in Tehran since 1979 are freed
1981 President Sadat of Egypt assassinated by Islamic fundamentalists	**1982** Israel invades Lebanon
1983 Islamic law imposed in Sudan	
1986 US bombs Libya in retaliation for terrorist attacks	**1988** End of Iran–Iraq War
1987 Famine in Ethiopia	
1989 Fundamentalists seize power in Sudan	**1990** (Aug 2) Iraq invades Kuwait; UN demands Iraq's immediate withdrawal
1989–90 Collapse of Communism in Europe	**1990** (Aug 7) US troops sent to Gulf
1991 Islamic Salvation Front poised to win Algerian general election; army cancels second round of voting	**1990** (Nov 29) UN resolution authorizes members to use "all necessary means" against Iraq
1991 Start of civil war in Yugoslavia	**1991** (Jan) UN deadline for Iraqi withdrawal passes; Operation Desert Storm begins with bombing of Iraqi troops and installations
1991 Unsuccessful coup attempt in USSR; disintegration of Soviet Union	**1991** (Feb 24) Allied land offensive in Iraq
1991 Croatia, Slovenia, and Bosnia declare independence from Yugoslavia	**1991** (Feb 28) Cease-fire in war in Iraq
1992 Civil war in Georgia, Bosnia-Herzegovina	**1993** Oslo Accords between Israel and PLO based on principle of "Land for Peace"
1994 Russian troops invade Chechnya	**1993** Islamic countries issue Cairo Declaration to curb fundamentalism
1995 Peace agreement (Dayton Accord) ends the Bosnian war; UN troops remain	**1995** Israeli-PLO agreement extends Palestinian self-rule within the West Bank
1998 US bombs Sudan and Afganistan in retaliation for al-Qaida bombing of US institutions in Kenya and Tanzania	**2000** Ariel Sharon's visit to Dome of the Rock inflames Israeli-Palestinian violence
1998 Slobodan Milosevic sends troops into areas controlled by Kosovo Liberation Army (KLA)	**2001** Sharon becomes Israeli premier; violence continues
1999 Kosovo Peace talks collapse; NATO begins bombing campaign	**2003** Claiming that Iraq is hiding weapons of mass destruction, US-led coalition forces invade Iraq in April and oust Saddam Hussein's Ba'ath regime
2000 Milosevic forced to step down	
2001 Milosevic arrested to face charges of war crimes in Bosnia and Kosovo	

1969 Yasser Arafat *becomes Chairman of the PLO. He has campaigned for the creation of a Palestiniian state and the recognition of Palestinian rights ever since.*

CENTRAL AND EAST ASIA

1955 Afghan government supports movement for separation of Pakhtunistan from Pakistan

1962 Land reform in Iran reduces power and influence of religious establishment

1973 Rebellion in Afghanistan

1979 Islamic revolution in Iran; deposition of shah; proclamation of Islamic republic
1979 Deposition of monarchy in Afghanistan; Soviet invasion and civil war

1989 Crushing of pro-democracy demonstrators in Beijing
1989 Soviet troops withdraw from Afghanistan
1990–91 Collapse of USSR; creation of Central Asian republics; Islamic revival throughout region

1995 Taliban militia reignites Afghan civil war
1996 Taliban forces capture Kabul

2001 Saudi millionaire Osama bin Laden identified as mastermind behind al-Qaida attacks on New York and Washington on September 11; US demands his extradition from Afghanistan
2001 US-led coalition declares "war on terrorism"; coalition forces attack and overthrow Taliban regime in Afghanistan in response to al-Qaida terrorist attacks

SOUTH AND SOUTHEAST ASIA

1952 First Indian general election won by Congress Party
1954 Sukarno abrogates union with Dutch and declares unitary state of Indonesia
1956 Pakistan constituted as Islamic Republic
1957 Malaya granted independence from Britain, despite ongoing Communist insurrection
1958 Abortive secessionist uprisings in Baluchistan, Pakistan

1963 Federation of Malaysia incorporates Singapore, Sarawak, and Sabah, along with Malaya
1965 Second inconclusive Indo–Pakistani war over Jammu and Kashmir
1965 Failed Marxist coup and military countercoup in Indonesia ends Sukarno regime

1971 Secession of E Pakistan leads to creation of Bangladesh. Third Indo-Pakistani war as India intervenes

1975 Indonesia annexes East Timor

1989– Revival of violent insurrection against Indian rule in Jammu and Kashmir

1998 Economic crisis in Indonesia leads to overthrow of government
1999 Referendum in East Timor produces overwhelming vote for independence
2001 Attack on Indian parliament by Muslim terrorists leads to increased tension between India and Pakistan over Kashmir

1967 Israeli trucks transport *Egyptian prisoners from the battlefield in the Six Day War. Israel defeated the combined forces of Syria, Jordan and Egypt.*

1989 Ayatollah Khomeini, *Iran's leader and symbol of the Iranian revolution is escorted to his grave amid scenes of uncontrollable grief.*

ISRAEL AND THE PALESTINIANS

THE CONFLICT BETWEEN ISRAEL and the Palestinians – the Arab population of the pre-1948 British mandated territory of Palestine – is crucial in Middle East politics. In 1947 the UN approved a plan to partition Palestine, to create separate Jewish and Arab states. This was accepted by the Jewish side but not the Arabs. When the British Mandate ended in May 1948, Arab states invaded Palestine but were pushed back well beyond the UN partition lines by Israeli forces. Nearly a million Palestinians became refugees. The 1949 armistices left only East Jerusalem, the West Bank, and the Egyptian-administered coastal Gaza Strip not in Israeli hands. Jordan declared East Jerusalem and the West Bank to be part of its territory, only renouncing this claim formally in 1988.

In the 1967 Six-Day War Israel took East Jerusalem, the West Bank, and Gaza. Jewish settlers began moving in, regarding these occupied territories as part of the biblical-era Land of Israel.

The Palestine Liberation Organization (PLO) led by Yasser Arafat claimed to be the Palestinians' "sole legitimate representative". It did not recognize Israel's right to exist until 1988, while Israel refused to "negotiate with terrorists". In 1993 the PLO concluded a historic "land for peace" deal with Israel, the "Oslo Accords." The two sides formally recognized one another, and Arafat and Israeli Prime Minister Rabin signed a Declaration of Principles in Washington D.C. A five-year timetable for "permanent status" negotiations would tackle the future of Jewish settlements in the West Bank and Gaza and the Palestinian demand for East Jerusalem as their capital. Palestinians were to get interim self-rule, initially in Gaza and Jericho (achieved in 1994), and gradually in the whole West Bank. This meant Palestinian police taking over responsibility for security from the Israeli military, who had been struggling since 1987 to end an insurrection led by the radical Islamic organization Hamas. The Palestinian National Authority (PNA) was established on Palestinian territory, based in Gaza. Arafat – its chairman – made a triumphal return in July 1994 and in 1996 won a mandate as president of the 88-member Palestinian Legislative Council.

The "Oslo B" accord extended PNA rule from Gaza and Jericho to six more West Bank towns in 1995. Mutual mistrust and violence, however, threatened to derail the peace process before it reached the stage of "final status" talks, and Arafat risked losing credibility among radical Palestinians. After Israel's 1999 elections, a Labour-led government under Ehud Barak established with the PNA an ambitious timetable for a permanent agreement. US diplomacy helped keep this plan alive until the eleventh hour, but heavy-handed Israeli retaliation to violent incidents in September–October 2000 provoked Palestinian rage and a return to the tactics of *intifada* (uprising). In a bitter climate of atrocity, retaliation, and counter-strike, Israeli policy hardened under a new government headed by Ariel Sharon, who was elected prime minister in 2001.

INDEX

ACKNOWLEDGMENTS

All translations from the Qur'an used in this book are from *The Koran Interpreted* by Arthur J. Arberry (OUP 1964)

The publisher would like to thank the following for their kind permission to reproduce their photographs: (Abbreviations key: t=top, b=bottom, r=right, l=left, c=centre, a=above)

Agence France Presse: 20bl, 40cl.
AKG London: 182clb; Biblioteque Nationale, Paris 66tl.
Max Alexander: 176cl.
Ancient Art & Architecture Collection/Ronald Sheridan: 50bl, 52bl, 71tr, 83tr, 92tl.
The Art Archive: HarperCollins Publishers 41; Museo Correr Venice/Dagli Orti 70bl; Real Biblioteca de lo Escorial/Dagli Orti 60clb; Topkapi Museum Istanbul/Dagli Orti 68cla; Victoria and Albert Museum London/Eileen Tweedy 66clb; Victoria and Albert Museum London/Sally Chappell 73.
Ashmolean Museum, Oxford/Geoff Dann: 27crb.
Bodleian Library: Ms Marsh 144 p. 167 95tr; Ms Pococke 375 fol.3v-4r 97crb.
Bridgeman Art Library, London/New York: Biblioteque Nationale, Paris, France 63crb, 65crb; Bibliotheque Nationale de Cartes et Plans, Paris, France 94cl; Chateau de Compiegne, Oisne 106cla; British Library, London 39tr, 64tl, 96bl; Cordoba, Andalucia, Spain 175tr; Institute of Oriental Studies, St. Petersburg, Russia 97tr; Jean-Loup Charmet 78tl, 104cla; Lauros-Giraudon 180cl; Louvre, Paris, France 60tl; Ma'daba, Jordan 49tr; Musee Conde, Chantilly, France 24tl; National Museum of India, New Delhi 74tl; Palacio del Senado, Madrid, Spain 61tr; Private collections 31bc, 76clb, 90clb, 177tr; School of Oriental & African Studies Library, University of London 37br; Topkapi Palace Museum, Istanbul Turkey 71cr, 95br, 178clb; University Library, Istanbul, Turkey 99.

British Library, London: Lawrence Pardes 29bc; 89br,172clb; Alan Hills 102tl; Janet Peckham 18bl.
Corbis: 3tr; Angelo Hornak 36tl; Arte & Immagini srl 91cr; Charles & Josette Lenars 6; Chris Hellier 92clb; Ed Kashi 100; Nik Wheeler 4; Paul Amasy 84cl; Roger Wood 72cl; Tiziana and Gianni Baldizzone 19tr.
Alistair Duncan: 21cr.
Mary Evans Picture Library: 77cra.
Werner Forman Archive: 85br, 93cr, 173cra, 173crb; Spink & Son, London 46.
Gables Collection: 179tr.
Sonia Halliday Photographs: 106clb; Biblioteca Nacional, Madrid 49bc; Biblioteque Nationale, Paris 16tl; Topkapi Palace Museum, Istanbul, Turkey 177crb.
Robert Harding Picture Library: 83crb.
Heeresgeschitliches Museum, Vienna: 179crb.
Hulton Archive: 183crb, 185tr; Keystone 79crb; Three Lions 107tr.
Imperial War Museum: 183tr.
Dinesh Khanna: 75cr, 174tl.
Neil Lukas: 175br.
Paul Lunde: 16bc, 32tl, 42clb, 88tl, 105cr, 171cl.
Christine Osborne: 13fp, 28tl, 31tr, 34tr, 87, 109; Camerapix 17br; Chris Barton 62tr; Julian Wurker 82cl; Patrick Syder 45cr, 55tr, 85br.
Popperfoto: Reuters 3bl, 43tr.
Ram Rahman: 74clb, 181tr.
Rex Features: 107crb, 184clb.
Peter Sanders: 14, 22cl, 26, 29cra, 35br, 38clb, 80, 171tr, 171crb.
Tony Souter: 45tr.
Jon Spaull: 56tl, 57, 59cr, 181crb.
Frank Spooner Pictures: Gamma 108tl, 185crb.
Linda Whitwam: 25br, 39br, 61crb.
Francesca York: 30cl, 33br, 44cal, 86clb.
All other images © Dorling Kindersley.

For further information see: www.dkimages.com